Taking *truth* next door

DAVID FAUST

Taking *truth* next door

Offering honest answers to 21st-century seekers

Standard PUBLISHING

CINCINNATI, OHIO

All Scripture quotations, unless otherwise indicated, are taken from the HOLY BIBLE, NEW INTERNATIONAL VERSION®. NIV®. Copyright © 1973, 1978, 1984 by International Bible Society. Used by permission of Zondervan Publishing House. All rights reserved.

Scripture quotation from THE MESSAGE, Eugene H. Peterson © 1993, 1994, 1995. Used by permission of NavPress/Pinon Press. All rights reserved. For copies call 1-800-366-7788.

Grateful acknowledgment is made for permission to reprint from

My Utmost for His Highest by Oswald Chambers, page 125. Edited by James Reimann, © 1992 by Oswald Chambers Publications Assn., Ltd. Original edition © 1935 by Dodd Mead & Co., renewed 1963 by the Oswald Chambers Publications Assn., Ltd., and is used by permission of Discovery House Publishers, Box 3566, Grand Rapids, MI 49501. All rights reserved.

God in the Dark by Os Guinness, copyright © 1996, pages 97, 103, 106. Used by permission of Good News Publishers/Crossway Books, Wheaton, Illinois 60187

Library of Congress Cataloging-in-Publication Data
Faust, David.
     Taking truth next door : offering honest answers to
21-century seekers / David Faust.
          p.   cm.
     Includes bibliographical references.
     ISBN 0-7847-1077-5
     1. Witness bearing (Christianity).   2. Evangelistic work.
3. Apologetics.   4. Christianity Miscellanea.   I. Title.
BV4520.F35   2000
248'.5–dc21   99-26406
                                              CIP

Edited by Theresa C. Hayes
Cover design by DesignTeam
Interior design by Robert E. Korth

Standard Publishing, Cincinnati, Ohio.
A division of Standex International Corporation

To my friends

Dan and Sue Burton,
who are serving Christ in Ethiopia

and

Luke and Tiffany Smith,
who are serving Christ in Australia

ACKNOWLEDGMENTS

The individuals whose questions form the basis for this book are real people. They graciously allowed me to interview them and include enough details to give the reader helpful glimpses of their personal lives and spiritual struggles. In some cases, their names have been changed to protect their privacy. Their stories are told in my short book for seekers, *Searching for Hope*, and repeated verbatim in this volume at the beginning of chapters three, four, five, seven, eight, ten, and eleven.

For the sake of consistency, I've chosen to tell all of the stories in the present tense. However, it's important to realize that all of these individuals have moved further along in their spiritual journeys since asking the questions contained in this book. Today, some of them are committed Christians (as I've tried to make clear in the chapters about them). In these cases, the questions are retrospective, reflecting the honest struggles these individuals experienced before coming to faith.

Thanks to Jim Eichenberger, Diane Stortz, Theresa Hayes, and others at Standard Publishing who have encouraged me by their careful editing, insightful suggestions, and prayerful vision for the impact of this project.

CONTENTS

What kinds of questions did Jesus face, and how did he respond to them? What kinds of questions are we likely to encounter when we talk with people about Christ? How can we answer these questions with gentleness and respect?

The evangelistic landscape has changed in today's postmodern culture. What new issues and attitudes confront Christians today as we attempt to share our faith?

When Ben found out I was a Bible teacher, he said, "The Bible? You can't believe anything in that book!" How can Christians help someone like him trust in the reliability of Scripture?

wonders why her dad died of a heart attack when she was only fourteen . . . and why she was raped when she was a teenager . . . and why her marriage broke up. She's angry with God. How can Christians help someone like her?

Chapter 9. What Is Faith, Anyway?

As we ponder the honest questions in this book, it appears that many in our culture not only are uncertain *what* to believe; they're also confused about *what it means to believe at all*. This chapter dispels some of the misconceptions, and offers a clear biblical explanation of what Christians mean when we talk about faith.

Chapter 10. Yoshi: What About My Family Traditions?

"I don't have personal faith in any gods," this retired Japanese businessman admits. Yet he clings firmly to the Shinto and Buddhist customs his family has followed for generations. How can we lead someone to Christ if he's unwilling to depart from the traditional religious beliefs that dominate his family or ethnic group?

Chapter 11. Tom and Danielle: Why So Many Phony Christians?

This husband/wife team ask a classic question: Why do so many Christians seem hypocritical? Who needs the church if the people in it are no more genuine than the people outside it?

Chapter 12. Truth, Freedom, and Tolerance

Three out of four Americans say they don't believe in absolute truth. Instead, the watchword of our time is "tolerance." How can we tell the truth in a culture that isn't even sure it believes in truth anymore?

Postscript: To Whom Shall We Go?

Where can we find peace of mind? Alcohol, money, power, material possessions—none of these things can satisfy the deepest needs of the human heart. The Bible's book of Ecclesiastes asks the same hard questions people are asking in our postmodern world. Christ holds the answer to our longing for peace and hope.

In the author's e-mail correspondence with Pat (the questioner described in chapter five), she asks some key questions about the meaning of Jesus' death and resurrection.

Two kinds of lesson plans: (1) suggestions for leading a discussion group for seekers who are willing to talk about faith, and (2) suggestions for a Sunday school class or believers' small group whose members are interested in learning how to reach postmodern people for Christ.

HOW THIS BOOK CAME TO BE

This was a hard book to write. Let me explain why.

It wasn't hard to write because of its format. I enjoyed talking with the people whose questions appear in this book. Ordinary people have fascinating stories to tell, and we make a big mistake if we don't listen carefully before telling others our own point of view. "Faith comes by hearing" (Romans 10:17), but many won't listen to us until first we've listened respectfully to them. I'm thankful for Ben, Cathy, Pat, Matt, Bev, Yoshi, Tom, and Danielle—for their candor, their insights, and their willingness to make themselves vulnerable in this public forum so others can learn from their private soul-searching.

Nor was this book hard to write because of the difficult questions I had to address—although I must admit, a few times I found myself initially stumped! When real people ask questions about faith, they don't speak in concise sound bytes. Their queries don't always fit neatly into our preconceived theological categories—or make catchy titles for the chapters of a book—which makes writing and editing more of a challenge.

The thing that made this book hard to write wasn't the weight of the material; it was the weight of the responsibility. I feel a strong sense of responsibility to people who don't know Christ. Many of them are searching earnestly for spiritual truth, and frankly, we in the church need to do a better job acquainting them with the God who loves them.

I also feel a strong responsibility toward Christians. There's never been a time when it was more urgent for believers to "give the reason for the hope that you have . . . with gentleness and respect" (1 Peter 3:15). Jesus said to go and make disciples, not stay and make ourselves comfortable. He calls us to engage the world in spiritual battle, not retreat from it in fear. His disciples can't afford to shrink back into the safe confines of our church buildings. We must boldly take our faith into the tough arena of public conversation. There, the hard questions of real people will require from us every ounce of mental energy and love we can muster. And there, with God's help, we can build relationships and engage in worthwhile conversations that lead people to the foot of the cross.

But, it's easier to talk about evangelism than to actually do it, so I've tried to give this book a practical angle based on my own experiences in talking with people about Christ. Throughout the months of writing, I've prayed for you, the reader—that you will do more than simply read this book and place it on your shelf. I pray that you will use the accompanying small book of questions (Searching for Hope), along with your own insights and experiences, to reach out to your friends and lead them to the Savior.

Since honesty is one of the themes of this book, I need to be honest about the limitations of what I've written. No volume except the Bible itself can address every question non-Christians ask. I've chosen to focus on some key issues people are asking about today. No doubt you could think of other important topics to add. This book isn't intended as a comprehensive training manual for evangelism. It's more of a "pre-evangelism" tool—a way to get started—a springboard for further discussion about matters of faith. Many Christians don't know how to initiate conversations about God and the Bible, so they never make an attempt. I hope this book helps you move beyond square one.

Frankly, I'm also concerned that someone might read the questions posed in this book, conclude that my answers are unsatisfactory, and find his own faith shaken. While I don't want to reinforce anyone's doubts, I think there's a greater danger if we don't talk openly about questions like these. Our unbelieving friends and neighbors ponder them more than we realize, and so do many Christians (more than we often admit). Talking about doubt is the first step toward overcoming it. Besides, since Christian faith is rooted in the truth, it will stand up under close, critical examination. If you're not satisfied with my answers, that's all right—as long as you keep digging into God's Word to find better ones of your own.

One final disclaimer. Our goal isn't to win arguments, but to win souls. Hopefully this book offers some fresh insights and new ideas you'll find helpful, but no humanly devised methods will convince people to accept Christ. The basic tools of evangelism remain unchanged: truth and love, the sword of the Spirit, the good news of a living Savior who lived, died, and rose for us. Our job is to plant and water gospel seeds in hope that God will give the increase. If this book helps you do that, then the effort has been worthwhile.

Dave Faust

December 25, 1998

HOW TO USE THIS BOOK

This is a different kind of book that combines several kinds of information into one volume. It's *an apologetics book* that explains some of the reasonable evidence that supports Christian faith. It's *an evangelism book* that offers practical suggestions for making disciples among postmodern people. And it's *a storybook* that introduces us to real people and their honest questions. Furthermore, this book has been written to supplement a smaller book, *Searching for Hope.*

Searching for Hope relates seven questions asked by real people whose interest in God ranges from nonexistent to curious but cautious. By giving this small book to seekers, you can open the door for discussions about faith. *Taking Truth Next Door* can then be used (alone or in group study) to prepare yourself for further conversations with your searching friends.

Chapters three, four, five, seven, eight, ten, and eleven begin with the questions printed in *Searching for Hope,* and continue with suggested ways to answer these questions.

Take It Personally

Underlying this book are certain assumptions about the approach Christians need to use in order to communicate our faith effectively in today's world and "take truth next door."

1. It must be *a personal approach*. First Peter 3:15 is every Christian's responsibility: "But in your hearts set apart Christ as Lord. Always be prepared to give an answer to everyone who asks you to give the reason for the hope that you have. But do this with gentleness and respect." All of us can initiate conversations about spiritual issues, respond to questions posed by our non-Christian friends, and explain why we have hope. Christians need to be better equipped so we can do more than refer others to the minister or give them a book that will "answer all of their questions." Postmodern people resist evangelistic approaches that seem canned, preachy, or manipulative. To communicate the gospel, we need to "take it personally" through one-on-one interaction with people whose trust we have earned.

2. It must be *a loving approach*. This book advocates an "apologetic of love." We need to defend our faith confidently and knowledgeably. But no persuasive argument will be successful without love. "Knowledge puffs up, but love builds up" (1 Corinthians 8:1). "By this all men will know that you are my disciples, if you love one another" (John 13:35). To lead others to Christ, we first need to listen to them, hear their stories and concerns, and try to understand where they're coming from.

3. It must be *a respectful approach*. When we legitimize a friend's honest questions instead of squelching them, we fan the flame of his spiritual curiosity and open doors for constructive dialogue. No one wins when our attempts at evangelism degenerate into angry tirades and personal attacks. "And the Lord's servant must not quarrel; instead, he must be kind to everyone, able to teach, not resentful" (2 Timothy 2:24).

4. It must be *a flexible approach*. Instead of requiring you to memorize a "one-size-fits-all" evangelistic formula, this book provides a variety of questions and biblical facts you can use as talking points depending on your friend's interests.

5. It must be *a patient approach*. Nowadays, most people come to Christ as a result of an ongoing process of relationship building and honest discussion rather than a one-time encounter.

6. It must be *a biblical approach*. Whatever outreach method we employ must keep the good news of Jesus Christ foremost. While we can offer evidence to support our faith, we shouldn't count on clever human arguments to achieve what only the Spirit of God can do as he works through the inspired Word. At the same time, we can learn a lot about evangelism from

the many examples found in Scripture (particularly in the book of Acts) that illustrate how believers interacted with non-Christians in the first century.

7. It must be *a time-tested approach*. The ideas presented in this book are based on lessons I learned during more than twenty years of ministry in local churches. The material has been further refined by my years of teaching college courses in Christian evidences and church growth. I've found that when it comes to personal evangelism, nothing beats a one-on-one approach that leads seekers to the Master Teacher who can answer their questions better than anyone else.

Suggestions for Using This Book and Its Companion Volume, *Searching for Hope: Seven Honest Questions*

Before undertaking any kind of outreach effort, pray and ask for God's wisdom and guidance. Let the apostle Paul's words in Colossians 4:5, 6 guide you: "Be wise in the way you act toward outsiders; make the most of every opportunity. Let your conversation be always full of grace, seasoned with salt, so that you may know how to answer everyone."

If you want to use the material in *Taking Truth Next Door* **for your own personal growth . . .**

• Read through the lesson plans provided on pages 215 through 256, especially the *Reflect* sections.

• If possible, discuss these lessons with an accountability partner.

If you want to use the material in *Taking Truth Next Door* **to help you reach out to your friends in evangelism . . .**

•Buy several copies of *Searching for Hope: Seven Honest Questions.* (These small books are available in packages of six.)

• Give a copy of *Searching for Hope* to one or more of your unchurched friends at work or school, to a neighbor, or even to a family member. Say something like this: "Please read this short book (or chapter ___ of this book) and then let's get together and talk about it. I'd like to hear your reaction to the questions posed in the book." Or you might want to say, "You remind me of _____, the person described in chapter _____. Does this person's question express where you're coming from?"

• Follow up. If your friend is interested, meet with him or her for a cup of coffee and discuss the question(s) raised in *Searching for Hope*. Read the material in *Taking Truth Next Door* before you meet. In some cases, a seeker will agree to meet with you on a regular basis for a one-on-one Bible study and discussion.

• Better yet, invite your friend (and others) to attend a discussion group for seekers, using the lesson plans provided on pages 215-256. This book can open doors for discussion about some of the basic questions non-Christians ask, but it can't take the place of ongoing Bible study and discipleship that help enfold a person into God's family, the church.

If you want to use *Taking Truth Next Door* **as a study guide for believers . . .**
• Purchase enough copies of *Searching for Hope* so that each member of the class or group can have at least three copies—one for his own use and at least two to share with friends.

• Purchase one copy of *Taking Truth Next Door* for each member of the class or group.

• Follow the lesson plans provided.

The lesson plans are designed so you can use them "as is." If you prefer, you may photocopy the lesson plan pages (for classroom use only).

CHAPTER 1

QUESTIONS PEOPLE ASK

For as long as I can remember, I have asked a lot of questions. Growing up on a southern Ohio farm, I liked it when my parents took my two brothers and me on trips in our 1962 Ford Galaxie 500. As we drove along, I'd fire question after question at my dad from my perch in the backseat. (I'm sure he appreciated them greatly.) "Where are we going, Dad?" "How much longer, Dad?" "Can we stop at Dairy Queen, Dad?"

I was fond of the "why" questions, too. "Why is the sky blue?" "Why do we have to go to bed so early?" "Why do my older brothers get to do things I don't get to do?"

It's interesting how things work out. As the years went by, my wife and I had three children of our own, and now *I'm* on the receiving end of the endless questions.

Serious Questions

My youngest daughter Mindy is especially curious. She asks questions like "What do lightning bugs do during the day?" and "Why don't birds get electrocuted when they sit on power lines?" But not all of her questions are childish. One night as I tucked her into bed, she looked up at me thoughtfully and asked, "Dad, how do we know that Jesus is real?" I was glad to see her spiritual curiosity, but inwardly I breathed an anxious sigh, for I recalled the painful questions I wrestled with in my own heart when I was a young man.

Even though I was brought up in a Christian home, the teen years filled my mind with heavy questions. "How do I know there really is a God?" "Does it really make sense to be a Christian?" "What about evolution?" "How do I know the Bible is true?" "Why do I believe what I believe?" "Is my faith really my own, or is it merely a reflection of my parents' faith?"

I don't think my spiritual curiosity was particularly unusual. At age seventeen my mind was absorbed with girls, basketball, music, and cars—but I also wondered about deeper issues. Frustrated with the hypocrisy I sensed in a lot of Christians, I hungered to know: Is Christianity a worthy choice, or is it simply a waste of time? As a teen, I'd never heard of H. G. Wells. But I would have been intrigued by his comment: "If there is no God, nothing matters. If there is a God, nothing else matters." Instinctively I understood that if a God who created the universe really existed, he deserved more than half-hearted lip service on Sunday morning. If God really loved me—if he heard and answered prayer—then I wanted to know him and converse with him. If God really guided the production of an inspired book filled with divine wisdom and truth, I wanted to understand it. If life after death was more than a fantasy, I wanted to claim it as my own and help others discover it too.

But I also dared to look at the other side of the coin. Frankly, I reasoned, if God was nothing but a hoax and a lie, then I didn't want to waste my life in religious game-playing.

During the summer before my senior year in high school, I began working for a tall, tan, muscular fellow named Ray. Now, Ray wasn't a theologian or a philosopher. He was a bricklayer, and a good one at that. He built houses and walls, fireplaces and chimneys. Ray gave me a job mixing mortar and carrying cement blocks for $2.50 an hour—not bad money for a seventeen-year-old in 1971. As we drove from job to job in Ray's red Chevy pickup truck, I asked him a lot of questions about life and faith. He didn't have all the answers, but he listened, and I listened to him as well. Ray's calm assurance about his faith earned my respect, and I noticed that the rugged men who worked for him tried to clean up their language when they were around him. I found Ray's commitment to Christ oddly reassuring, even though I continued to struggle with my own private doubts.

Sometimes that's all it takes—just one real Christian who really believes, just one person living a consistent life of faith—to make a difference in a seeker's heart.

At age eighteen I decided to attend a Christian college, not because I wanted to become a minister but because I wanted to find answers to satisfy my growing curiosity about my faith. During those college years I experienced the wonderful reality that God "rewards those who earnestly seek him" (Hebrews 11:6). Sometimes the rewards came in the form of wise words from godly instructors who patiently guided me through my valleys of uncertainty. They made me feel as if I were riding in the backseat of my dad's 1962 Ford again as I asked question after question and soaked up anything that might help me understand or explain my faith.

And along the way, an interesting thing happened. The more answers I discovered, the more I found myself wanting to help other people with *their* spiritual journeys.

So I became a minister—and ended up in New York, of all places! I was a farm boy from Ohio, suddenly thrown into the challenging fray of a diverse urban culture. In my daily work I encountered skeptics, agnostics, free-thinkers, and New Agers. I met Jehovah's Witnesses, Mormons, and followers of Sun Myung Moon's Unification Church. I got acquainted with Jewish rabbis who seemed shocked when they learned that I honestly believe Jesus is the Messiah promised in the Hebrew Scriptures.

After ten years in New York, I moved to Cincinnati to teach in a Christian college; and during that time I also led in planting University Christian Church, an urban congregation with a strong outreach to university students. There I dialogued with Hindus and Muslims, preached to eager-minded young scholars studying engineering, mathematics, music, and art, and led a small group attended by graduate students from the university medical school. As I listened to their comments, I discovered an interesting fact. My new friends were asking the same kinds of questions I'd started asking as a teenager: "Is the Christian life really worth living?" "Is God for real?" "Is the Bible true?"

Questions Jesus Faced

Along the way, as I continued to study my Bible, I also noticed how often people asked *Jesus* the tough questions.

Jesus' first recorded words in the New Testament were a response to the question of his mother, Mary. His family had gone up to Jerusalem to celebrate the Passover feast when he was twelve years old, and his parents inadvertently left him behind while they traveled a day's journey back toward their home in Nazareth. After searching for three days, they finally found him in the temple courts, sitting among the teachers who were amazed at his understanding and his answers. With a motherly combination of relief and rebuke, Mary asked, "Son, why have you treated us like this? Your father and I have been anxiously searching for you." And Jesus answered her question with two questions of his own: "Why were you searching for me? Didn't you know I had to be in my Father's house?" (Luke 2:49). Mary and Joseph didn't understand what he meant, but young Jesus hadn't responded to them with insolence or rebellion. Despite his brilliance—he was the rare twelve-year-old who really did know more than his parents!—Jesus returned to Nazareth and continued to honor and obey Mary and Joseph (Luke 2:50-52).

During Jesus' public ministry, people constantly asked him questions. Some questions were *sincere*, asked by people who at least appeared to have a genuine interest in the truth. "What must I do to inherit eternal life?" asked the rich young ruler (Mark 10:17)—a good question, even though the young man later responded by walking away from the Lord. "How can a man be born when he is old?" wondered Nicodemus (John 3:4)—and Jesus' intriguing answer proved convincing enough that Nicodemus later defended Jesus and apparently became a disciple (John 7:50-52; 19:38-42). When they came upon a man who'd been born blind, Jesus' disciples asked, "Who sinned, this man or his parents, that he was born blind?" (John 9:2). We might not have phrased the question quite the same way, but it's a legitimate issue nonetheless. Who hasn't wondered about the problem of evil and the cause of suffering?

Others came to Jesus with *insincere* questions cleverly designed to trap him in his words and make him look foolish. His debates with shrewd, hostile opponents make one of today's presidential press conferences look mild by comparison. Trying to stir up doubt and controversy, the Pharisees asked Jesus' disciples, "Why does your teacher eat with tax collectors and 'sinners'?" (Matthew 9:11). Touching the sensitive nerves of nationalistic pride and hatred of taxation, others asked Jesus, "Is it right to pay taxes to Caesar or not?" (Matthew 22:17). Even the important question, "Teacher, which is the greatest commandment in the Law?" came from a lawyer whose main intent was simply to test Jesus (Matthew 22:34-36). The Lord answered each inquiry with amazing wisdom and disarming honesty.

Questions Jesus Asked

Jesus was good at *asking* questions, too. He began a life-changing conversation with the Samaritan woman at the well with a simple request: "Will you give me a drink?" (John 4:7), and before their encounter was over she began to comprehend what he meant when he offered her "living water." In his Sermon on the Mount, Jesus humorously illustrated the futility of judging others by asking, "Why do you look at the speck of sawdust in your brother's eye and pay no attention to the plank in your own eye?" (Matthew 7:3). In response to the query, "Who is my neighbor?" Jesus told his well-known story about the good Samaritan, and then drove home the point with a question of his own: "Which of these three [the priest, Levite, or Samaritan] do you think was a neighbor to the man who fell into the hands of robbers?" (Luke 10:36). So adept was Jesus at responding to public scrutiny and debate that the day finally came when "no one dared to ask him any more questions" (Matthew 22:46).

Jesus even knew when *not* to answer a question! He amazed Governor Pilate when he refused to answer the accusations false witnesses flung at him (Mark 15:5; John 19:9). Likewise, during Jesus' trial, King Herod, who hoped to see him perform some miracle, "plied him with many questions, but Jesus gave him no answer" (Luke 23:8, 9). Pardon the mixed metaphor, but to engage in serious dialogue with an old "fox" like Herod would be nothing more than throwing pearls to pigs (Luke 13:31-33; Matthew 7:6).

On one occasion, the Jewish chief priests and elders demanded, "By what authority are you doing these things? And who gave you this authority?" Jesus wisely replied, "I will also ask you one question. If you answer me, I will tell you by what authority I am doing these things. John's baptism—where did it come from? Was it from heaven, or from men?" Good question. But instead of answering it immediately, Jesus' adversaries slinked away and held a committee meeting. They discussed it among themselves and said, "If we say, 'From heaven,' he will ask, 'Then why didn't you believe him?' But if we say, 'From men'—we are afraid of the people, for they all hold that John was a prophet." So they dismissed their meeting, marched back to Jesus, and announced their conclusion: "We don't know." And Jesus said, "Neither will I tell you by what authority I am doing these things" (Matthew 21:23-27). End of discussion!

Jesus wisely understood the balance expressed in two proverbs: "Do not answer a fool according to his folly, or you will be like him yourself" (Proverbs

26:4)—in other words, there are times when it's best not to answer a question asked with impure motives. But sometimes we must speak up. "Answer a fool according to his folly, or he will be wise in his own eyes" (Proverbs 26:5).

When necessary, Jesus was always ready to wrestle with tough issues in the give-and-take of public dialogue. He didn't shrink back from debate, but always handled himself with wisdom and grace. So should we.

Questions We Will Face

Since we are called to follow in the footsteps of Jesus, we need to look carefully at the kinds of questions he faced, for they serve as prototypes for the kinds of questions we may encounter as well. I've discovered that people usually ask questions that fall into four or five major categories.

1. **Philosophical questions.** "Wait a minute," you may say. "I'm not a philosopher. I probably know more about Play-Doh® than Plato! I don't sit around pondering the meaning of life." Don't sell yourself short. You don't have to be a card-carrying member of the American Philosophical Association to wonder about questions like "Where is the God of justice?" (Malachi 2:17), "If a man dies, will he live again?" (Job 14:14), or even "What is truth?" (John 18:38). Admittedly, some Christians don't like to talk about philosophy, because the word rarely appears in the Bible, and when it does, it's used in a negative sense to describe hollow and deceptive human ideas that oppose the revealed Word of God (see 1 Corinthians 1:20 and Colossians 2:8). But at its root, the word *philosopher* simply means "lover of wisdom" (Greek *philos* plus *sophia*). And since God wants us all to be lovers of wisdom (as the book of Proverbs makes clear), we need to pay attention to the philosophical trends of our culture so we'll be prepared to think wisely and "take captive every thought to make it obedient to Christ" (2 Corinthians 10:5).

2. **Theological questions.** You don't consider yourself a theologian? Neither did Tony. When I met him, he was employed as a detective for the New York City Transit Police. A tall, tough-looking individual with a thick Italian accent and a gun strapped to his ankle, Tony wasn't exactly St. Thomas Aquinas. His daily work meant investigating subway suicides and muggings. But when Tony and his wife started coming to my home for Bible studies, their questions were hard-hitting and heartfelt: "Why is there so much evil in the world? How can anybody be hopeful anymore, when

people can be so cruel? Does God really care?" Accustomed to seeing life at its worst, Tony couldn't be satisfied with a naive, unquestioning faith.

Jesus dealt deftly with tricky theological questions like, "Lord, are only a few people going to be saved?" (Luke 13:23, 24). And in his ministry with new Christians, the apostle Paul found it necessary to respond to numerous inquiries about doctrinal issues like the Lord's Supper, spiritual gifts, and the resurrection (see 1 Corinthians 11–15). To handle questions like these, we need to be diligent students of Scripture who "correctly handles the word of truth" (2 Timothy 2:15).

3. **Ethical questions.** First-century Christians wondered, "Is it better to marry or remain single? Is it OK to eat meat that previously was offered as a sacrifice to idols?" (see 1 Corinthians 7, 8). Like them, Christians today continue to face questions about tough issues like abortion, assisted suicide, genetic engineering, and homosexuality.

4. **Hypothetical questions.** There always have been some people around who ask questions simply for argument's sake, not because they really want to know the answer. Have you ever encountered someone like that? Perhaps it's a coworker filled with casual curiosity who quizzes you about your faith but always manages to shrug off your invitations to attend a Bible study or church service. Maybe it's a classmate who loves to get the professor to "chase rabbits" by diverting the class lecture down some point-less side alley. Or maybe you have a skeptical friend who delights in asking theoretical brainteasers like "If God can do anything, can he make a rock so big he can't lift it?"

Some folks simply enjoy a stimulating argument. They would agree with the eighteenth century philosopher Joseph Joubert, who said, "It is better to debate a question without settling it than to settle a question without debat-ing it."

Jesus faced a classic hypothetical question when some men came to him and described the following situation:

"'Teacher,' they said, 'Moses told us that if a man dies without having children, his brother must marry the widow and have children for him. Now there were seven brothers among us. The first one married and died, and since he had no children, he left his wife to his brother. The same thing happened to the second and third brother, right on down to the seventh.

NEW TESTAMENT CHRISTIANS WHO DEFENDED THEIR FAITH

PAUL

• He "proved," "explained," and "gave evidence" that Jesus was the Christ (Acts 9:22; 17:3).

• He often "reasoned" with others about the gospel (Acts 17:2, 3, 17; 18:4, 19; 19:8).

• He considered himself ready to "defend" or "confirm" the gospel (Philippians 1:7, 16).

• When people believed his message, they were "persuaded" (Acts 17:4; 18:4).

PETER AND JOHN

• They insisted, "We cannot help speaking about what we have seen and heard" (Acts 4:20).

• Peter urged, "Always be prepared to give an answer to everyone who asks you to give the reason for the hope that you have" (1 Peter 3:15).

• John wrote, "We proclaim to you what we have seen and heard" (1 John 1:3).

APOLLOS

• He "vigorously refuted the Jews in public debate, proving from the Scriptures that Jesus was the Christ" (Acts 18:28).

The question isn't "*Did* New Testament Christians defend their faith?" but simply, "*How* did they do so (and how can we)?"

Finally, the woman died. Now then, at the resurrection, whose wife will she be of the seven, since all of them were married to her?'"

A complicated scenario indeed! But wait a minute—who were the people who came to Jesus with this clever question? They were "the Sadducees, who say there is no resurrection." Here they were, asking a complicated riddle about life after death, when they had already presupposed that no resurrection was possible in the first place (Matthew 22:23-28)!

Cutting to the heart of the real issue, Jesus replied, "You are in error because you do not know the Scriptures or the power of God." However, Jesus didn't evade their question. At the resurrection, he explained, "people will neither marry nor be given in marriage; they will be like the angels in heaven" (and angels, evidently, are quite content to be single!). Then the Lord quickly returned to the bigger issue: "But about the resurrection of the dead—have you not read what God said to you, 'I am the God of Abraham, the God of Isaac, and the God of Jacob'?" In other words, when God spoke to Moses at the burning bush hundreds of years after Abraham, Isaac, and Jacob died, he still could identify himself as their God—for these men were still living in God's presence even after death. Jesus then put to rest this hypothetical question when he pointed out that God "is not the God of the dead but of the living." And the crowds "were astonished at his teaching" (Matthew 22:29-33).

5. **Personal questions.** At some point, everyone wonders about the significance of his or her own life—and death. The book of Ecclesiastes begins with this brutally honest refrain: "'Meaningless! Meaningless!' says the Teacher. 'Utterly meaningless! Everything is meaningless!'" (Ecclesiastes 1:2). Let's face it. Life does seem meaningless at times—especially if there's no divine reference point to help it all make sense. Many of our friends and neighbors face each new morning with the kind of inner "dis-ease" (a lack of ease) Moses warned that the people of ancient Israel would experience if they denied God: "There the Lord will give you an anxious mind, eyes weary with longing, and a despairing heart. You will live in constant suspense, filled with dread both night and day, never sure of your life. In the morning you will say, 'If only it were evening!' and in the evening, 'If only it were morning!'" (Deuteronomy 28:65-67).

Anxiety and discontent are nothing new. But "dis-eases" like these have reached a new level of intensity in today's culture. In extreme cases, despair boils over like a volcano when misguided youths explode in violence and open fire on teachers and classmates at school. More often, the despair just lingers like a cold fog, stealing hope from the hearts of young and old who sense that life should consist of more than the routines of work to do and bills to pay, punctuated by the short-lived, counterfeit joy of occasional parties and holidays. *There must be more to life than that,* they think. And they're right.

Honest Answers

While serving as a minister in New York, I received a phone call one day from a woman named Nana. "You don't know me," she began, "but I've heard that you're willing to speak to different groups about Christian faith."

"Yes," I replied, privately wondering what I was about to get myself into!

"My husband, Charles, and I have a little group of friends who share a common interest in finding out more about different faiths," Nana continued. "Would you be willing to come and talk to our group about what it means to be a Christian?"

"Sure," I said. And a few days later, my wife and I sat in Charles and Nana's house dining on authentic Greek food—lamb, feta cheese, stuffed grape leaves. After dinner we headed downstairs to their large basement, where to my amazement, Charles and Nana's "little" group of friends continued to grow until about fifty people crowded into the room and sat on folding chairs. As they greeted me, some of the guests identified themselves as atheists, others as disenchanted Catholics; some were Jewish; others said they were Greek Orthodox; and others simply called themselves seekers.

Soon, our hosts quieted everyone down and Charles announced, "Everybody, this is Dave Faust. He's come here tonight with his wife, Candy, to talk to us about his faith as a Christian." Then turning to me warmly, he said, "Dave, tell us what you believe."

Now, I hadn't prepared a fancy speech! Thinking quickly, I came up with a simple outline that focused on three key points: why I love Jesus, why I love the Bible, and why I love the church. Not particularly controversial topics—or so I thought. But after I spoke for about half an hour, the group kept me standing on the floor for another ninety minutes of polite but vigorous questions and answers. Like Paul at Athens, I was "bringing some strange ideas to [their] ears, and [they wanted] to know what they mean"

SECOND-CENTURY CHRISTIANS WHO DEFENDED THEIR FAITH

Many early Christians faced misunderstanding and opposition. They were accused of atheism because they refused to join in the official emperor worship demanded by Rome. They were accused of cannibalism because unbelievers misunderstood the Lord's Supper and spread rumors about those strange people who gathered to "eat the body" and "drink the blood" of Christ. Some even accused Christians of sexual immorality because they loved one another deeply and ate together in meals called "love feasts," and perverted minds were quick to assume the worst about what happened there. Others charged them with causing rebellion against the Roman government because Christians insisted "Jesus (not Caesar) is Lord." According to the New Testament, believers were accused of "advocating customs unlawful for . . . Romans to accept or practice" (Acts 16:21), and saying "there is another king, one called Jesus" (Acts 17:7).

A thoughtful group of second-century Christians rose up to defend the church against these verbal attacks. Known in church history as "The Apologists," brave men like Quadratus, Aristides, and Athenagoras defended and explained their faith. The best known of these Apologists was Justin (A.D. 100-165), who wrote a bold defense of the Christians and addressed it to the emperor, Antonius Pius. Justin's *First Apology* argued that Christians were politically harmless and explained what really happened at their worship services: they sang, prayed, shared the Lord's Supper, baptized their converts, and urged good citizenship. Justin eventually was arrested, however. He defended his faith before a judge, then was executed. We know him best as "Justin Martyr." It wasn't easy to defend the Christian faith in those days, nor is it today.

(Acts 17:20). By the time my wife and I said our goodbyes and left that night (with an invitation to return again at a future date) I was more convinced than ever that spiritual curiosity is alive and well in our culture.

I've never forgotten those curious questioners in Charles and Nana's basement. I think Simon Peter had people like them in mind when he urged,

"But in your hearts set apart Christ as Lord. Always be prepared to give an answer to everyone who asks you to give the reason for the hope that you have" (1 Peter 3:15). *The reason for our hope.* That's what our friends and neighbors seek from us. Not impressive-sounding intellectual arguments. Not some canned, artificial evangelistic sales pitch. Not hollow, pious-sounding religious answers to questions no one's really asking.

They want to know why they should bother to get up in the morning and face another day. They want to know if God is real—and if he is, what difference does he make in ordinary life? In their honest moments of introspection, they want to know if life after death is more than just a pipe dream.

To people like these, we Christians dare to make an audacious claim. We say there is indeed a God who is there, and that the reality of God makes all the difference.

We say there's hope.

People like Charles and Nana—people in your family and your neighborhood—want to know why.

We need to give them honest answers. We need to take the truth next door.

QUESTIONS FOR PERSONAL REFLECTION:

1. The thought of defending my faith makes me feel . . .

2. One situation in which I defended my faith was . . .

3. One question I'd like to ask God is . . .

RESOURCES FOR FURTHER STUDY:

Norman Geisler and Ron Brooks, *When Skeptics Ask* (Victor, 1990).

Gregory Boyd and Edward Boyd, *Letters From a Skeptic* (Victor, 1993).

CHAPTER 2

COMMUNICATING OUR FAITH TO 21ST-CENTURY PEOPLE

"I've been talking to people about Christ for years," says Ron, "but lately it seems like I've been running up against some new roadblocks when I try to share my faith."

"When I try to back up my ideas with Scripture, my friends shrug and say, 'That's just your opinion,'" sighs Carol. "They say the Bible is outdated, and that we all can just make up our own ideas about what's right and wrong. Why doesn't anyone seem to respect the Bible as the Word of God anymore?"

Jenny agrees. "My friends at work seem interested when I talk about God," she points out, "but they get really defensive whenever I talk about *obeying* God—or even going to church. What are they afraid of? Why do they put up so many walls?"

Basic human needs will always remain the same. We're made in God's image, and to paraphrase Augustine, "Our hearts are restless until they find rest in God." We're sinners who need God's forgiveness and grace. But a lot of people these days seem pretty resistant to the old, old story of Jesus and his love. What's going on, anyway?

"Be prepared in season and out of season," the apostle Paul told his young friend Timothy (2 Timothy 4:2). But what season is it right now?

Students prepare for exams, athletes prepare for games, soldiers prepare for battle. What challenges should Christians prepare to face as we take the good news to today's—and tomorrow's—world?

In the days of King David, some capable men from the family line of Issachar rose to prominence in Israel. These men of Issachar "understood the times and knew what Israel should do" (1 Chronicles 12:32). How well do we understand our times? Do we know what God's people should do? It's important to analyze the cultural context in which God calls us to communicate our faith. After all, as someone has said, if you want to lead a lost sheep to Jesus, it helps to know what bush the sheep is stuck in.

Evangelism's New Landscape

Analysts often characterize our current culture as "postmodern," but to be honest, words like postmodernism give me a headache.[1] The experts can't even agree on what the term means.

Some see it mainly as *an era* or a time period. Theologian Thomas C. Oden, for example, argues that the "modern age" began in 1789 with the French Revolution when French patriots stormed the wall of the Bastille Prison in Paris, and ended in 1989 with the dismantling of Germany's Berlin Wall.[2] We've been in the postmodern era ever since.

Others see postmodernism more as *a belief system.* During the modern age, most people assumed rational knowledge was certain, objective, good, and attainable. Modernists expected science and education to lead to a better society and solve many of humanity's problems. Postmodernists, however, have become disillusioned by science and education. They recognize that human reason can take us only so far. Postmodernists assume that truth is not necessarily rational or objective; often they are more interested in emotion and intuition than in logical proofs. And they've grown up in a culture saturated for the last twenty or thirty years with the assumption that nothing is absolutely true. As professor Allan Bloom of the University of Chicago put it, "There is one thing a professor can be absolutely certain of: almost every student entering the university believes, or says he believes, that truth is relative."[3]

Still others think postmodernism mainly means *an attitude* or mood. Do you see any of the following characteristics in people you know?

1. *Pessimism and anxiety.* In the early 1900s, modernists made optimistic, almost utopian predictions about a bright future to be ushered in by education and technology. But after two World Wars, the Holocaust, Vietnam, and endless scandals in Washington, DC, it's harder to be optimistic today. Generally, today's young adults can expect lower incomes, a higher percentage paid to Social Security than any generation before them, and a slower transition to adulthood—which often means more years spent living at home with their parents. As one observer notes, "When the Boomers were twentysomething, they were ready to save the world; Busters feel they are barely able to save themselves."[4]

2. *Fear of commitment.* Since 1955, the median age for marriage in the United States has risen from twenty-one to twenty-six. Distrusting institutions and disliking authority figures, postmodern people are much more cautious about making commitments. They view political parties and religious groups with increasing cynicism. Local church membership is often considered unimportant or irrelevant. According to Alan Ahlgrim, a church-planting strategist who ministers with Rocky Mountain Christian Church in Colorado, "In the twenty-first century, 'spirituality' will be up; church attendance will be down."

3. *Longing for authenticity.* When I helped to plant Cincinnati's University Christian Church in 1989, we chose as one of our slogans, "Real People, Real Faith." Without fully comprehending the depth of it, we had stumbled onto an important touchstone for communicating with today's generation. Ironically, the same culture that disputes the very existence of "truth" is searching desperately for people who are "real."

As Ahlgrim points out, "Postmodernists don't seek perfection from their leaders; they seek identification with them."

After growing up amid headlines about hypocritical television evangelists and crooked politicians, exposed to hundreds of advertising messages per day, and weary of telephone solicitations read from a script, people in our culture respond with understandable caution when confronted with a message we say will change their lives. But they also respond with surprise and delight when someone shows them authentic love with "no strings attached." They expect phoniness; they suspect sales pitches; they respect honesty.

4. *Desire for community.* "Relationship" remains a key buzzword. Surrounded by computers and calculators, bombarded by talk radio shows

and talking-head TV news reports, our neighbors still want to experience what the Bible calls *koinonia* or "fellowship"—a shared life, a shared journey of faith and love. In our fast-paced world of fax machines and Federal Express, we long for meaningful connections with others who will listen, care, and pray for us.

Behind all the e-mail addresses and the shallow chitchat are faces, feelings, and families—real people who can't be content in isolation. Ahlgrim says, "High tech means [people need] high touch."

5. *Dislike for dogmatism.* Eighty-one percent of Generation Xers do not believe in absolute truth.[5] No wonder so many are reluctant to receive any message that sounds preachy, narrow, or intolerant. The one Bible verse most people in our culture can quote? "Do not judge, or you too will be judged" (Matthew 7:1).

6. *Interest in the arts.* Music has always been in fashion, but today it sparkles with crystal clarity from convenient CD players and state-of-the-art personal sound systems. Attention spans are shorter, and communication styles tend to be more right-brained, nonlinear, and feelings oriented than in the past. Visually oriented young people who cut their teeth on a TV remote control may not want to slow down and read a serious book or engage in a logical debate.

7. *Acceptance of diversity.* In the 1970s it was considered innovative when TV shows like "The Jeffersons" and "Sanford and Son" featured African-American stars. But surrounded by increasing numbers of immigrants from Asia and Latin America, and brought up with "The Cosby Show" at the top of the ratings, today's generation takes ethnic diversity for granted.

The bottom line? These subtle but profound cultural trends have changed the evangelistic landscape considerably in the last two decades. No wonder Christians run into some new roadblocks when we try to share our faith!

Christian apologist Ravi Zacharias sums up the results of postmodernism in five major shifts:

1. Philosophy has moved to the existential.
2. Art has moved to the sensual.
3. Religion has moved to the mystical.

4. Education has moved to the skeptical.

5. Individuals have moved to the transcendental (that is, each person acts as if he is his own "god").[6]

OBSTACLES OR OPPORTUNITIES?

It's tempting for Christians to react to all of this with dismay or even despair. Some believers talk as if our task is impossible—as if our neighbors are unreachable. Yet in many places large numbers of seekers are coming to Christ. Maybe it's time to quote the old proverb, "The man who says it cannot be done should not interrupt the man doing it."

The Scripture urges, "Let us not become weary in doing good, for at the proper time we will reap a harvest if we do not give up" (Galatians 6:9). Instead of giving up, we need to ask, *"What does it take to communicate the gospel of Christ in a culture where many of our neighbors no longer take the Christian worldview for granted?"*

Nearly two thousand years ago, the apostle Paul confronted the complex culture of Ephesus—a city of more than 250,000 residents—and he decided to stay there for a while "because a great door for effective work has opened to me, and there are many who oppose me" (1 Corinthians 16:9).

"Open doors"? Yes, for Ephesus lay at the center of a network of Roman roads, enjoyed the greatest harbor in its region, and served as a political and economic gateway to all of Asia Minor.

"Many who oppose me"? Yes, for Ephesus was filled with sexual immorality, occultism, and pagan religion.

Open doors and opposition often go together. We must have the faith to focus on the open doors, not the forces that oppose us. It's almost as if Paul relished the opportunity to serve Christ in a place where obstacles abounded. The darker the darkness, the brighter even a small light can shine.

The Challenges

If you want to shine for Christ among twenty-first century people, here are some trends to understand.

DRIFTING FROM
THE TRUTH

According to Christian philosopher Dr. Norman Geisler, in the twentieth century, departures from biblical faith took two major directions. Modernism (theological liberalism) led to a skeptical, analytical view of God and the Bible, while postmodernism tends toward more of a mystical, experiential approach. Modernism "invaded" America from Europe with the rationalistic philosophies of secular humanism; postmodernism "invaded" America from Asia with the pantheistic New Age philosophies of Eastern religions like Hinduism. Modernism stressed education (the great frontier: outer space); postmodernism stresses meditation (the great frontier: inner space).[7]

MODERNISM	**POST-MODERNISM**
↓	↓
Skepticism	**Mysticism**
↓	↓
Secular Humanism	**New Age, Pantheism**
↓	↓
"Invaded" America from Europe	**"Invaded" America from Asia**
↓	↓
Stressed Education	**Stresses Meditation**

People are still interested in spirituality, but they are attempting to redefine what spirituality means. While many react to Christianity with a "been there, done that" shrug, there's a renewed fascination with "spiritual" topics like angels, prayer, forgiveness, and meditation.

People are still interested in the Bible, but often they do not really know what it says. In our culture most people own Bibles, but how many people really study God's Word with consistency and depth? Biblical illiteracy is rampant among adults, and as Sunday school attendance has declined over the last two decades, fewer children have learned even the basic lessons of the Bible. Ninety-three percent of American homes contain at least one

Bible. But fifty-four percent of Americans can't name the authors of the four Gospels; sixty-three percent don't know what a Gospel is; fifty-eight percent can't name five of the Ten Commandments; and ten percent think Joan of Arc was Noah's wife.[8]

Additionally, in recent years postmodern scholars have applied new approaches to biblical interpretation that question the ability of human language to convey accurate meaning to the reader. (Ironically, scholars write and sell five-hundred-page books to persuade us that language is ultimately meaningless!)

The good news? Many of our friends and neighbors own copies of the Bible and possess a healthy curiosity about it. The bad news? As a whole, our culture no longer stands willing to accept the Bible as a clear, authoritative guide for understanding what is right and wrong.

People still long for meaningful personal relationships, but have lost confidence in traditional family ties. Divorce, sexual abuse, and other dysfunctions in the home have left huge scars on our culture, making it more difficult for Christians to explain what we mean when we speak of the church as "the family of God"—and even more crucial that we model healthy relationships in our own homes and congregations.

People are increasingly committed to the concept of pluralism. In one sense, pluralism merely refers to the growing diversity of race, heritage, religion, and value systems in Western culture, and the value of toleration for this diversity. It's even engraved on our coins and bills: *"E pluribus unum"*—"out of the many, one." American Christians have flourished in our free land where various ethnic groups find freedom to live and worship as they choose.

But in a postmodern world, this pluralism has a new wrinkle. Now, many people understand pluralism to mean an insistence that no belief system can claim to be superior to any other.[9] As a result, our neighbors find themselves confronted with a bewildering variety of competing religions—a spiritual buffet where you can choose whatever soul food you like. The cover of *Life* magazine (December 1998) asked, "When You Think of God, What Do You See?" The author of the accompanying article concluded, "I don't confine myself to the faith of my fathers anymore. All the religions are spread before me, a great spiritual smorgasbord, and I'll help myself, thank you."[10]

As theologian D.A. Carson observes in his critique of postmodern thought, The Gagging of God, "Nowadays . . . if any religion claims that in some measure other religions are wrong, a line has been crossed and resentment is immediately stirred up. . . . Exclusiveness is the one religious idea that cannot be tolerated."[11]

The Open Doors

Do these trends sound like obstacles, or opportunities? Certainly they present some challenges to today's Christian. But Jesus Christ hasn't lost his power. He is "the same, yesterday and today and forever" (Hebrews 13:8). What if we adopt a positive approach and look for some open doors amid the challenges of postmodernism?

Today's spiritual curiosity may be misguided, but it is a good thing. Many are recognizing and abandoning the hollow, empty religious traditions and stubborn denominational loyalties that have held sway in our culture for decades. Isn't it good that most of our neighbors still believe God answers prayer, and that they're questioning the rationalism and naturalism that long have held Western culture in their grip?

Isn't it encouraging to see that people still hunger for genuine Christian love? Our love must be demonstrated in real life. Can we host effective small groups in our homes, build one-on-one friendships with seekers, and create mentoring programs in which older Christians or successfully married couples take younger people under their wings and support them with love and kindness? Can we address the current fascination with art through coffee houses, drama presentations, and quality music? Can we find ways to bring more Christian input into the media?

Can we learn to communicate cross-culturally and reach across ethnic lines to build bridges for the gospel? Can we develop preaching and teaching styles that include thought-provoking stories and allow for discussion, interaction, and feedback? Can we develop personal evangelism methods that build trust over time instead of demanding immediate decisions? Can we learn not only to answer the question, "Is there a God?" but also explain "Which God?"

In Can Man Live Without God? Ravi Zacharias points out three levels on which philosophical dialogue occurs: theory, art (or media such as TV, movies, and music), and *"table talk"* (the ordinary conversation that happens around the kitchen table, in restaurants and dorm rooms). On the level of theory, Zacharias insists, we need to argue vigorously and persuasively for the truth. Through the arts, we need to illustrate the truth. Around the kitchen table, we need to apply the truth to life.[12]

Speaking the Truth in Love

Mitra was brought up in a multicultural home (her dad was a Muslim), and her husband Craig received a nominal exposure to Christianity as a boy; but neither of them felt settled in their faith.

One day they visited a worship service at the church where I was preaching at the time. The church's youth minister, Dan Giese, and his wife, Vivian, befriended them. They rode bikes together in the mornings. Other friends from the church, Mark Taylor and Tom Powell, visited in their home and answered some of their questions. Each Sunday they listened intently to my sermons. Finally one Sunday, Craig and Mitra walked forward at the end of the worship service to declare their desire to accept Christ as their Savior and Lord. As we prepared for their baptisms, I asked what had made the difference as they considered their decision. Their answer was simple and certain: "Friends who cared enough to get to know us and help us learn about Christ."

Come to think of it, the Bible tells us to "speak the truth in love" (Ephesians 4:15). That's a time-tested method that works in any culture—even in a changing world where real people are searching for honest answers.

QUESTIONS FOR PERSONAL REFLECTION

1. What changes have you observed in our culture during the last ten years? Which ones do you consider positive? Which ones do you consider negative?

2. Do you think these changes affect the way Christians need to communicate the good news of Christ? If so, how? If not, why not?

RESOURCES FOR FURTHER STUDY

David S. Dockery, editor. *The Challenge of Postmodernism* (Victor, 1995).

William Mahedy and Janet Bernardi, *A Generation Alone* (InterVarsity, 1994).

James W. Sire, *The Universe Next Door* (InterVarsity, 1976, 3rd ed. 1997). This book has been around for a long time, but it still has an eye-opening ability to give Christians a greater awareness of the importance of a person's worldview—and it can help us communicate with others who have rejected our Christian worldview.

FOOTNOTES

[1] I venture to offer this chapter's analysis of postmodernism with an important caution: Many people in our culture resent any effort to label or categorize them. Consider, for example, the worn-out expression "Generation X," the label for the Baby Busters born in the 1960s and 70s. The unknown factor "X" carries a negative connotation of blankness, blandness, a lack of identity, and a sense of negation. Gen Xers have been branded as lazy, cynical, amoral, soft, and financially irresponsible—by other generations that have their own flaws as well.

Let's be fair. We shouldn't paint all members of any generation with the same wide brush. In this chapter on postmodern culture, it's not my intention to slander the many hard-working, sharp-thinking, Christ-honoring young adults in our culture. Like anyone else, they deserve our respect. In fact, I think it's a good idea for Christians to avoid overusing the Gen X label, if we even choose to use it at all. In an article in *American Demographics* (December 1996, p. 27) called "Gen X–Not," Marc Spiegler advises advertisers to use the Gen X designation sarcastically or not at all. "People in their twenties," he writes, "have suffered through so many negative labelings that they're label-phobic. Any kind of label, no matter how seemingly innocuous, will go over wrong." Let's be careful not to apply sweeping generalizations to a generation that despises labels in the first place!

[2] Thomas C. Oden, "The Death of Modernity and Postmodern Evangelical Spirituality," in *The Challenge of Postmodernism*, David S. Dockery, editor (Victor, 1995), p. 24.

[3] Allan Bloom, *The Closing of the American Mind* (Simon and Schuster, 1987), p. 25.

[4] Andres Tapia, "Reaching the First Post-Christian Generation," *Christianity Today*, September 12, 1994, p. 19.

[5] Tapia, p. 21.

[6]Ravi Zacharias, "An Ancient Message, Through Modern Means, to a Postmodern Mind," *Just Thinking*, Fall, 1998, p. 3.

[7]For this comparison of modernism and postmodernism I am indebted to Dr. Norman Geisler who presented a lecture on these ideas at an apologetics conference in Orlando, Florida, on March 2, 1995.

[8]Russell Shorto, "Belief by the Numbers," *The New York Times* magazine, December 7, 1997, p. 61.

[9]Gary Philips, "Religious Pluralism in a Postmodern World," *The Challenge of Postmodernism* (Victor, 1995), p. 258.

[10]Frank McCourt, "When You Think of God, What Do You See?" *Life*, December, 1998, p. 64.

[11]D. A. Carson, *The Gagging of God: Christianity Confronts Pluralism* (Zondervan, 1996), pp. 32, 33.

[12]Ravi Zacharias, *Can Man Live Without God?* (Word, 1994), p. 14. Used by permission.

CHAPTER 3

BEN: IS THE BIBLE REALLY TRUE?

In Australia to speak for a church-sponsored retreat, I strolled into the retreat center's dining hall where lunch was being served. Still adjusting to jet lag, but eager to experience Australian culture, I sat down next to a young man and struck up a conversation. I soon learned that my new friend Ben was twenty-three years old. We talked about cricket, rugby, and American football ("footy," or "gridiron," as the Aussies call it) while sipping creamy pumpkin soup.

Ben asked me what I do in America. When I told him I'm a Bible teacher, a skeptical look swept across his face. "The Bible!" he said. "You can't believe a *thing* that's in that book!"

Calmly I said, "Well, I disagree. I think you *can* trust the Bible. But would you like to talk about this some more?"

He would, and we did. I wondered why Ben was attending the retreat in light of his skepticism. But I soon discovered that he was willing—even eager—to talk about spiritual things. And later, when I decided to write a book filled with honest questions people ask about Christian faith, I knew I needed to include Ben's story.

What's Beyond the Border?

"I'm willing to talk about these things," Ben says, "but Christians annoy me when they try to push their opinions on me. If I want to know something, I'll ask them."

"When I was about eight I went to Sunday school," he remembers. "But it started at 9:00, and I just wanted to stay in bed. The only reason I went was that my mother pushed me to go. Finally I told her I just didn't want to go anymore."

Does he believe in God? "I don't believe in him, but I don't disbelieve in him either. I have no idea whether he's real or not. I have a lot of questions about the very beginning of life—you know, how did we get here in the first place?—and about whether there is such a thing as an afterlife. I don't really believe in life after death. I don't see how we're any different from animals. As far as I know, when you die you go six feet under the ground and have worms crawling out your eyes."

"Everything has to start somewhere," Ben continues, "no matter what it is. Basically the world is like a picture in a frame. It has to have a border where it finishes. And what's outside the border, nobody knows. Nobody's been able to go that far into space."

Show Me the Facts

What is his biggest question about Christian faith? "People always say that God has told them this, that, or whatever, and I really can't see how. I guarantee that you can't actually hear him. You can't actually see him. You can't actually touch him. Some people say, 'I just know in my heart that he's told me to do this.' But the way I see it, that's just a gut feeling they have because they want to do something."

But what about the Bible? Does he believe it's God's Word?

"I don't take anybody's word for anything, straight up!" Ben immediately responds, and the swift barrage of comments that follows makes it clear that this topic hits a nerve. "If the Bible is true, prove it to me. I don't believe it. Anybody could have written it. I wouldn't trust it. There's no actual proof for it. 'Have faith'—that's what I've been told many times. But I don't believe in something I have no proof for. It doesn't matter what it is."

"A lot of what people recorded in the Bible might have actually happened," he concedes. "They might really have stoned someone or stabbed someone or whatever. But people living in those times could have just written it down and made a story out of it. The writers don't really give any proof of God.

"All other history books are based on facts—physical events that actually happened. But the whole God thing isn't like that. There's no reason to believe that God came down and spoke to Moses on the mountain. I don't see how that actually happened."

Hard to Believe

Softening his tone a bit, Ben goes on. "The Bible has a lot of good things in it that relate to life. But I don't think you can see it as reliable.

"And another thing. If you get ten different people to read the Bible, you might come out with ten different versions. Even though they're reading the same words, they interpret them in an entirely different way. That makes it harder to believe. I do have to admit that the Christian interpretation seems a lot better than some of the other ones I've heard about. But if God actually wrote the Bible, he'd make it so that everyone could understand it in the same way. If he wanted somebody to know something, he'd make it plain.

"I find it hard to believe the prophecies of the Bible,

too," he continues. "With Saddam Hussein causing trouble in the Middle East, people keep pointing to the Bible and predicting there's going to be doomsday or World War III, but nothing's happened so far."

How much of the Bible has he read? "Maybe half of it."

Ben works for a boat-building firm during the week. And despite his doubts, he still goes to church occasionally on the weekends. He has a lot of friends there, including the minister. "I'm sort of the 'resident atheist,' I guess," he smiles.

He doesn't consider himself an enemy of Christians, but at least for now he can't accept their faith as his own.

"I think the Bible tells us some good points to live by," he concludes, "but a lot of stuff in there is hard to believe. And some of it even seems impossible."

RESPONDING TO BEN

IS THE BIBLE REALLY TRUE?

Ben hasn't found the answers he craves, but at least he's asking some worthwhile questions. How can we help him trust in the reliability of God's Word? Let's start with some information about the uniqueness of the Bible–some basic facts no one can deny.

The Bible at Least Deserves a Fair Hearing

There are plenty of other religious books a person can read. But it's hard to find *any* other book (of any kind) that has the credentials of the Bible.

Jesus said his words would never pass away (Mark 13:31), and the Bible has fulfilled that prophecy. It's proved indestructible, surviving *through time* (even though most of it was written on perishable materials like leather and papyrus), *through persecution* (Roman emperors like Diocletian ordered copies of the Bible destroyed), and *through criticism* (what other book has endured so much scrutiny?). It has survived the negligence of its friends (Christians who seldom read it), the animosity of its enemies (Communist governments who have suppressed its publication and distribution), and false systems that have been built upon it (like cults that twist its meaning, or slave owners who tried to use the Bible to justify slavery). Critics keep pounding on the Bible, but like an anvil, God's Word endures while the skeptics' hammers wear out.

Individual lives and entire cultures have been changed by the Bible's message. Go to some of the world's finest educational institutions and you'll find they were founded by Bible-believing people. Visit (as I have) poverty-stricken nations like Haiti and Ethiopia, and observe the vast amount of medical and vocational assistance being offered in Jesus' name by missionaries and native Christians. Visit a law library and ponder the fact that many of our nation's laws are grounded in moral principles as old as the Ten Commandments. Consider the impact of biblical themes on great music and art, from Handel's *Messiah* to Michelangelo's statue of David. Look around at the hospitals, schools, and senior care facilities in your town begun and supported by Bible-believing people—and notice how Bible believers so often show up to help with disaster relief and other forms of community service. And who can count all the individuals whose lives have been made whole because of their faith? Even the English language has been influenced by Scripture, for many of our everyday expressions originated in the Bible: "the handwriting on the wall" (Daniel 5:5), "the apple of my eye" (Deuteronomy 32:10; Psalm 17:8), "an eye for an eye" (Exodus 21:24), "scapegoat" (Leviticus 16:6-10, 20-22), the "Good Samaritan" (Luke 10:25-37), "thorn in the flesh" (2 Corinthians 12:7).

The Bible has earned the admiration of literary scholars for its poetry (Psalm 23), its in-depth evaluation of deep subjects like the problem of evil (Job), its impartiality and frankness about its heroes and their flaws (reporting honestly about Noah's drunkenness, Abraham's lies, David's adultery, and Peter's denials of Christ). And it has received tributes from great thinkers like Abraham Lincoln ("I believe the Bible is the best gift God has ever given to man") and Sir Isaac Newton ("There are more sure marks of authenticity in the Bible than in any profane history").

While all of this will not convince a skeptic that the Bible is God's Word, it demonstrates that it's unreasonable to ignore or belittle this great Book. If God were to reveal himself through a written book, we would expect that book to be unique, and that's exactly what we find in the Bible. Its basic message is simple enough for a child to understand, yet challenging enough that a scholar can never fully plumb its depths. This Book deserves a fair hearing.[1]

Just the Facts

The famous evolutionist Aldous Huxley once said, "Facts do not cease to exist because they are ignored." Unfortunately, many people have never been shown the multitude of facts that support the truthfulness of the Bible.

Unlike legends or fairy tales that start with "once upon a time," the events recorded in the Bible occurred in real places and many of them have been substantiated by other historical documents. Moses lived in Egypt and walked on Mount Sinai. Jesus was born in Bethlehem, grew up in the village of Nazareth, and walked the streets of Jerusalem. He healed a lame man by the pool of Bethesda; he sailed with his disciples on the Sea of Galilee; he sat with a Samaritan woman beside Jacob's well in Samaria. The apostle Paul visited Rome, Ephesus, and Athens. Since these places still exist, the accuracy of the Bible events such as travel times, relation of one locale to another, and even the end result of a predicted destruction (Nineveh, for example) can be verified today. The Bible's history lays itself open for critical examination.

Luke, a medical doctor who wrote the Gospel of Luke and the book of Acts, has earned wide respect for his historical and geographical accuracy. Luke's frequent mention of well-known government officials and regional boundaries invite historical scrutiny, and strong evidence supports the beloved physician's precision time after time. According to Bible scholar Norman Geisler, altogether "Luke names thirty-two countries, fifty-four cities, and nine islands without making a single error" in geographical placement, and he gives correct titles for a wide variety of government officials, like "governor" and "tetrarch" (Luke 3:1), "politarch" or "city official" (Acts 17:6), "proconsul" (Acts 18:12-17), and "protos" or "chief official" of the island (Acts 28:7).[2]

A few years ago, I decided to put the Bible to my own little historical test. I read through the book of Acts and jotted down any references I found

WHY CALL IT "THE BIBLE"?

Bible comes from the Greek *biblos*, which meant a "book" (literally a "roll" or "scroll," since ancient books were rolled onto sticks instead of bound like modern volumes). *Biblos* is the first word in the Greek New Testament, for Matthew 1:1 refers to the "record [or book] of the genealogy of Jesus Christ." The word also refers to the "book of Moses" (Mark 12:26), the "book of the words of Isaiah" (Luke 3:4), and even the occult books used by the sorcerers in Ephesus (Acts 19:19). John used a similar word, *biblion* ("little book") when he observed that Jesus performed many more miraculous signs than John's Gospel could contain (John 20:30), and Paul used it when he asked Timothy to bring him his scrolls—some small personal copies of portions of the Scripture (2 Timothy 4:13).

When we call it "the *Holy* Bible," we mean it's the Book of books—a volume like no other—the special, unique, verbal message of God in a permanent, written form.

to people or events that might have some corroboration outside the New Testament. Then I spent several hours in the dusty recesses of a library reference room, checking to see whether other ancient historians backed up Luke's testimony. What I discovered strongly reinforced my conviction that the Bible is telling the truth. Here are some samples:

1. Candace, queen of the Ethiopians (Acts 8:27), was mentioned by the ancient writer Strabo (Book XVII, 54), who said she was "ruler of the Ethiopians in my time—a masculine sort of woman, and blind in one eye."

2. The famine that occurred during the reign of Emperor Claudius (Acts 11:27, 28) was corroborated by the Jewish historian Josephus who lived from about A.D. 37 to 100 (*Antiquities*, Book III, 15.3).

3. Herod Agrippa's gruesome death (Acts 12:19-23) was described in gory detail by Josephus (*Antiquities*, Book XIX, 8.2). The Bible says the king was struck down and eaten by worms because he accepted worship instead of giving praise to God. Josephus says the king didn't rebuke his flatterers

when they called him a god, and "a severe pain also arose in his belly, and began in a most violent manner."

4. Roman historical biographer Suetonius corroborated the fact that the emperor Claudius expelled the Jews from Rome (Acts 18:2; *Life of Claudius*, Book VIII, 25).

5. Acts 24:24 mentions Governor Felix and his wife, Drusilla. According to the Roman historian Tacitus, Drusilla was the granddaughter of Cleopatra and Antony (*History*, Book V, 9). Everybody's heard of Antony and Cleopatra, but did you realize their granddaughter was mentioned by name in the Bible?

In the Bible lands today, you can visit archaeological sites that illustrate how the story of the Bible intertwines with other historical events. Wade through Hezekiah's tunnel, first mentioned in 2 Kings 20:20. View the more than two-thousand-year-old Isaiah scroll found among the Dead Sea Scrolls, which provides important evidence for the text of this ancient book. Sit in the great theater in Ephesus mentioned in Acts 19:29. Walk through the marketplace in Corinth where members of the Corinthian church shopped, and stand on the Areopagus in Athens where Paul preached. The Bible's historical accuracy offers impressive evidence that the Book deserves our trust.

ANCIENT PROPHECIES AND MODERN DISCOVERIES

Other important lines of evidence support the truthfulness of the Bible as well.

Prophet Sharing

In the book of Acts, Christians often pointed to fulfilled prophecies as evidence to support their preaching about Christ. These prophecies could not have been mere guesswork.

For one thing, anyone who claimed to be a true messenger of God had to speak with complete accuracy or risk being executed by stoning (Deuter-

AMAZING PROPHECIES
FULFILLED

Space won't allow a thorough study of all the Bible's amazing predictions. But here are two favorite passages I like to study with people like Ben.

Psalm 22, written by King David, provides an accurate description of Jesus' crucifixion centuries before it occurred:

- "My God, my God, why have you forsaken me?" (v. 1; compare Jesus' words from the cross recorded in Matthew 27:46)
- Mocked, insulted (vv. 6-8; compare Matthew 27:38-44)
- Bones out of joint (v. 14—a painful effect of crucifixion)
- Hands and feet pierced (v. 16; again predicting the manner of Jesus' death)
- Lots cast for clothing (v. 18; compare John 19:23, 24)

Isaiah 53 foretells the crucifixion of Christ with such vivid details that it almost reads like a page from the New Testament!

- Pierced for our transgressions (vv. 5, 6; compare 1 Peter 2:21-25)
- Silent before his accusers (v. 7; compare Matthew 27:14)
- Assigned a grave with the wicked (v. 9; compare Matthew 27:38)
- With the rich in his death (v. 9; compare Matthew 27:57-61)
- After his suffering, "will see the light of life," and bring redemption to countless generations of "transgressors" (vv. 10-12; compare Matthew 28:1-10)

onomy 18:20-22). Needless to say, a man or woman aware of this part of Moses' law would think twice before presuming to speak on God's behalf.

Furthermore, biblical prophecies dealt with information far beyond the range of scientific calculation or ordinary guessing, and often included

GRATEFUL FOR
THE BIBLE

During a mission trip to Ethiopia, I was the guest of a gracious family who invited me to their tiny hut for dinner. As we tore large pieces of injerra (thick bread) from a common plate and dipped it into a spicy dish called chicken wut, I talked with a man named Sima who sat next to me on a wooden bench.

"How did you become a Christian?" I asked.

"I learned about Christ from American missionaries who came here in 1963," he responded. Proudly, he pointed to the leather-bound volume lying on the bench beside him and his voice grew soft and somber. "They gave me this Bible when I accepted Christ," he said, "but I had to hide it for seventeen years because of the Communists. They would have taken it from me, or punished me for owning it."

I thought about the bookshelf in my study at home, where not just one Bible but several, in different translations, are openly displayed and ready for use.

"You must be relieved now that you can worship more freely," I told Sima. He scratched his chin.

"Actually," he said thoughtfully, "in some ways we were probably better off then. The Christians had to be more committed."

Poking another chunk of injerra into the chicken mixture, he sighed, "We have it too easy now."

Easy? I wondered. By American standards, Ethiopian Christians have it anything but easy. Many of them worship in simple church buildings with dirt floors where crowds gather to sit on crude wooden benches. Surrounded by unspeakable poverty and hindered by unsympathetic government policies, they still pray, sing, and study the Bible with a zeal that would put many Americans to shame.

Do we appreciate our Bibles as much as Sima appreciates his?

remarkably specific details. For example, the prophet Isaiah twice mentioned a Persian ruler named Cyrus who ruled from 538 to 530 B.C., even though strong evidence suggests that Isaiah wrote his book around 700 B.C.—more than a century before Cyrus was even born! (See Isaiah 44:28; 45:1; and Ezra 1:1-4 which includes Ezra's historical record of Cyrus's deeds.)

Consider the track record of prophets like these:

Elijah: He predicted a major drought. There was neither rain nor dew for three and a half years, until Elijah announced that it was going to rain (1 Kings 17 and 18; see also James 5:17, 18).

Nahum: He predicted numerous details about the downfall of the enormous Assyrian capital city of Nineveh that came true in astonishing detail! These facts are easily verifiable today (Nahum 1-3).[3]

Ezekiel: He predicted numerous details about the downfall of the city of Tyre long before they happened (Ezekiel 26).[4]

Daniel: He not only could *interpret* dreams with amazing accuracy; he could even tell *what* someone else dreamed in the first place! This amazing feat convinced even a pagan king that God was the source of Daniel's information (Daniel 2).

Micah: He foretold the Messiah's birthplace with enough clarity that King Herod's advisors could point the magi toward Bethlehem (Micah 5:2; Matthew 2:1-6).

Ben complains that "people keep pointing to the Bible and predicting there's going to be doomsday or World War III, but nothing's happened yet." But when Christians speak of biblical prophecy, we're not making lame speculations about what an erratic Iraqi leader might do. We're talking about facts that shine from the pages of history like permanent miracles for us to behold. Actually, Ben's comment sounds perilously similar to another prophecy made in Scripture: "In the last days scoffers will come. . . . They will say, 'Where is this "coming" he promised? . . . Everything goes on as it has since the beginning . . .'" (2 Peter 3:3, 4). By simply saying the word, God created the universe and later destroyed the earth with the great flood of Noah's day. And by that same powerful word, God has stated that the present heavens and earth are going to be destroyed (2 Peter 3:6, 7). We don't know when this will occur, but based on the Lord's track

WHY I BELIEVE THE BIBLE IS THE WORD OF GOD

All Christians need to be able to explain in a clear, concise fashion why we believe the Bible. Here's a little outline I've used for years.

C LAIMS. The Bible claims to be God's Word (2 Timothy 3:16; 2 Peter 1:21). By trusting that the Holy Spirit inspired the Scriptures, we're simply accepting the testimony of the biblical authors themselves, who said without hesitation or embarrassment things like "this is what the Lord says" or "what I am writing to you is the Lord's command" (1 Corinthians 14:37).

H ISTORICAL ACCURACY. The writers of Scripture didn't tell us "cleverly invented stories." They were eyewitnesses who reported the facts (2 Peter 1:16).

R EMARKABLE STYLE. The Bible's wisdom, beauty, and spiritual power impress even those who read it merely for its literary value. Charles Dickens called the New Testament "the very best book that ever was or ever will be known in the world."

I NDESTRUCTIBILITY. Written long before modern printing presses, the Bible has survived centuries of hand copying with an unparalleled record of textual accuracy. "The word of the Lord stands forever" (1 Peter 1:25).

S CIENTIFIC AND PROPHETIC ACCURACY. A biblical author like Isaiah, for example, wrote about the water cycle long before scientists understood it (55:10, 11), and described numerous details about Jesus' life long before he came to earth (53:1-12).

T OTAL UNITY. Finally, I'm impressed by the internal harmony of the Bible. Written by dozens of different authors over hundreds of years, it relates one consistent message about God's will and his plan for our salvation.

Did you notice that my outline is an acrostic for the word *CHRIST*? Most of all, I appreciate the Bible because I love the Son of God revealed within its pages. Jesus himself loved the Scriptures so much that he quoted them frequently and prayed, "Your word is truth" (John 17:17).

record of accuracy, we're wise to be prepared. It's going to happen (Mark 13:32-37).

Jesus' teachings about the end of the world are interwoven with predictions that have already been fulfilled about the destruction of Jerusalem, which took place in A.D. 70 under a Roman general named Titus (Matthew 24). The Bible honestly acknowledges that false prophets will arise (Jeremiah 23:16-32; Matthew 7:21-23; 24:4, 5, 24). This fact does not negate God's ability to know the past, the present, and the future, as he claims in his Word (Isaiah 46:9, 10).

The Bible's prophecies underscore the reliability of the entire volume. As the apostle Peter put it, "For prophecy never had its origin in the will of man, but men spoke from God as they were carried along by the Holy Spirit" (2 Peter 1:21).

Science Facts, Not Science Fiction

In 1994, an Australian Parks and Wildlife Service officer named David Noble stumbled onto a grove of thirty-nine trees in the Wollemi National Park rain forest preserve near Sydney. The trees, nicknamed "Wollemi pines," have been dubbed one of the most important botanical finds of the twentieth century because they represent a plant species experts thought had become extinct centuries ago. One environmental expert commented, "The fact that such a large plant can go undiscovered for so long is a clear indication that there is more work to be done before we can say we understand our environment." Ironically, *Wollemi* is an aboriginal word that means "look around you."[5]

Look around you? Yes, that's what Christians say to do: look at nature, and look at the Bible, and you will discover that God's works do not contradict God's words. The same God who created the universe also inspired the Scriptures. What God has *said* in the Bible harmonizes with what he's *done* in creation.

Our word *science* comes from the Latin *scientia*, which means *knowledge*. God was the first scientist. In fact, as theologians point out, God alone is capable of "*omni*science" (*omni* means "all"). He's the "omni-scientist," the only one who possesses all knowledge of nature. "The fear of the Lord," the Bible points out, "is the beginning of *knowledge*" (*scientia* in the Latin version).

Christian faith isn't unscientific or anti-scientific. For one thing, Christians acknowledge the contributions of science. We benefit as much as anyone else from eyeglasses, dental care, and heart bypass surgery. We drive cars, cook with microwaves, and write books with the help of computers. God is the one who created physical laws for us to discover and use. To engage in good science, as astronomer Johann Kepler said, is "to think God's thoughts after him."

But unlike those who practically make a god out of science, we insist that science has its limitations. Because today's foregone conclusion often becomes tomorrow's discarded theory, the truly scientific mind must be humble about its conclusions, not arrogant. Some folks seem to live by two basic rules: 1. Science holds the answers to all the questions of life, and 2. Anyone who does not believe Rule Number One is not scientific. But if science alone were the key to life, Solomon would have discovered it, since he possessed unsurpassed knowledge of botany, biology, and other sciences (1 Kings 4:29-34). Yet all his scientific knowledge left him empty and still grasping for the meaning of life. Science and the Bible can be useful allies, however, for the very questions science alone cannot answer—questions about the worth and purpose of human life, our origin and destiny—are the very questions the Bible seeks to answer.

Does the Bible have anything to say about modern science? More than we often realize. The first book of the Bible indicates that the stars are uncountable (Genesis 15:5). Another early text, Job 26:7, speaks of the earth being suspended in space, and Isaiah 40:22 mentions the circle of the earth. Today we know how blood circulates water, oxygen, and nourishment to the cells of our bodies, but centuries ago God's Word stated that "the life of the creature is in the blood" (Leviticus 17:11, 14). The idea that the eternal God has always been alive fits well with the scientific law of biogenesis, the principle that says all life comes from previously existing life. And the order and complexity of nature fit better with the concept of a wise Creator than with the macro-evolutionary hypothesis that credits creation to an impersonal force, plus time, plus chance.

In fact, the Bible provides a helpful frame of reference for science, for unlike other religious worldviews, the Scripture insists that the physical world is real (not an illusion), and it was created good (Genesis 1), but it is not God (and so it's a legitimate object of study and innovation, not an object of worship).

But Isn't It All Simply a Matter of Interpretation?

Ben voices a common frustration many people feel about the Bible when he complains, "If you get ten different people to read the Bible, you might come out with ten different versions. Even though they're reading the same words, they interpret them in an entirely different way." Many skeptics are quick to dismiss the Bible by saying, "It's all a matter of personal interpretation."

In one sense, it *is* a matter of interpretation, for we do have to carefully apply our minds to the task when we study the Bible. (If this were not the case, non-Christians would have another reason to argue that Christian faith is intellectually unacceptable.) But it's unfair to conclude that Scripture is impossible to understand. Actually, biblical interpretation (also known as *hermeneutics*) is a highly developed discipline—too broad to examine thoroughly here. But let me offer some basic suggestions as a starting point.

1. Focus on what you CAN understand, not what you CAN'T. Bible study is a growth process. I've been married to my wife, Candy, since 1975. I know her a lot better now than I used to; years from now, I'll know her better still. It's much the same as we get acquainted with God. Be inquisitive; be patient. Admittedly, there are plenty of difficult passages in the Bible, and equally honest believers sometimes disagree about their meanings. But the basic gospel, and the foundational moral teachings of the Bible, are quite clear.

2. Ask God to help you. Even the Bible itself acknowledges that some of its writings are hard to understand (see 2 Peter 3:15, 16). But the Bible isn't written in some sort of secret code; it's written in human language, and we can grasp its meaning if we study it according to ordinary rules of grammar and logic. God wants to give us wisdom and help us understand his will. That's why he gave us the Bible in the first place (see 2 Timothy 3:14-17; James 1:5).

3. Study the Bible with an open mind. As much as possible, we need to lay aside our preconceived ideas and take a fresh, unbiased look at the Scriptures. Don't read the Bible through colored glasses. Denominational or cultural biases make Bible students look for "proof texts" for their favorite theological causes or political agendas instead of discerning the whole counsel of God. Someone who doesn't think miracles are possible will explain away historical records of miraculous events without giving them a fair examination. As Dr. Charles Webster, a Christian family physician in Seattle, correctly points out,

SCRIPTURE STATS

* Total books in the Old Testament: thirty-nine, originally written in Hebrew (with small portions in Aramaic, a dialect of Hebrew).

* Total books in the New Testament: twenty-seven, originally written in Greek.

* Portions of the Bible have been translated into more than twenty-two hundred different languages and dialects, far more languages than any other book.

* The Bible was the first major book ever printed (by Johann Gutenberg in 1456).

* The Bible has even made it to the moon! (In 1970, a microfilm packet containing Genesis 1:1 in sixteen languages and a complete Revised Standard Version Bible were placed on the moon by astronaut Edgar Mitchell of the Apollo 14 moon mission.)

* The Bible possesses an amazing internal harmony despite the diversity of its authorship. It's actually a library of sixty-six books, written over a period of approximately fifteen hundred years by thirty to forty different authors. It contains historical narratives, poetic songs, personal letters, fascinating character studies, short stories, parables, witty proverbs, mind-boggling visions, and frank descriptions of real people who often failed more than they succeeded. Yet despite their varied literary styles and personalities, the writers focused on one key theme (God's unfolding plan of redemption) and dealt with controversial issues without contradicting themselves.

"If someone has already decided that one plus one doesn't equal two, then he will never agree that one hundred plus one hundred equals two hundred."

4. Let the Bible speak for itself. Correct interpretation of the Scripture requires *exegesis*, deriving the meaning of Scripture out of (*ex*) the text itself—not *eisegesis*, which means reading your own meaning into (*eis*) the text. "The Bible is its own best interpreter," someone has said. Often a question raised in one section of Scripture will be answered by other verses that deal with the same subject.

5. Use common sense. Keep Bible verses in context. Note who is speaking, when, where, and why. Use a Bible dictionary, Bible encyclopedia, concordance, or other reference tool to make sure you know the correct meanings of words. Study biblical events in their historical context; for example, it makes a big difference whether a biblical principle was given under the old covenant of the Jews or the new covenant initiated by Jesus Christ. And pay attention to the literary form: Is the text meant to be literal or figurative? Is it poetry or prose? Is it a personal letter, a legal document, a proverb, a parable, or a prophecy? These are weighty issues, but they're not impossible to handle if we use common sense.

6. Focus on the book's main theme. God's Word speaks with spiritual power (1 Thessalonians 2:13; Hebrews 4:12; James 1:18; 1 Peter 1:23-25), but it's not merely a rule book. It's a message about God's redeeming love and his plan for our salvation. It's a living message about the living Christ who died for our sins and rose from the dead. Jesus himself is the heart of the Bible's message (Luke 24:44-47; 1 Corinthians 15:1-4). When you read the Bible, make sure you don't miss the good news!

7. Apply it to your life. Once you grasp that a biblical passage is meant for you to obey, don't hesitate to put it into action. Be a doer of the word, not just a hearer (James 1:22, 23).

If we follow basic principles like these, the Bible won't cause division and confusion. It will give us encouragement and hope. That's why the apostle Paul urged Christians to pray, "May the God who gives endurance and encouragement give you a spirit of unity among yourselves as you follow Christ Jesus, so that with one heart and mouth you may glorify the God and Father of our Lord Jesus Christ" (Romans 15:5, 6).

Not Just an "Imaginary Mate"

"What would it take for you to believe?" asked Luke, the Australian minister who has become Ben's good friend. "Factual proof and evidence," Ben responded. "If somebody actually has facts and evidence to support what he's saying, then you can't really argue with that."

But there's more to the story. A few years ago, Ben was almost killed in a car accident. His car was hit broadside by another car, and emergency workers had to cut Ben out of his vehicle. For two years, he was out of work while he recuperated from his injuries and learned how to walk and talk again. He'd been an apprentice cabinetmaker with only one year left in his apprenticeship, but after the accident he had to give up that career and support himself in a less satisfying job with a boat-building company.

"I feel frustrated with God," Ben says. "If God is there, why doesn't he answer me, talk to me, show himself? In a time of desperation, I prayed to him, but nothing happened and things kept turning out wrong. It felt like I was talking to an imaginary mate."

Honest questioners like Ben need all the facts we can give them about the Bible. But they also need us to be real "mates"—real friends—as we patiently introduce them to the God who cares. The Bible is a letter from a loving Father—a letter inviting us home and guiding us until we get there.

You can see some beautiful stars in Australia—different ones than you see in the northern hemisphere. It's called the Land of the Southern Cross, because one constellation looks like a cross shining brightly in the sky.

Wherever Ben is tonight, I hope he's looking up.

QUESTIONS FOR PERSONAL REFLECTION

1. If you were telling a person like Ben why you believe the Bible is God's Word, what would you say? How would you begin your explanation?

2. Do you think Ben's painful experience with his auto accident might have something to do with his unwillingness to believe the Bible? Why, or why not?

RESOURCES FOR FURTHER READING

F. F. Bruce, *The New Testament Documents: Are They Reliable?* (Eerdmans, 1978).

Gary Habermas, *The Historical Jesus* (College Press, 1996).

FOOTNOTES

[1]For more discussion of the uniqueness of the Bible and its implications, see Josh McDowell, *Evidence That Demands a Verdict* (Campus Crusade, 1972), pp. 17-28, and William R. Kimball, *The Book of Books* (College Press, 1986), pp. 19-100.

[2]Norman Geisler and Ron Brooks, *When Skeptics Ask* (Victor, 1990), p. 201.

[3]For further explanation of Nahum's prophecy about Nineveh, see James Montgomery Boice, *The Minor Prophets, Vol. 2* (Zondervan, 1986), pp. 57-72.

[4]For a detailed explanation of Ezekiel's prophecy about Tyre, see James Smith, *Ezekiel* (College Press, 1984), pp. 306-317, and Josh McDowell, *Evidence That Demands a Verdict* (Campus Crusade, 1972), pp. 285-291.

[5]Peter James Spielmann, "Grove of Prehistoric Pines a Startling Australian Find," *The Cincinnati Enquirer*, December 15, 1994.

CHAPTER 4

CATHY: DOES FAITH FIT IN THE REAL WORLD?

"It wasn't hard for me to climb the corporate ladder," Cathy says with a calm assurance that sounds like self-confidence, not arrogance. "It was just a matter of understanding the system, and then manipulating it and using it to my advantage."

A bright, attractive thirty-nine-year-old, Cathy has accomplished a lot; but don't let the apparent ease of her success fool you.

Determined to Succeed

Her family didn't make things easy for her. Growing up with an alcoholic dad, Cathy took on the role of family peacemaker. Even when her dad wasn't drinking, he often was emotionally abusive to the family, so she lived with constant tension.

Nor was it easy for her to get an education. Determined to prove herself, she worked full-time during the day as a business secretary, then she attended university classes at night. "I was the first person on either side of my family to graduate from college," she points out.

Cathy also found time to volunteer as a social activist, supporting feminist causes like NOW and pro-choice political candidates.

"Getting involved in these causes was necessary to my survival as a woman," Cathy recalls. "I felt that the world didn't want me to succeed as a woman or to be independent, own my own home, and enjoy the comforts of life, without being married."

In her work as a secretary, Cathy was just as capable as her better-paid male supervisors, and she was determined to make as much money as they made and to live as comfortably as they did. During her final college semester, she developed some specific expectations about the first career job she would get after graduation, including a list of ten benefits she wanted her employer to offer her.

"There was a certain profile I was looking for, and until I could find a company that could check off all ten things, I wasn't willing to settle for anything less. Looking back, that sounds pretty arrogant," Cathy laughs, "but that's really how I felt. I had an incredible chip on my shoulder!" After about forty interviews, she landed a sales job with a consumer food products company—the beginning of a thirteen-year climb up the corporate ladder.

For Cathy, this part was easy. She liked sales. "If you do well in sales, you get credit for it, and you are responsible for the results," she explains. "It was a way to put the spotlight on me and say, 'Look at what I can do.'" She was promoted three times in two and one-half years.

Changing Goals

"I was surprised how easy it was for me to move up the corporate ladder," says Cathy. "But at the same time, it was unfulfilling. Growing up in a blue-collar family, I always thought the white-collar world held something special—a lot of prestige and respect. There was a mystique about professionalism. But once I got involved in that world, I realized that people are people, no matter how much money they make. Even though I was being promoted, my career was not fulfilling. It was really devastating. I was accomplishing the career goal I had set for myself, but it wasn't satisfying. For a while, I was afraid to set another goal. I thought, 'What if I work another six or seven years toward a goal, and then when I get there, I don't feel fulfilled?'

"Then my goals began to change. Instead of reaching a certain title or even earning more money, I wanted to reach a higher level of recognition or excellence in my work in sales. When I was about twenty-eight or twenty-nine years old, I began to think, 'Look, I'm now working as hard as I can work. I'm traveling. I'm having fun and doing exciting things. I'm an independent, successful, professional person. Yet there still seems to be a hole inside my heart.' It was frightening when I realized, 'I don't think I can continue to do this forever.'"

Ruefully, she admits, "I'd think about where my life was headed, but I didn't do anything about it. I'd see older people who worked hard all their lives, and they weren't as sharp. Some of the reality of my own frailty began to sink in. I'd think, 'Is that what life is about?' But then I'd just go have another gin and tonic and play a little harder."

"During this time I was removed from anything remotely related to faith in God. I never gave any thought to it. If I had to put a label on it, I'd probably say I was an agnostic. I knew that there were churches, but I didn't think there was anything in them that would interest me. Churches were for families—for married men and women who had children. They were not the place for professional career women to go."

Shrewd, or Sincere?

The marketing director at work was a Christian. One day he told her, "If you ever want to go to church, my wife and I go every Sunday and we would be glad to have you join us." He seemed sincere, but when Cathy told him "OK" it was only because she needed to stay on his good side to advance her career. She didn't have any interest in going to church, but she wanted him to be her friend for business reasons.

She was curious enough to wonder, though, "What goes on at church? Why do people go there?"

Later the marketing director told her that his wife led a Bible study. Would she like to go?

No, Cathy didn't want to go. But she didn't want to disappoint her colleague, so she told him, "I don't know anything about the Bible. Maybe one of these days I might go." As soon as she returned to her office, Cathy answered the phone. It was the marketing director's wife, saying, "I understand you'd like to go to the Bible study. It's this Thursday night at 7:00. Here are the directions—look forward to seeing you there!"

"I was terrified," Cathy admits. "But then I told myself, 'Look, I can go just this once. It'll be over by 8:30, so I'll still have time to have a few drinks with my friends.'"

Thursday night she walked uneasily into the house where a group of women sat in the living room for a Bible study. "I went there thinking, *I'm not going to like anybody there. And no one will be like me, and I won't be anything like them.* But they turned out to be surprisingly open with me. I was surprised that they didn't seem afraid of me, and the roof didn't fall in!"

"The Bible study topic that week was *love*. The leader said that love is not merely a noun, it's a verb. It's something you do—an action word. I thought, 'At least they're not a bunch of idiots. They know the difference between a noun and a verb!' But as they talked about love, they explained that the reason we know Jesus loves us is not because of what he says but because of what he did by dying on the cross for us.

"I thought, 'That's logical. It makes sense! It's like A plus B equals C. It has nothing to do with me, and it will never have anything to do with me, but it does makes sense.' I couldn't personalize what those women were saying, but I was intrigued by the logic of it.

"I'd heard about Jesus Christ. I knew that we celebrated Christmas to recognize Jesus' birth, and that he died on the cross. But it was a story. I never understood *why*. It had no reality to it. Nobody ever had explained to me the reason for Jesus' life and death. And I wondered, 'How can you possibly know that it's true?' Not that I was skeptical about the Bible. I just didn't know anything about the Bible. I'd never seen anyone who lived by faith."

Living, or Surviving?

As Cathy's spiritual journey has continued, she's found some new questions to ask.

"I've started going to Bible study every week. It's a safe place to ask questions. The women there don't care what I've done in the past, and they don't make me feel foolish for asking questions. But I don't feel worthy to go to church. The way I look at it, those people who go to church live squeaky-clean lives, and I don't. I live a fast life, and they don't. They don't have fun, and they don't know what is out in the world. They live in closed, protected environments. They kind of go off by themselves. They are cloistered people, with no sense of reality.

"I've attended the Bible study for a year and a half, but I still haven't found the nerve to go to church. The Bible study has helped me a lot, but I still wonder how to put my two worlds together. It's always seemed to me that you can either be a shrewd businessperson, or a person of faith. You can't be both, can you?

"The women at my Bible study talk about living by faith, and they talk about eternal life. But what I want to know is, how can you talk about really living, when you're just trying to survive?"

DOES FAITH FIT IN THE REAL WORLD?

Squeaky-clean lives? Closed, protected environments? Cloistered people with no sense of reality? No fun? That sounds a lot different from most of the Christians I know. For that matter, it sounds a lot different from the people we encounter in Scripture. Many words come to mind when I think of Simon Peter. Brash, rough-cut, fast-talking. But "squeaky clean"? I don't think so.

First-century Christians in big cities like Corinth or Ephesus were surrounded by sexual immorality, occult religions, and pagan philosophies every time they ventured out into the marketplace. Cloistered? Hardly.

The apostle Paul's travels sound like a modern adventurer's itinerary: Athens, Jerusalem, Cyprus, Rome. He was beaten, stoned, shipwrecked, and endangered by everything from bandits to false teachers. He labored and toiled so much that he often went without sleep, and he knew how it felt to be hungry, thirsty, cold, and naked (2 Corinthians 11:24-27). A "closed, protected environment"? No way.

Although they lived in a different culture than ours, Bible characters faced pressures much like the ones we face today. If you think Cathy climbed the career ladder rapidly, what about David? He ascended all the way from shepherd to soldier to king by age thirty (2 Samuel 5:4). At the peak of his career, Solomon enjoyed unparalleled material blessings, but like Cathy, even in the midst of his success he felt empty and unfulfilled (1 Kings 4:20-28; 10:14-29; Ecclesiastes 2:1-11).

FILLING THAT "HOLE IN THE HEART"

Living by faith doesn't remove us from the so-called "real world." It puts us squarely in the middle of it. In fact, since God is real and his Word is true, the true realist is the person who takes God seriously.

But we have to admit, a lot of people have the impression that believers are somehow out of touch with the real world. "It's fine for you to believe in God and go to church if you feel the need for something like that," they say. "But me? I don't feel the need for it. And even if I did, I just don't see how I'd fit with all those people who go to church."

(To a Christian, it sounds strange when someone says, "I don't feel the need for God." Isn't that a bit like saying, "Well, it's fine if you feel like you need to breathe air—but me? I don't need air to survive!")

Cathy recognized that something was missing. "There's a hole in my heart," she said. But she still struggled to see how faith in Christ fit in her everyday world.

Other folks aren't so polite about it. They hint, with a bit of condescension, "Isn't faith in God just a crutch? A comforting intoxicant for those too weak to face life on their own? If you're strong, hard-working, and self-sufficient, why do you need to lean on God? Shouldn't you just take responsibility for your own life instead of depending on God to take care of you?"

Some Historical Background

These questions have deep roots in our culture. As the influential psychiatrist Sigmund Freud (1856-1939) analyzed the religious beliefs of his patients, he came to an interesting conclusion that he described in a short book called

The Future of an Illusion. Essentially Freud argued that, instead of men and women being created in the image of God, it's really the other way around: we created God by wishing for a divine Father-figure, a protector to help us when we're afraid.[1]

If Freud is right, then faith in God is little more than wishful thinking, a product of human weakness and fear. Furthermore, this view implies that as we become more mature, we should grow out of our childish dependence on God and learn to face life bravely on our own.

Karl Marx (1818-1883) added his own twist to this argument. Religion, he insisted, is "the opiate of the masses"—a way to keep ordinary people pacified in drug-like contentment while the rich and powerful exploit them.

Like the old cereal commercial that said, "Trix are for kids," many people assume that faith and Sunday school are for kids. But the tough, real world? Where you have to watch out for Number One and claw your way to the top? In that harsh world, you'd better put away childish things and fend for yourself.

Consider the following comments from a university student whose column appeared in a University of Iowa newspaper:

"I don't believe in God. I think God is nonsense. The Bible is pure fiction, written by men to codify men's dominance. Jesus, if he did exist, was a mere human being. He was not a 'god.' The whole idea of God is a construct, a product of wishful thinking. . . . Whenever I hear someone say the words 'sin' or 'God,' I want to scream: 'You dummy—wake up! God/Allah/Santa Claus/the Easter Bunny—they're all the same—imaginary!'"[2]

Another university student wrote:

"Organized religion is the root of all evil. . . . Religion is a form of dependency. . . . Socially, all organized religion does is provide a support network and a place to go in time of need or spiritual unrest. . . . It's nothing but a revolving door so that the church can make some more money off you. The first eighteen years of my life I went home to my parents. . . . Generally, I was forgiven and felt better to boot. Now that I am on my own spiritually, I haven't needed to be saved, healed, or forgiven."[3]

How can we respond to all of this? Is faith in God simply for weak people who have lost touch with the real world? Let's take a closer look.

FAR MORE THAN A CRUTCH

The "God-is-just-wishful-thinking" school of thought actually takes a very negative, uncomplimentary look at humanity. If faith is based on our fear, ignorance, and immaturity, then how do you explain the fact that people of great learning, courage, and maturity believe strongly in God?

It's all too easy to paint all believers (and all unbelievers) with the same broad brush until we end up with caricatures instead of reality. As Clark Pinnock has written, "Many of the things [Freud] said about neurotic religion, of course, were true and perceptive, but nowhere in his writings is the slightest indication that he recognized religion at its best and what it can mean to honest people every bit as intelligent as himself. His charge is wide of the mark as far as the gospel is concerned."[4] J. B. Phillips wrote in his book, *Your God Is Too Small*, "No one would accuse [Christianity's] Founder of immaturity in insight, thought, teaching, or conduct, and the history of the Christian Church provides thousands of examples of timid half-developed personalities who have not only found in their faith what the psychologists call integration, but have coped with difficulties and dangers in a way that makes any gibe of 'escapism' plainly ridiculous."[5]

But how can we help someone like Cathy see how the world of faith connects with the "secular" world of business, politics, entertainment, and finances? Here are some suggestions.

Acknowledge That We Do Need God

Yes, many people do treat God as a crutch. But that's a reasonable thing to do, since all of us are "crippled." If we're honest with ourselves, there comes a point at which most of us feel overwhelmed by life's problems.

Cathy began to realize this when she moved up the corporate ladder, but then felt unfulfilled. Notice her comments: "I'm an independent, successful, professional person. Yet there still seems to be a hole inside my heart." Even an atheist leans on something. As Edward Young once said, "By night an atheist half believes in God." The question is, which crutch will you choose? Will you lean on God, or as Cathy put it, will you just "go have another gin and tonic and play a little harder"?

Years ago I heard Peter Sweisgood, executive director of the Long Island

Council on Alcoholism, speak shortly after he returned from attending a conference on alcoholism in Moscow. Commenting on Russia's growing problem of alcohol abuse, he remarked, "I think they are beginning to realize that religion is not the opiate of the masses. Alcohol is the opiate of the masses."

Christians freely admit our need for God. Doesn't it make sense that the created would desire fellowship with the Creator? Is it a surprise when a child reaches for the security of her father's arms? Isn't it logical that imperfect people would want to honor a perfect God? As someone has said, "God is not a crutch—he's a stretcher! We couldn't even limp into Heaven without him."

C. S. Lewis argued that for every need, something exists to fulfill that need. Ducks feel the need to swim; and there is such a thing as water. Human beings feel the need to eat; and thankfully, there is such a thing as food. So if we feel the need for God, isn't it logical to think there is a God who can fulfill that need?[6]

CHALLENGE SOME FALSE ASSUMPTIONS

Many people who reject Christ and the church do so not because of strong evidence, but because they filter the evidence through some deeply ingrained presuppositions. Cathy assumed that "churches were made up of men and women who had children—they were not the places for professional career women to go." But once she actually began attending a home Bible study, she discovered a number of Christian women whose lives were remarkably like her own. Here are three other false assumptions we need to clear up.

False Assumption 1:
If you live by Christian values, you won't make it in the real world.

Try telling that to NFL Hall of Famer Anthony Munoz, widely respected as one of football's greatest offensive linemen—and respected for his integrity and Christian principles.

Try telling it to Lowell "Bud" Paxson, who has dedicated his growing television network to the glory of God. Paxson says, "Each of us has three threads, or elements, of life we need to get through the needle's eye: the business or career thread, the spiritual thread, and the family thread."[7]

Perhaps you could introduce someone like Cathy to Christian friends who have bridged the gap by living out their Christian values while pursuing excellence in their careers.

We also may need to redefine what it means to "make it" in the world. God doesn't define success the way the world does. Jeremiah was successful in God's eyes even when no one wanted to hear his prophecies. John the Baptist was successful in God's eyes even when he was put to death by King Herod's sword. Jesus was successful even when the crowd called for his crucifixion and mocked him as he suffered on the cross. Paul was successful—and content—even when he was beaten, stoned, and imprisoned for preaching Christ.

False Assumption 2:
Christians believe in God mainly because he gives us comfort.

Make no mistake about it: God does comfort us. "He gives strength to the weary and increases the power of the weak" (Isaiah 40:29). He is "the Father of compassion and the God of all comfort, who comforts us in all our troubles, so that we can comfort those in any trouble with the comfort we ourselves have received from God" (2 Corinthians 1:3, 4).

Some folks think of God solely as a comforter, while others see him mainly as a threat. Some see him as a kind Father, others as a harsh judge. But the important issue is what the Bible says about God, not our preconceived ideas about him. Not only does the Bible tell us that God exists; it tells us what kind of God he is—and he is not the kind of God we would invent, even if we tried.

Pagan gods? Their worshipers tried to appease and manipulate them to gain a better harvest or win an important battle. The gods of the Greeks and Romans? Those so-called deities displayed the same moral frailties common to human beings—selfishness, unrestrained anger, lust. That's what happens when people create their own gods.

But the God of the Bible is holy, all-knowing, all-powerful, eternal, and unchanging. It's unlikely we would "invent" a God like that—especially since he is also a sovereign God who requires our obedience and compliance to his will. Christians voluntarily surrender to Someone wiser and more powerful than we are, while atheism tries to "kick sand in the face of God."[8]

God is more than a comforter—more than a soft-spoken Savior who soothes our hurts. He's also our Master and Ruler, the Lord of Heaven and earth. He's a God of grace and mercy, but he's also the all-knowing presence who is always "looking through the keyhole" of our lives, aware of our every thought and our every move—a God from whom there is no escape (Psalm 139:1-7).[9] "Everything is uncovered and laid bare before the eyes of him to whom we must give account" (Hebrews 4:13). Who could invent a God like that? Who would even want to?

Christians don't create a god who makes us feel good; we accept the authority of God who rules our lives whether we're comfortable or not.

Instead of wishing God into existence, it's more reasonable to think that some folks try to wish God *out* of existence because they don't want to be subject to his moral restrictions. According to Romans 1:18, people "suppress the truth by their wickedness." "God's invisible qualities—his eternal power and divine nature—have been clearly seen, being understood from what has been made, so that men are without excuse" (Romans 1:20). But sin hardens hearts and sears consciences, making it harder to believe the self-evident reality that God exists.

False Assumption 3:
The Christian life is boring.

Sure, some Christians *are* boring. So are some worship services, some sermons, and some Bible classes.

But the life of an all-out, sold-out, Spirit-filled, service-minded Christ-follower is anything but dull!

Christians don't emerge from the baptistry wearing special spiritual space suits that insulate us from the stresses of life. In fact, the water is barely dry before we discover we've embarked on a major adventure of self-sacrifice—and often, greater pain—as we serve our Lord in the rough and tumble of daily life.

Christians aren't the ones who've chosen the easy way. It takes guts to follow the road less traveled and commit ourselves to Jesus' kind of humble service and self-discipline.

Jesus never told his disciples, "Lean on your crutch and follow me." He did say, "Take up your cross and follow me." A cross is hardly a crutch.

And yet, like Jesus himself who endured the cross "for the joy set before him" (Hebrews 12:2), Christians have fun, laugh at life's absurdities, and enjoy good humor—all with the added joy of sensing that somehow the God of grace is chuckling along with us!

THE GOOD NEWS ABOUT CATHY

Cathy finally began to understand this. In fact, she's come a long way since initially asking the questions she voiced at the beginning of this chapter. Gradually, as she continued meeting week by week with her Bible study group, she realized, "The answers are in here. There's a purpose for life—a reason I was born."

Some of the lessons were hard for her to swallow, though. For example, how did an independent-minded, results-oriented person like Cathy respond to the biblical idea of submitting her will to the Lordship of Christ?

"I used to call submission the 'S' word when I first became a Christian. But once I agreed to believe that the Scripture really is the truth, then I understood that it is *for* me and it will help me, not hurt me. As I began to hear about submission and humility, those were painful lessons. There was a period when I wondered, 'Does that mean I can't speak up? Does that mean I don't have an opinion, and I can't think?' Fortunately, the woman who mentored me said, 'No, you need to be all that God has created you to be.' I learned that being a Christian doesn't mean you're just a doormat, or that you acquiesce to everything.

"I learned there's a difference between wanting what God wants, and wanting what you want. If God has given you gifts, you use them—but for his purposes, not for your own."

Someone Died So You Can Live

Today Cathy is a strong Christian. What advice would she offer believers who want to reach people like her? "Don't approach people with an attitude that says you're trying to change them. Their defenses will go up. Encourage them, love them, and bring them to God who will change them. A lot of us want to bring people to church for their exposure to Christ. But for me, I felt safer in someone's home where I could ask questions and explore who Christ is.

"When you're the product of a painful past, you approach life with a need to survive, not to live. I didn't see how applying skills to survive had any connection to this life that seemed to exist in the church.

"But then I found out that Someone already died so that I can live," Cathy says, as her usually confident voice suddenly trembles with heartfelt emotion.

"Every man and woman needs to hear that."

QUESTIONS FOR PERSONAL REFLECTION:

1. Do you think of God as a crutch for you to lean on? Why, or why not? What other "crutches" do people lean on when they feel weak?

2. Do you think some Christians are, in fact, out of touch with the "real world"? Why do you think this perception is so common among unbelievers?

RESOURCES FOR FURTHER STUDY

Bill Hybels, *The God You're Looking For* (Zondervan, 1997).

Terry L. Miethe and Gary R. Habermas, *Why Believe? God Exists!* (College Press, 1993).

FOOTNOTES

[1]Freud argued that belief in God grows out of our childhood relationship with our parents. We must grant, of course, that there is some truth to this. Parents do shape a child's view of God during the child's early years, and Christian parents do their best to introduce their children to the true God. But according to Freud's view, faith in God springs from a childish wish for a heavenly protector to shield us from "the crushingly superior force of nature" (famines, earthquakes, hurricanes, and diseases); to assure that justice is done when other people violate our rights; and to help us cope with death, "the painful riddle, against which no medicine has yet been found, nor probably will be." "When the growing individual finds that he is destined to remain a child forever, that he can never do without protection against strange superior powers," Freud wrote, "he lends those powers the features belonging to the figure of his father; he creates for himself the gods whom he dreads, whom he seeks to propitiate, and whom he nevertheless entrusts with his own protection. Thus his longing for a father is a motive identical with his need for protection against the consequences of his human weakness." Religious doctrines, Freud concluded, "are illusions and insusceptible of proof. No one can be compelled to think them true, to believe in them." See Sigmund Freud, *The Future of an Illusion*, edited by James Strachey (W. W. Norton & Company, 1961), pp. 20-34.

[2]Tom Hunter, "The God Myth: The Emperor Unclothed," University of Iowa *Daily Iowa* (September 14, 1993).

[3]William Brown, "Organized Religion Thrives on Dependence, Based on Lies," University of Cincinnati *News Record* (February 17, 1993).

[4]Clark Pinnock, *Reason Enough* (InterVarsity, 1980), p. 112.

[5]J. B. Phillips, *Your God Is Too Small* (Macmillan, 1961), pp. 33, 34. Christian counselor Dr. Gary Collins made a similar point in a workshop on "Healthy and Unhealthy Religion" at the July, 1992, North American Christian Convention in Anaheim, California. He pointed out that part of Sigmund Freud's problem was, he saw many unhealthy Christians in his psychiatric practice, and jumped to the unwarranted conclusion that *all* Christians are unhealthy.

[6]C. S. Lewis, *Mere Christianity* (Macmillan, 1950), p. 120.

[7]Steve Rabey, "PAX TV Off the Ground," *Christianity Today* (October 5, 1998), p. 15.

[8]R. C. Sproul, *Reason to Believe* (Zondervan, 1982), p. 73.

[9]*Ibid.*, pp. 70, 71.

CHAPTER 5

PAT: WHO IS GOD, ANYWAY?

"I'm pretty good at generating questions," grins Pat. "If I start to offend you or if you think I'm getting too heated, tell me right away, OK?"

When I tell her I'm writing a book filled with honest questions people ask about faith, her reaction is immediate and enthusiastic.

"Religion is one of my primary interests," she smiles thoughtfully, "but I'm one of those who needs to look at things in her own way and draw her own conclusions. Ideas have to ring true in my gut as well as pass the head test before I can sign on to them.

"I'm not looking to be converted to anything," she's quick to insist. "What I'm looking for is the truth. I probably won't find it until I'm dead, but that's OK."

The BFWT

A self-described "computer geek" and "fiendish gardener," thirty-four-year-old Pat has been married seven years to a forty-six-year-old chemist who frequently surveys her collection of salvaged computer hardware and sighs, "How many more of these are you going to bring home?"

They have no children. "Just an extremely spoiled and rather obese yellow Labrador retriever," laughs Pat.

"I was a biology major in college—in the pre-med program," she says, "but I didn't have the money or the intestinal fortitude to go through that much school. Biology still interests me, though."

Pat also is interested in spirituality, but she's cautious about opening up what she calls the "Religion Zone." As she puts it, "I'm not crazy about religious discussions that generate more heat than light, and I find the use of any religion as a means to kill, maim, discriminate, or generally behave like an idiot, particularly abhorrent!

"I have some nasty baggage regarding the religious right," she adds. "When my sister first told me she had become a Christian, I immediately was afraid that she would be out bombing abortion clinics the following day!

"I've read a ton of stuff: bits of the Bible, some assorted Buddhist and New Age writings, and *Black Elk Speaks*, the life story of an Oglala Sioux holy man."

What does she think about God?

"I've been turned off to the words *God* and *Jesus* because of the bad things people have done while invoking those names," she says. "I tend to refer to God as the 'Big Fuzzy White Thing' (BFWT), because that term doesn't have the baggage, and it's more gender-neutral. That's more how I think of him/her/it."

Pieces of the Truth

"I don't have many cast-in-concrete beliefs," says Pat. "There are really only two it will take a lot to get me to relinquish.

"One is reincarnation. I have no proof, but it makes a lot of sense. Why base judgment of a person for all eternity on one lifetime, when they might have been plunked down in rotten circumstances and died young? If I were designing a universe, I'd rotate beings through all sorts of different circumstances so that they would learn more.

"My other main belief is the feeling that all religions have a piece of the truth, but they don't see the whole picture. Isn't there a tale about an elephant behind a curtain with people reaching through, grabbing different parts of it and judging what animal it is, based on what piece they are holding onto? That's sort of how I feel."

Pat has other questions, too. "The necessity of Jesus. Why isn't a relationship with the BFWT enough? What is the point of Jesus? Example? Teacher? Savior? Lunatic? None of the above?

"The exclusivity of Christianity. If you think of God as a room, Christians believe there is only one door into the room and Christianity is it. I'm not saying Christianity isn't a door," she's quick to point out, "I just don't understand why it's the only one. And I won't accept something simply because the Bible says it."

Let's Talk About It

Pat has spent a lot of time thinking about all of this, and there's a lot at stake in the way we deal with issues like these. If there really is a God who cares about us—who created us, who answers prayer, who offers hope—it only makes sense to get acquainted with him and find out what he expects of us.

But a lot of times, discussions about faith degenerate into quarrels. Nobody listens, and nobody learns.

Can't we talk about our faith—and our questions—in an atmosphere of honesty and respect?

That's what Pat and I have been doing lately.

"Some people see no value in a journey unless they reach a destination," says Pat. "I'm the opposite. I think the journey is often more interesting than the destination."

RESPONDING TO PAT

WHO IS GOD, ANYWAY?

I don't want to pigeonhole anyone, but I think it's fair to say that my friend Pat typifies the postmodern quest for spiritual truth. She's sampled a wide variety of religions, but is unwilling to commit firmly to any of them. She's uncomfortable with Christianity because it seems too exclusive, and she's especially turned off by what she terms the "religious right." She wants a faith that makes sense, yet she admits she believes in reincarnation even though there's no proof for it. To further complicate matters, she's unsure about the trustworthiness of the Bible; so if we try to use the Bible to defend our faith, she may accuse us of circular reasoning, or she may not listen to us at all.

In my discussions with Pat, we kept coming back to one key question: "Who is God, anyway?" She refers to God as the "Big Fuzzy White Thing" (BFWT), and she's turned off by the very names of God and Jesus. If we can help Pat understand who God is, then we'll be able to clear up some of her other concerns as well.

Getting Started

With someone like Pat who already has her defenses up, you can't come across as preachy or manipulative. As we began our conversation, I complimented her honesty and thanked her for opening the door to her "Religion Zone."

Even though she plainly disagrees with my Christian beliefs, she's not looking for a quarrel. She told me, "It's not my intent to 'flame' you. What to me might be just a spirited, rousing, fun debate might be a horrible ulcer-producing argument to you."

I reassured her that I didn't think it was likely she could offend me or give me ulcers as we discussed her questions.

"Even a heated argument isn't all bad," I pointed out, "because at least it shows that people care deeply about the topic they're discussing.

"I have trouble understanding the blasé, 'who cares' attitude so many people seem to have about matters of faith," I continued. "To me, issues like the existence of God and the reliability of the Bible are too important to ignore. I don't want to fritter away my life on 'matters that don't matter' if there really is a God who answers prayer and gives purpose to life. And if Christian faith is true, as I believe, then it will stand up in the give-and-take of serious examination. Jesus never avoided the hard questions, nor should we."

I also thought it wise to tell Pat how I feel about the word *religion*.

"Frankly, I'm not crazy about that word," I told her. "I know what people usually mean by it, but you might be surprised to learn that the word rarely appears in the Bible. And when it does, the Scripture simply says, 'If anyone considers himself religious and yet does not keep a tight rein on his tongue, he deceives himself and his religion is worthless. Religion that God our Father accepts as pure and faultless is this: to look after orphans and widows in their distress and to keep oneself from being polluted by the world' (James 1:26, 27). Watch our words. Take care of parentless children and widows. Avoid hypocrisy and the things that pollute our souls. I'm not sure a lot of people would define 'religion' like that. But my guess is, if believers put that kind of faith into practice, you wouldn't have to worry about so-called Christians who 'use religion as an excuse to kill, maim,' and so on.

"I don't think of myself as a 'religious person,'" I continued. "I'm a Christian. A believer in God. A disciple of Christ. I don't have a halo over my head. I don't sit in a corner praying twenty-four hours a day, and I don't try to do 'good works' so God or others will be impressed with me. I'm a normal guy with a mortgage, a car payment, and some dismay that my teenage daughter can run faster than I can now that I'm middle-aged! But I also believe that Jesus is who he claimed to be, that the Bible is true, and that there's hope for me when I die. If you want to call that 'religion,' OK. But I'd rather just talk about 'faith.' To me, following Christ is simply a way of life, not a 'religion' I practice."

This made sense to Pat. As we began our discussion, I also asked her for some more specifics: "If you don't mind my asking, what exactly is your 'baggage' from the 'religious right'?" She had a lot to say. For example, she had a bad experience as a fourteen-year-old student in a church's confirmation class. The minister said she shouldn't be confirmed because she had too many questions. But to please her parents, she went ahead and gave "the right answers" so she could be confirmed. Instead of finding the answers she needed, she learned to "stuff" her questions and to be suspicious of anything Christian.

Pat had said, "Some people see no value in a journey unless they reach a destination. I'm the opposite. The journey is often more interesting than the destination." I challenged her to look at this a different way.

"I agree with you in part," I ventured. "But what if the point of life is to appreciate BOTH? In other words, what if God created us with the capacity to enjoy the journey, while at the same time, there really is a destination or goal he has in mind for us? What if he gave us a road map to guide us? And better yet, what if God himself wants to accompany us on the journey?"

GETTING TO KNOW GOD

As my dialogue with Pat has continued, here are some steps I've taken to help her understand what I believe about God, and why I believe it. If you know someone like Pat, perhaps some of these ideas will help you as well.

Ask Your Friend to Describe the God in Whom She Does Not Believe

Like Pat, many people hold a distorted, unbiblical concept of God. It can help a lot if you explain that you don't believe in that kind of "god" either.

Some folks think of God as sort of a cosmic Clint Eastwood—a harsh judge just waiting for a chance to say, "Go ahead, make my day." To others, he's a cuddly divine Bill Cosby—kind, wise, often humorous, usually rather passive—certainly not someone to fear. Still others see him as a Star Wars-style "Force." In *Your God Is Too Small*, J. B. Phillips pointed out that many people believe in a divine being who is little more than a "Parental Hangover," a "Pale Galilean," a "God-in-a-Box," or some other inadequate "god."[1]

Pat thinks of God as the "BFWT"—the Big Fuzzy White Thing. Not exactly a biblical designation for the Almighty, but at least it's a place to start. And we have to start where our friends are, not where we'd like them to be.

Tell Your Friend About the God in Whom You Believe

We can't explain everything about God. If we could comprehend him fully, he wouldn't be God. To fit all knowledge about the infinite God into our finite brains would be like trying to fit the ocean into a teacup. Nevertheless, we do know a lot about God because he has revealed himself to us through the world he created, through the Word he inspired, and most of all, through his Son Jesus Christ (Hebrews 1:1-4). He's far more than a vague, nameless deity.

Here are some of the attributes or personal qualities of God described in Scripture.[2]

1. Alive, and the giver of life. God is the "living God." He's not a lifeless idol, but a divine being who has always been alive and always will be alive. All life ultimately depends on his creative and sustaining power (Matthew 16:16; John 1:4; 1 Timothy 4:10; Hebrews 10:31).

2. Spirituality and personality. "God is spirit," Jesus said (John 4:24), not an impersonal force. Among other things, this means he is self-conscious, rational, intelligent, thoughtful, and capable of entering into loving relationships. He is the great "I AM" (Exodus 3:14).

3. All-knowing and all-powerful. He knows every detail of our lives (Psalm 139:1-6; Hebrews 4:13). And "with God all things are possible" (Matthew 19:26)—that is, he has unlimited power to do all things that are consistent with his nature and purpose (Psalm 115:3; Jeremiah 32:17). We require several hours of sleep every night—a consistent reminder of our human weakness and mortality. But God never runs out of energy! He never slumbers nor sleeps (Psalm 121:3, 4).

4. Eternal and ever-present. We live by the clock and measure our time in years, months, days, and hours. But God has no beginning or end. He was there when time began (Genesis 1:1), and he is immortal (1 Timothy 6:15, 16; Jude 25), "the Alpha and the Omega, the First and the Last, the Beginning and the End" (Revelation 22:13). He cannot be limited by space, for he created space (Deuteronomy 10:14), and there's no place we can go to escape from his awareness (Psalm 139:7-10; Jeremiah 23:23, 24).

5. Holy, holy, holy. He is set apart, distinct, different from all else. His heavenly angels stand in awe of his glory (Psalm 99:5; Isaiah 6:3; Revelation 4:8). He is separate from all sin, impurity, or unholiness (Habakkuk 1:13; 1 Peter 1:14-16).

6. Truthful and faithful. He never lies. Because it's his nature to be truthful (Titus 1:2; Hebrews 6:18), God always keeps his promises. We can rely on him completely (Lamentations 3:23; Hebrews 10:23).

7. Righteous and just. Always fair and good, he is the perfect standard of all that is right (Deuteronomy 32:3, 4; Daniel 4:37; Psalm 96:13). "God is light; in him there is no darkness at all" (1 John 1:5).

8. Jealous and angry. God's jealousy is not the spiteful ill will or envy we consider a sin. It's a protective jealousy—the kind of earnest concern a devoted husband rightly feels for his wife, or the vigilant way a loving father watches out for anyone who would harm his children (2 Corinthians 11:2, 3). God isn't just a passive, mild-mannered deity. He possesses intense concern for the welfare of his people (Exodus 20:5; 34:14). Furthermore, his jealousy is a righteous anger toward sin—the natural reaction of his holy nature against all that is hurtful and wrong (Romans 1:18; 2:6-10; Revelation 20:7-15). Finally, God's jealousy refers to his rightful expectation that he alone deserves our worship and honor. God is rightfully, justly jealous when we give our attention and loyalty to someone or something besides him. Our reverence is his due, and he is angry when we give it elsewhere. He alone is God (Exodus 20:5; 34:14).

9. Loving and gracious. God always acts with intelligent goodwill toward the objects of his love. So generous is his giving, so profound his personal sacrifices, the Bible even says "God is love" (1 John 4:8-11; see also John 3:16; Romans 5:5; 2 Corinthians 13:11-14; and Titus 3:4-7). Through Christ, he graciously gives us far more than we deserve, and mercifully spares us from punishments we do deserve (Ephesians 2:1-10; 1 Timothy 1:16; 1 Peter 5:10).

10. Unchanging. God is not fickle or unreliable. He is steadfast and constant (Malachi 3:6; James 1:17).

When we begin to understand God in biblical terms, we fall in awe before his majesty. To put it mildly, the God described in the Bible is far more than a "Big Fuzzy White Thing."

Tell Your Friend Why You Believe the God Described in the Bible Really Exists

Why do you believe in God? Can you put your reasons into words? Philosophers have offered complicated answers, but people like Pat want answers that ring true on a gut level and pass the head test before they can accept them.

I started with a personal testimony. I told her, "I can understand why you might question God. But to me, he's inescapable, even when I try to run from him. Even in my lowest times of doubt and discouragement, my mind can't completely deny him. My emotions cry out for him. My strength fails without him. Jesus said the greatest commandment is to love God with all our heart, soul, mind, and strength. This makes sense to me, because when I'm honest, I realize every part of my being longs for relationship with my Creator."

Then I told her, "At the risk of over-simplifying a complex subject, here are some of the reasons I believe the God revealed in Scripture is the true and living God."

The universe requires a Creator. "In the beginning God created the heavens and the earth" (Genesis 1:1). He preceded all creation; he planned it; he has a purpose for it; he put it all together by his power. Whether you look through a telescope or through a microscope, at the orbits of the planets or at the wings of a hummingbird, you can see order and complexity in nature that point to the hand of God.

Because of Pat's interest in biology, this argument makes sense to her. "Nature," someone has said, "is God's Braille to a blind world." The true God must be higher than his creation; so Christians can't accept pantheism (the idea that "everything is God") or any kind of idolatry that reduces God to a part of nature itself. (See Romans 1:18-20.)

Life requires a Designer—especially human life. A single molecule of human DNA contains roughly the same amount of information as a volume of an encyclopedia. A single living cell functions like a tiny factory. Your human body contains a highly complicated computer (brain), pump (heart), furnace (stomach), camera (eye), musical instrument (ear), communication network (nerves), all designed to move around on a flexible but sturdy structural framework (bones), under a protective covering (skin) that allows perspiration to escape when you exercise but keeps water from pouring into your body when you bathe or swim. In recent years, scientists have spent thousands of hours and millions of dollars to analyze and map the DNA of a common earthworm. If it takes so much human effort to map what's already there (in one of earth's simplest creatures), wouldn't it require a divine effort to create what *wasn't* already there (including all the varied forms of life with all their complexity)?

Even if an evolutionary theory could satisfactorily explain (and none has) how we humans developed such amazing bodies through purely natural means, it would only have scratched the surface of the problem. Where did we get the spiritual part of our being? How did we develop what Christian apologist Francis Schaeffer used to call our "mannishness"? Where did we get our minds, wills, morals, emotions, and aspirations? How did we even come up with the idea of God, if we are not made in his image? Don't we instinctively recognize that we are "fearfully and wonderfully made," and that God has "set eternity in the hearts of men"? (See Psalm 139:13, 14; Ecclesiastes 3:11.)

When Pat suggested that "all religions have a piece of the truth," I told her, "I agree with you in one sense. I think everyone is born with an intuitive awareness that God exists. We have a moral law within us. Even the

Bible acknowledges this (Romans 2:14, 15, for example). We all have an innate longing to know God because we're made in God's image."

"I like that 'moral law within' statement," Pat agreed. "I tend to run things past an internal compass in my gut when I'm not sure what's right."

The Bible requires a Revealer. We need to be careful not to engage in circular reasoning ("I believe in God because the Bible says so; I believe the Bible because God revealed it.") But it's not circular reasoning to say something like this: (1) There's sufficient reason to believe God *exists* even if we didn't have the Bible. (2) But without the Bible, how could we know what God *expects* of us? How could we know about his grace and his plan for our salvation? (3) If God exists, it's reasonable to think he would communicate with creatures made in his image. (4) The Bible has proved reliable in countless areas (like historical details) where we can check its accuracy (see my answer to Ben in chapter three), so it's reasonable to trust its accuracy in areas we can't check.

I've concluded that the Bible is not a book mere men could have written on their own. They wrote it with assistance from God. (See 2 Timothy 3:16, 17, and 2 Peter 1:20, 21.) If Pat disagrees with this conclusion, she then must explain how a magnificent book like the Bible could be produced by ordinary people without any divine help.

Challenge Your Friend to Think About the Consequences of Her Worldview

Non-Christians often put Christians on the defensive. But sometimes we need to turn the tables and compel our unbelieving friends to face the consequences of their beliefs. Here are some questions we can ask:

1. If God is nothing but a Big Fuzzy White Thing (BFWT), what does that make *you*? Are you simply a grown-up germ that emerged from the slime through eons of evolution—as someone said, "from the goo to you by way of the zoo"? Apart from the biblical view that we are created in the image of God, is there really any reference point for human dignity?

2. Are your views really logical, or are they simply wishful thinking? I asked Pat, "Aren't you making a big leap of faith to believe in reincarnation simply because it 'seems right' to you, even though you admit there's no proof for it?"

THE COMMON SENSE OF CAUSE AND EFFECT

A story requires an author.

A song requires a composer.

A painting requires an artist.

A computer code requires a programmer.

A law code requires a lawgiver.

A meal requires a cook.

A child requires a parent.

Doesn't the universe require a designer?

3. Do you have any hope of life after death? If so, on what do you base your hope? Christians believe in eternal life because we hold that Jesus really rose from the dead. If you don't accept his resurrection, do you have any reasonable basis for hope? How can you live without it?

4. Do you have strong, positive convictions to believe in, or are you mainly just reacting against traditional views of God you find difficult to accept?

For example, it seems to me that there's something fundamentally negative about being an "atheist" or an "agnostic." Does it make sense to build your whole philosophy of life on something you deny? To define yourself by a God you don't believe in, or a God you claim not to know? If someone asks me what I am, I don't say, "I'm an *a-Buddhist*," or "I'm an *a-Hindu*." Now, I'm *not* a Buddhist or a Hindu; but I'd rather not describe my beliefs primarily in reference to what I *don't* believe. I am a Christian, a follower of Jesus, a willing servant of the Most High God. That's ennobling, positive, uplifting.

Dare to ask your non-Christian friend whether she really has any peace of mind. This little slogan is trite but true: "No God, no peace. Know God, know peace."

Focus the Discussion on Jesus Christ

In my conversations with Pat, the ultimate question I wanted her to consider was simply, "Who is Jesus Christ?" A Christian's strongest argument for the existence of God is what I call "the Jesus argument." If Jesus is who he claimed to be, then we not only know that there is a God; we also know what God is like.

How can we be sure God isn't just a Big Fuzzy White Thing? Because two thousand years ago he came to earth in the person we know as Jesus of Nazareth!

Philip, one of Jesus' disciples, spoke for a lot of honest questioners when he said, "Lord, show us the Father and that will be enough for us." Do you recall what Jesus said in response? "Don't you know me, Philip, even after I have been among you such a long time? Anyone who has seen me has seen the Father. How can you say, 'Show us the Father'?" (John 14:8, 9).

The God of the Bible isn't just a fuzzy mystical power; he is the Word who "became flesh and made his dwelling among us." And while "no one has ever seen God," the fact is, God's Son "has made him known" or explained him to us (John 1:14, 18). As the apostle Peter wrote of Jesus, "Through him you believe in God, who raised him from the dead and glorified him" (1 Peter 1:21).

Jesus of Nazareth claimed attributes, powers, and honors which belong only to God. His followers believed him to be God. John wrote, "The Word was God" (John 1:1). Paul said, "For in Christ all the fullness of the Deity lives in bodily form" (Colossians 2:9). The doubter Thomas eventually called him "my Lord and my God" (John 20:28). Statements like these appear even more impressive when you recall that Jesus' original disciples were Jewish monotheists who understood that it would be blasphemy for a mere man to claim to be God.[3]

As C. S. Lewis pointed out in *Mere Christianity*, "A man who was merely a man and said the sort of things Jesus said would not be a great

Pat says, "If you think of God as a room, Christians believe that there is only one door into the room, and Christianity is it. To me, this invalidates genuine revelatory experiences that others have encountered in other belief systems." She's willing to agree that Christianity is one "door," but not the "only one."

Here are some points I discussed with her:

1. Christians aren't trying to make our faith exclusive. We're trying to be consistent with the teachings of Jesus who claimed to be the only way to the Father (John 14:6; 1 Timothy 2:5).

2. It's odd that we'd be called "exclusivists," for actually, unlike many religious systems that are tied to a specific ethnic group, Christianity says God loves all people equally and invites everyone to come to him through Christ (Matthew 28:18-20). Centuries before it was popular to be inclusive, Jesus started a church where everyone has equal standing and there is no Jew or Gentile, male or female, slave or free (Galatians 3:26, 27).

moral teacher. He would either be a lunatic—on a level with the man who says he is a poached egg—or else he would be the Devil of Hell. You must make your choice. Either this man was, and is, the Son of God, or else a madman or something worse. You can shut him up for a fool, you can spit at him and kill him as a demon; or you can fall at his feet and call him Lord and God. But let us not come with any patronising nonsense about his being a great human teacher. He has not left that open to us."[4]

Keep the Discussion Going

I've been dialoguing with Pat for months, but she remains unconvinced. *[Note to the reader: If you'd like to read more, the appendix of this book (page 203) contains some excerpts from my ongoing e-mail correspondence with Pat.]*

3. Sometimes misguided Christians have acted as if their own manmade rules are equal to God's rules, thus making the "narrow road" appear more narrow than it really is. Don't confuse bigotry with real Christianity.

4. In many other areas of life, truth is narrow. Why can't we accept this reality in matters of faith? (For example, Pat's husband is a chemist. He must do his work within certain narrow boundaries or the results will be explosive! Likewise, as a computer geek, Pat knows she can send a sensible e-mail message only by pressing the right keys. Why wouldn't the God who created an orderly universe ask us to respond to him within certain prescribed limits?)

5. Jesus talked about the "narrow gate" that leads to life (Matthew 7:13, 14). That road is narrow enough that everyone needs to hear about Jesus and accept him as Savior (Acts 4:12; 1 John 2:23). But that road is also wide enough that God wants everyone to come to a knowledge of the truth and wants no one to perish (1 Timothy 2:3, 4; 2 Peter 3:9; 1 John 2:2).

(For more on this question, see chapter twelve, "Truth, Freedom, and Tolerance," on page 183.)

I'm going to keep in touch. Who knows? Perhaps I've planted a gospel seed someone else will water. Perhaps in time, Pat will find her heart softening to the Word of God. I hope she doesn't wait too long. But in the meantime, I want to keep the lines of communication open so she knows I'm there to talk if she's interested.

Don't be discouraged just because someone rejects your Christian testimony at first. If you had lived in the first century, would you have thought there was any chance that Saul of Tarsus, the church's archenemy, would eventually become a Christian? If you noticed how so many Jewish leaders opposed the gospel, would you have expected that eventually a large number of priests would be obedient to the faith? That's exactly what happened (Acts 6:7).

Never underestimate the power of the gospel. "It is the power of God for

WHAT ABOUT REINCARNATION?

A lot of postmodernists are turning to belief in reincarnation, the idea that we go through many cycles or lifetimes of birth, death, and rebirth. This view is rooted in Eastern religions (especially Hinduism). Space will not permit a thorough discussion of this question in this book, but here are some questions to ask:

Isn't reincarnation intellectually unconvincing? It lacks the kind of historical evidence that supports the resurrection of Christ, whose risen body was witnessed by hundreds of people (1 Corinthians 15:1-6).

Isn't it emotionally unsatisfying? Doesn't it lead to despair if you think you're stuck in an ongoing cycle of lifetimes? How can you offer comfort to a person who's suffering if he's simply paying the price for sin in a past life? And if you aren't sure what form you will take in a future life, how can you have any real hope?

Isn't it spiritually demoralizing? Doesn't it make you feel depersonalized to think there is no personal God who cares about you, and you're simply at the mercy of impersonal fate? Christianity offers a personal relationship with a real heavenly Father, not a philosophy that tells you to lose your identity and become one with the universe.

Isn't it morally uninspiring? How can reincarnation motivate you to be a better person? After all, there's no proof a "good" person will come back in a better form—and who says what's "good" or "better" anyway, if there is no God?

Isn't it socially unworkable? The poor, the sick, the homeless—aren't they simply working out the consequences of bad karma? Why help them avoid the results of their own misdeeds? Have cultures dominated by belief in reincarnation developed superior ways of life?

And of course, it's unbiblical. "Man is destined to die once, and after that to face judgment" (Hebrews 9:27).

THE CLAIMS OF CHRIST

Jesus claimed to be "equal with God" (John 5:17, 18), insisted that he should be honored the same way we honor God the Father (John 5:23), and said, "I and the Father are one"—which his listeners immediately recognized as a claim of equality with God (John 10:30-38). Furthermore, Jesus claimed for himself attributes, powers, and honors which belong only to God:

1. Moral perfection (John 8:29, 46; 2 Corinthians 5:21; 1 Peter 2:22)

2. Eternal existence (John 8:58; 17:5; Hebrews 1:8; Revelation 1:4, 8, 17; 22:13)

3. Power to forgive sin (Mark 2:1-12)

4. Power to bestow life (John 11:25)

5. Authority to judge (Matthew 25:31-46; John 5:26, 27)

Additionally, it's quite significant that Jesus accepted worship when his followers praised him (Matthew 8:2; 9:18; 14:33; 15:25; 28:9, 17; John 9:35-38). It's wrong, of course, to worship Satan (Matthew 4:10). It's wrong to worship men, for even a great man like Peter refused to let Cornelius fall at his feet (Acts 10:25, 26). It's wrong to worship angels (Revelation 19:9, 10; 22:8, 9). But it's right to worship Jesus, the Lamb of God (Revelation 5:12). Thus, he's not a mere man or an angel; he is God.

the salvation of everyone who believes" (Romans 1:16). Like a sharp sword, God's "living and active" Word "penetrates even to dividing soul and spirit, joints and marrow; it judges the thoughts and attitudes of the heart" (Hebrews 4:12). God says, "My word . . . will not return to me empty, but will accomplish what I desire and achieve the purpose for which I sent it" (Isaiah 55:11).

We will reap a harvest if we don't give up (Galatians 6:9). That's why we need to keep giving honest answers to honest questioners like Pat.

QUESTIONS FOR PERSONAL REFLECTION:

1. Do you think you'd enjoy talking about your faith with someone like Pat? Why, or why not?

2. If you believe in God, what convincing reasons can you offer to support the reasonableness of your faith?

RESOURCES FOR FURTHER READING

Bill Hybels, *The God You're Looking For* (Zondervan, 1997).

Jack Cottrell, *God the Creator* (College Press, 1983); *God the Ruler* (College Press, 1984); and *God the Redeemer* (College Press, 1991).

J. I. Packer, *Knowing God* (InterVarsity, 1973).

FOOTNOTES

[1]See J. B. Phillips, *Your God Is Too Small* (Macmillan, 1973).

[2]For a helpful in-depth discussion of the attributes of God, see *God the Creator*, by Jack Cottrell (College Press, 1983).

[3]For an interesting contemporary look at the historical evidence for the claims of Christ, see *The Case for Christ*, by Lee Strobel (Zondervan, 1998). A still-useful older book that introduces people to Christ is *More Than a Carpenter*, by Josh McDowell (Tyndale, 1986).

[4]C. S. Lewis, *Mere Christianity* (Macmillan, 1952), p. 56.

CHAPTER 6

STRANGE IDEAS

I like to keep things plain and simple. Just ask my wife and kids. They know my favorites. Ice cream? Vanilla. Christmas present? A comfortable T-shirt or a funny videotape. Car? Anything that requires no maintenance while consistently transporting me from point A to point B.

Whenever possible, I also like to keep things simple when I talk about my faith. Somewhere I read that when Jesus' words are translated into English in our modern Bibles, 84.4 percent are translated by one-syllable words, 14.2 percent by two-syllable words, and only 1.4 percent by three-syllable words.

No wonder the common people listened to Jesus gladly. He used words they could understand. He didn't speak in a stain-glassed voice or bog down his lessons with theological jargon. He used everyday objects and topics of discussion (like lamps, garden seeds, coins, fish, bread, water, birds, trees, salt, children—even the weather!) to explain deep spiritual truths. He illustrated his points with real-life examples about workers who want fair pay, brides and grooms who rejoice on their wedding day, fathers who give gifts to their children and long for wandering sons to return home, and farmers who bring in the harvest.

When people asked Jesus straightforward questions, he responded with answers both simple and profound. But the problem is, many of today's questions don't sound very simple. A popular book making the rounds among Christians today asks, "What would Jesus say?" and conjectures how the Lord might speak to some of our current celebrities. What *would* he say to honest questioners of the twenty-first century? What would his apostles say?

By now, some readers of this book may even be wondering, "Is this approach to evangelism really biblical—to start with the questions of unbelievers? Are these strange new ideas?" But the fact is, we can find a helpful model for communicating with postmodern people right in the book of Acts.

The New Testament Christians used different approaches with Gentiles than they did with Jews. What can we learn from these first-century believers? How we can take the good news of Christ into the streets where many of our friends, like the men of ancient Athens, think we're bringing "strange ideas" to their ears (Acts 17:20)?

SOME LESSONS FROM THE PAST

The apostle Paul describes his approach to evangelism in 1 Corinthians 9:19-22 when he writes, "Though I am free and belong to no man, I make myself a slave to everyone, to win as many as possible. To the Jews I became like a Jew, to win the Jews. . . . To those not having the law [that is, the Gentiles] I became like one not having the law. . . . I have become all things to all men so that by all possible means I might save some."

What is Paul saying here? Is he advocating a wishy-washy compromise of God's truth? That we become spiritual chameleons who simply adopt the standards of our changing culture and blend with the world around us? No way! To make sure no one misunderstands, Paul hastens to add a disclaimer: "I do all this for the sake of the gospel, that I may share in its blessings" (1 Corinthians 9:23). Firmly committed to the truth of Christ, Paul never advocated anything less than the complete and accurate gospel message. But he was willing to adapt the method of its presentation because he was determined to communicate the message with maximum effectiveness to every culture. Even though he was free in Christ, he was willing to walk in the shoes of others—to understand their worldview and present the gospel in words they could understand.

WORLDS APART

TWO DIFFERENT CULTURES IN THE FIRST-CENTURY WORLD

JEWS	GENTILES
Familiar with the Hebrew Scriptures	Didn't know Amos from Adam
Respected the moral standards of God's law	Didn't know or respect God's law
Monotheistic worldview— believed in one God	Polytheists—had a "god" for almost everything
Familiar with Messianic prophecies	Had never heard of Isaiah, let alone his predictions about the suffering Lamb of God
Familiar with the Spirit and power of God and his miracles	Familiar with philosophical approaches to religious questions
"Demand signs" (1 Corinthians 1:22)	"Look for wisdom" (1 Corinthians 1:22)

Eugene Peterson's *The Message* paraphrases Paul's words as follows: "Even though I am free of the demands and expectations of everyone, I have voluntarily become a servant to any and all in order to reach a wide range of people: religious, non-religious, meticulous moralists, loose-living immoralists, the defeated, the demoralized—whoever. I didn't take on their way of life. I kept my bearings in Christ—but I entered their world and tried to experience things from their point of view. I've become just about every sort of servant there is in my attempts to lead those I meet into a God-saved life. I did all this because of the Message. I didn't just want to talk about it; I wanted to be *in* on it!"[1]

A Closer Look at Paul's Approach

The people Paul encountered could be divided into two main groups: the Jews (those "with the law") and the Gentiles (those "without the law"). There were profound differences between these two groups of people.

The Jews were familiar with the Hebrew Scriptures which they had learned from childhood and their rabbis had taught for generations. They were monotheists (that is, they believed in the one true God). Since they were familiar with the Messianic prophecies written by Isaiah, Jeremiah, Daniel, and other prophets of God, they were filled with eager anticipation of the Messiah's coming. They were familiar with the Spirit and power of God, and the miracles performed through the ministries of Spirit-filled men like Moses and Elijah. Thus, Paul says, "Jews demand miraculous signs" (1 Corinthians 1:22).

The Gentiles, on the other hand, were unfamiliar with the Scriptures. They were polytheists (that is, they believed in many gods). They knew little or nothing about Messianic prophecies or a future intervention by a coming Savior. The Gentiles were familiar with philosophical approaches to God. Thus, Paul says, "Greeks look for wisdom" (1 Corinthians 1:22).

Many religious seekers today still fit into one of these two categories. Like the first-century Jews, some are familiar with the Bible but not satisfied with it. Preoccupied with spiritual gifts and special powers, they "demand miraculous signs" and want personal verification that God really exists before they will believe. Others, like the first-century Gentiles, know little about the Bible but they "look for wisdom"—that is, they're constantly searching for a new system of thought that will explain everything according to human logic and reasoning. But to both groups Paul says, "We preach Christ crucified: a stumbling block to Jews and foolishness to Gentiles" (1 Corinthians 1:23).

The Jews considered Christ's crucifixion a *stumbling block* for a number of reasons: How could prophecy's powerful King suffer and die? And wasn't crucifixion an especially humiliating, shameful manner of death? After all, according to the Law of Moses, a special curse was pronounced on anyone who was "hung on a tree" (Deuteronomy 21:23).

The Gentiles, on the other hand, considered Christ's crucifixion *foolishness*—an oddity. Why should they fall in worship at the feet of a Jewish peasant, especially one who died by such a miserable punishment? Except for extreme cases of treason, Roman citizens were exempt from crucifixion. In 63 B.C. Cicero said, "the very word 'cross' should be far removed not only from the person of a Roman citizen, but from his thoughts, his eyes and his ears." The mere mention of such a horrible punishment, Cicero argued, "is unworthy of a Roman citizen and a free man."[2] Furthermore, Christians proclaimed that Jesus not only died on the cross, but he also rose from the dead. Many of the Greeks denied the possibility of resurrection and rejected any idea of life after death (see Acts 17:32 and 1 Corinthians 15:12).

Maybe we don't have it so bad in our postmodern society after all. If ever a culture appeared resistant to the gospel, it was the *premodern* world of the first century!

But the gospel message still had its effect. Thousands of Jews and Gentiles gladly embraced it. They discovered that Christ is indeed "the power of God and the wisdom of God. For the foolishness of God is wiser than man's wisdom, and the weakness of God is stronger than man's strength" (1 Corinthians 1:24, 25).

SOME PRINCIPLES FOR TODAY

What does all this have to do with reaching postmodern people? A lot! When presenting the gospel to Jews, the apostles followed a pattern that looks something like this:

Old Testament prophecy and history

+

Crucifixion and resurrection of Jesus

They could approach Jews with confidence that members of this audience already believed in God, held a high regard for the Scriptures, and shared their basic worldview. They could begin with Scripture and use it to

HITTING THE STREETS WITH THE GOSPEL

The New Testament shows that Christian faith wasn't just something to talk about inside the comfortable confines of a church building. Believers answered questions and proclaimed their faith in a wide variety of settings:

Open-air gatherings (Acts 2:14-41)

On the road (Acts 8:26-39)

Houses of worship (Acts 13:14-48)

Riverside meeting sites (Acts 16:13-15)

Prisons (Acts 16:22-34)

Shopping malls or marketplaces (Acts 17:16-21)

Government hearing rooms (Acts 17:22-31; 25:1-26:32)

Private homes (Acts 18:26; 20:20)

Lecture halls (Acts 19:9)

Passenger ships (Acts 27:1-26)

make convincing points. This is exactly what Simon Peter did on the Day of Pentecost. He quoted from the book of Joel and from the Psalms, then drove home the point by insisting that "God has raised this Jesus to life, and we are all witnesses of the fact." Not only that, but "God has made this Jesus, whom you crucified, both Lord and Christ" (Acts 2:14-36). Paul followed a similar pattern when he preached in a Jewish synagogue in Pisidian Antioch, except there he also included a more extensive overview of Old Testament history (Acts 13:14-43).

But when they approached Gentiles, the apostles faced an audience who held a worldview radically different from their own. They could not assume that their listeners held any belief in the true God, any familiarity with God's written Word, or any respect for the authority of Scripture. So instead of quoting Scripture, they began by laying a "theistic foundation"– by talking first about the fact of God's existence and who he is. Among the Gentiles the pattern looks more like this:

**Monotheism 101
(basic lessons in
getting acquainted
with the true God)**

+

**Crucifixion and
resurrection of Jesus**

To unsophisticated pagans in Lystra (Acts 14:14-17) and to sophisticated pagans in Athens (Acts 17:22-31), the apostles proclaimed a message about the true God, his kindness to all mankind, and his expectations. This message *harmonized* with biblical truth, but *did not assume prior commitment* to biblical truth. But just as the messages to Jewish audiences eventually brought listeners to confront the Christ of the cross, at Athens Paul concluded by insisting that God gave proof of his message "by raising him [Jesus] from the dead" (Acts 17:31).

All of this leads to three important implications for Christians today.

1. It's vital *to find common ground with seekers* as we strive to reach them for Christ. This does not mean we compromise with evil or betray our Christian values. By "common ground" I simply mean establishing a point of contact, a place of common understanding—some points you and your non-Christian friend can agree upon as a starting point for discussion. (Someone has called it "a landing strip" where you can come down with the gospel.) True to their convictions, yet willing to "become all things to all men," the apostles used different starting points depending on their listeners' worldview.

2. A key issue in determining where to begin is *the position of the non-Christian with regard to the Bible*. In today's postmodern culture, there are still many people around who believe in God (more than ninety percent

of Americans say they do), and many of them have a certain degree of respect for the Bible. Even some of those who don't have an active faith in Christ at least possess a "Christian memory"—that is, they have a positive orientation toward God because of their interactions with Christians in the past. (Perhaps they had a kind relative who quoted Scripture, or they attended Sunday school when they were children.) With people like these, we can go directly to the Scriptures to show God's plan of salvation and his will for our lives.

But in a postmodern culture characterized by increasing ignorance of the Bible and foggy ideas about God, and in which fewer children have been brought up attending Sunday school, we may have to do more foundational work.

Before presenting the plan of salvation, we may need to teach Monotheism 101. We'll need to answer questions like, "Who is God? Why should we believe the Bible is God's Word? What is the basic message of the Bible? What makes it different from other books?" In a postmodern world, we can't assume our friends know and believe the foundational truths familiar to most Christians.

Increasingly, our culture is becoming more "Gentile" than "Jewish," more like Athens than Jerusalem. The church can't afford to ignore this fact.

3. No matter the audience, *we must present the facts of Jesus' death, burial, and resurrection*—the very core of the gospel. Whether the apostles spoke to Jews or Gentiles, they emphasized the death and resurrection of Christ and invited their listeners to respond to the good news. Jesus' cross and empty tomb will never lose their relevance. Although the starting points may differ as we encounter different people and their questions, our goal must be the same with everyone: to introduce them to Christ and his life-changing power.

That isn't going to be easy in a postmodern world. But it's the message we must believe and proclaim, for in every culture the gospel is still the power of God for salvation (Romans 1:16).

QUESTIONS FOR PERSONAL REFLECTION

1. Before becoming a Christian, was your mindset more "Jewish" (familiar with God and the Bible, aware of God's principles of right and wrong), or more "Gentile" (unfamiliar with God and the Bible, unaware of God's ethical standards)?

2. Into which category do you think most of your current acquaintances fit? How will this affect the way you handle the questions they ask you?

RESOURCES FOR FURTHER STUDY

F. F. Bruce, *The Defense of the Gospel in the New Testament* (Eerdmans, 1977).

Zustiak, Gary, *The NeXt Generation* (College Press, 1996).

FOOTNOTES

[1] Eugene Peterson, *The Message*. Used by permission.

[2] Cicero, *In Defence of Rabirius* V.16, p. 467. See also John R. W. Stott, *The Cross of Christ* (InterVarsity, 1986), p. 24.

CHAPTER 7

MATT: WHAT ABOUT DOUBTERS LIKE ME?

When I arrived at the church building a half-hour before the Saturday morning wedding ceremony, the bride greeted me at the front door—in blue jeans and a T-shirt!

"Nice tuxedo," I teased the groom as he strolled up to me, looking as if he were dressed for a weekend barbecue instead of a formal wedding. Matt laughed and shook my hand. We sat on one of the church's well-worn oak pews and talked about how happy he was to be marrying Anne.

Finally, about fifteen minutes before the ceremony was to begin, Matt went downstairs and donned a tuxedo. And when the service started a few minutes later, Anne walked down the aisle, smiling and looking beautiful in her long white dress.

The Mystery Book

Matt and Anne attend a small college in Tennessee, but soon they'll move to Boston for graduate school. Matt has always been a thinker.

"When I was growing up in Indiana, I almost never

attended church," he says. "My parents had good jobs, they were busy making a living—and they seemed happy and content without any particular religious commitment.

"Not that they held any outright antagonism toward Christianity," Matt explains. "It's just that they were focused on other priorities. My family just maintained sort of a friendly lack of interest in spiritual things. I remember that my dad sometimes showed some mild fascination with preachers he heard on TV and radio. He listened to them frequently enough that I suspected he was genuinely curious about their message.

"My parents owned a big family Bible—one of those huge volumes some folks keep on the coffee table and use to record weddings and birthdays. Mom says that when she was pregnant with me, she sometimes read it. But for most of my boyhood, it was simply a 'mystery book'—too imposing for me to read and understand."

No Joke

When Matt was in high school, two of his friends invited him to some of their youth group activities at church. Matt enjoyed teasing them. He'd say, "Hey, Amy, who do you think wrote the Bible?" And when she said, "God did," he'd laugh.

His best friend, Ryan, went to church every Sunday—but mainly just because his mother made him go. Once in a while Matt went with him, and the two of them would sit in church with smirks on their faces, quietly ridiculing what was happening around them.

"We made fun of the sermon, the prayers—how fake the people sounded. It all seemed really goofy to us. It had no connection to real life. It all seemed like a big joke."

Then one day the church's youth minister invited him to

accompany the youth group on a mission trip to Panama City, Florida, and Matt decided to go. "It sounded like a cheap and easy way to have some fun and meet some girls," Matt chuckles.

To his surprise, the trip affected Matt deeply. For the first time, he found himself seriously considering the possibility that Christianity really was true.

A turning point came when a young man gave a short talk about some of Jesus' words from the Bible: "I am the vine; you are the branches. If a man remains in me and I in him, he will bear much fruit; apart from me you can do nothing."

"For some reason, those words really touched me," Matt recalls. "'Apart from me you can do nothing.' I realized I had been trying to do everything on my own."

Before returning home to Indiana, he was baptized in the Gulf of Mexico.

"After that," Matt says, "Christianity certainly was no joke."

Still Questioning

But his questions didn't go away. In fact, now that he was a Christian, the questions intensified.

"When I returned home from the trip to Florida and told my parents what I'd done, at first they thought I'd been brainwashed. They questioned me at length about what I'd done. They allowed me to keep attending worship services and youth group events, but they kept a friendly distance and watched to see if this was merely a phase I was going through."

Meanwhile, Matt wrestled with a new set of doubts.

"After accepting Christ, I knew that Christianity seemed to be working," he says. "I could easily admit, 'It's true for me.' But I wanted to know, is it more than just true for me? Is it TRUE—period? To me, it seemed that there was a big gulf between seeing something as reasonable and seeing it as really true. Just because something seems sensible, that doesn't prove it's right. Even if Christianity seems more reasonable than the other worldviews out there, does that necessarily mean it's true? I wanted to be faithful to the truth, wherever it led me."

He began to read books on philosophy—some written by Christians, others written by non-Christians.

Many of the Christians, it seemed to Matt, tended to overstate their case and make it sound like they had an air-tight case for faith even when they didn't. Other Christian writers were so cautious and hesitant about their conclusions, they offered little help at all. "They said things like, 'It's highly probable that God exists,'" Matt sighs. "Who wants to commit his life to something that's 'highly probable'? Furthermore, non-Christian philosophers do make some interesting points, offering plausible alternatives of their own."

Even though he's continued to go to church, Matt's studies have left him frustrated and anxious, troubled by nagging doubts.

"To me, these questions aren't just a minor irritation. I need to know if Christianity is really true. What am I supposed to do with all these doubts?"

WHAT ABOUT DOUBTERS LIKE ME?

Doubt is a difficult issue for Christians. As someone has said, "We shouldn't dig up in doubt what we planted in faith." Certainly we don't want to question the trustworthiness of God. Yet we have to admit that many of us—even deeply committed believers—do struggle with doubt. Some Christians are reluctant to admit that they have any questions at all, for they see doubt as treason against faith or even an unpardonable sin.

But the simple fact is, we can't resolve our doubts unless we identify and face them; and in the process, we will become better-equipped to assist friends like Matt who wrestle with doubt.

The stakes are high. Bertrand Russell, a famous opponent of Christianity, believed in God until he was eighteen. But during adolescence, he began to doubt his faith and nobody offered him any help. Years later, Russell described his youthful struggles as follows: "I became exceedingly religious and consequently anxious to know whether there was any good ground for supposing religion to be true. For the next four years [beginning when he was fourteen] a great part of my time was spent in secret meditation upon this subject, [but] I could not speak to anybody about it for fear of giving pain. I suffered acutely, both from the gradual loss of faith and from the necessity of silence."[1] Bertrand Russell was left with the tragic impression that he dare not even mention his honest questions about faith.

A DEEPER LOOK AT DOUBT

The word *doubt* comes from the Latin *dubitare*, which is also where we get our word *dubious*. Its root is an old Aryan word meaning "two." (Notice the similarity between *doubt* and *double*.) Doubt is double mindedness, a divided state of mind in which a person wavers between believing and disbelieving. "He who doubts," wrote James, "is like a wave of the sea, blown and tossed by the wind. . . . he is a double-minded man, unstable in all he does" (James 1:6, 8). In English, we say that a doubter is "sitting on the fence." The

Chinese have a similar expression; they use the humorous analogy of a "person having a foot in two different boats."[2]

As Matt has discovered, doubts don't necessarily go away simply because you accept Christ. In fact, he has a lot of company in the Bible, where numerous individuals asked honest questions and wrestled with doubt in one form or another.

Old Testament Questions

Even though you accept the fact of God's existence, you may find yourself wondering at times about the acts of God—why he says what he says and does what he does. For example . . .

Abraham and Sarah. When God informed them that they were going to have a baby in their old age, Sarah laughed. (After all, you don't see a lot of ninety-year-old women in the maternity ward.) Later, when their son was born, they named the boy "Isaac," which means "he laughs" (Genesis 18:9-15; 21:3).

Moses. At the burning bush God called Moses to lead his people out of Egyptian bondage, but Moses came up with one excuse after another: "Who am I to do this? What if the people don't believe me? I don't speak very well, Lord, so why don't you send someone else?" As someone has said, Moses' attitude was, "Here am I, send Aaron!"

Gideon. After the Midianites and other groups ransacked his homeland, Gideon found himself threshing wheat in the stifling discomfort of a winepress. God's angel appeared and said, "The Lord is with you, mighty warrior." But if there was anything Gideon didn't feel like right then, it was a mighty warrior. So he answered the angel with an honest question: "But sir, . . . if the Lord is with us, why has all this happened to us? Where are all his wonders that our fathers told us about . . . ? But now the Lord has abandoned us and put us into the hand of Midian" (Judges 6:11-13).

Job wondered about the goodness of God and asked, "If I have sinned, what have I done to you, O watcher of men? Why have you made me your target? Have I become a burden to you?" (Job 7:20).

David felt abandoned by God and asked, "How long, O Lord? Will you forget me forever? How long will you hide your face from me?" (Psalm 13:1).

Solomon keenly understood how empty life can seem at times. He asked, "Who knows what is good for a man in life, during the few and meaningless days he passes through like a shadow? Who can tell him what will happen under the sun after he is gone?" (Ecclesiastes 6:12).

Habakkuk wondered why God postponed his answers to prayer and sometimes refused to intervene at all. He asked, "How long, O Lord, must I call for help, but you do not listen? Or cry out to you, 'Violence!' but you do not save? Why do you make me look at injustice? Why do you tolerate wrong?" (Habakkuk 1:2, 3).

New Testament Questions

Zechariah. This aging priest found it hard to believe the angel's promise that Elizabeth, Zechariah's wife, would bear a son (Luke 1:18-20).

John the Baptist. From prison, John sent messengers to ask for reaffirmation that Jesus really was the Christ—even though he'd already received special confirmation from God about this matter (Matthew 11:2, 3; 3:13-17).

Jesus' brothers. At one point in Jesus' ministry, even James, Jude, and other members of his own family didn't believe in him (John 7:1-5; compare Mark 3:21; 6:1-3).

Martha confessed her faith in God's power to raise the dead, but she hesitated when Jesus said to open her brother's sealed tomb after four days (John 11:27, 38-40).

Thomas is famous for the way he demanded empirical evidence of Jesus' resurrection (John 20:24-29), but he was not really very different from the rest of the apostles who refused to believe the first reports that Jesus was alive again (Luke 24:9-12).

Other disciples. After Jesus' resurrection, in the verse immediately before the Lord's famous Great Commission, Scripture notes that "when they saw him, they worshiped him; but some doubted" even then (Matthew 28:17).

If you ever struggle with doubt, please note: the fact that the people closest to Jesus still had trouble believing him shows that they were not mindless sheep, blindly following anyone who came along with a tantalizing new message. The fact that Christ did not act as they expected him to gave them problems precisely because they were thinking, reasoning people. Like us, they wanted God to act as they thought he should, and they found it hard to accept him on his own terms.

DOUBTERS WE'RE LIKELY TO ENCOUNTER

Why do people doubt? For many different reasons. We make a serious mistake if we assume that all doubt is the same and all doubters require the same treatment. People like Matt need us to listen respectfully to their honest questions in order to discern the source of their doubt.

Some folks doubt because of *lack of information;* they simply don't know the facts that could help them believe. When Matt was growing up, his parents' big family Bible was little more than a "mystery book" to him. He doubted simply because he hadn't been informed. Others, like the two disciples Jesus encountered on the road to Emmaus, might be somewhat familiar with the Bible, but they are "slow of heart" to understand its deeper meaning (Luke 24:25).

Others doubt because of *perplexity.* Jesus' disciples, for example, didn't know how to react at first to his strange-sounding predictions about his coming crucifixion (Mark 9:30-32). People with troubled hearts (John 14:1) can find themselves immobilized by uncertainty and indecision.

Sometimes doubt results from *weariness;* we grow "faint of heart," exhausted by physical or emotional stress. After the dramatic victory over the prophets of Baal on Mount Carmel, when the Lord sent fire from Heaven to consume the sacrifice and prove that he alone was God, Elijah ran for his life from the wicked Queen Jezebel. It should have been the prophet's finest hour—a mountaintop experience to savor—but instead he found himself exhausted in the desert, sleeping under a broom tree and asking God to take his life (1 Kings 19:1-5).

Actually, it isn't surprising that some of Matt's greatest doubts arose

WORDS FOR DOUBT OR UNBELIEF IN THE GREEK NEW TESTAMENT

Distazo: to have two positions, to waver in opinion (Matthew 28:17)

Diakrino: to separate thoroughly, judge between, decide, discern; also to stagger, waver, or hesitate (Acts 10:20; 11:12)

Airo: to lift, take up or away, suspend; hang in midair; to suspend judgment (John 10:24)

Aporeo: unable to proceed or more forward; uncertain what to do; not sure which way to go (John 13:22; Galatians 4:20; 2 Corinthians 4:8)

Diaporeo: not knowing which way to turn; perplexed, puzzled (Acts 2:12; 5:24; 10:17)

Meteorizomai (the root of our word *meteor*): to raise up in midair, fluctuate; to be anxious or "up in the air" about something (Luke 12:29)

Dialogismos: a dialogue, discussion, dispute, or debate (Luke 24:38; Romans 14:1; Philippians 2:14; 1 Timothy 2:8)

Apistos: faithless, unbelieving (John 20:27; Revelation 21:8)

---

after he became a Christian. Jesus himself faced intense temptation shortly after his baptism (Matthew 3:13–4:11). C. S. Lewis wrote about what often happens after a person comes to faith: "I can tell that man what is going to happen to him in the next few weeks. There will come a moment when there is bad news, or he is in trouble, or is living among a lot of other people who do not believe it, and all at once his emotions will rise up and carry out a sort of blitz on his belief. . . . Now faith, in the sense in which I am here using the word, is the art of holding on to things your reason has once accepted, in spite of your changing moods."[3]

Another kind of doubt springs from a sense of personal *inadequacy.*

This is the "fearful heart" that comes from focusing on one's own weaknesses rather than the Lord and his strength. It's actually *self*-doubt—the frightening, almost paralyzing, this-job-is-bigger-than-I-am kind of hesitation that even caused great men like Moses, Jeremiah, and Paul to hesitate and ask, "Who is equal to such a task?" (Exodus 4:10-14; Jeremiah 1:6, 7; 2 Corinthians 2:16). If you've ever tried to tackle a task that looked too big to accomplish, you understand the doubt of inadequacy.

Then there's the doubt of *disillusionment*—the "wounded heart" that results from being let down by another Christian or a church leader you trusted. If you've been deeply hurt, you might choose the security of doubt over the risk of facing further disappointment. For example, when Jesus appeared to his disciples after rising from the dead, at first "they still did not believe it because of joy and amazement" (Luke 24:41). It seemed too good to be true. Os Guinness points out, "What they were seeing was the one thing in all the world they wanted most. That was precisely the trouble. They wanted it so much that to believe it and then discover it was false would have been profoundly disillusioning."[4]

While it's not necessarily a sin to feel weary, perplexed, or disillusioned, some other forms of doubt plainly cross the line into sin, for they involve willful or "volitional" doubts.

For example, there is stubborn *unbelief* or "hardness of heart." Did you ever meet a person who willfully refuses to accept the truth no matter how much evidence you offer him? Someone who will never be convinced no matter what you do?

Once his friends began to tell him about Christ, Matt accepted the Lord even though he still had plenty of questions. But not everyone is willing to do that. It can be exasperating when you encounter outright spiritual blindness. Even Jesus was deeply distressed by those who stubbornly refused to believe even after he'd presented them with large amounts of evidence (Matthew 11:20-24; Mark 3:5; 16:14).

Similarly, there is the doubt of *unsubmissiveness*—the "rebellious heart" that will agree with Christians in theory but still won't respond in faith and obedience. Scripture has another word for this attitude: "stiffnecked." What a vivid word picture for stubbornness! When you have a stiff neck, you find it hard to turn and look at things from a different point of view. For folks like these, their intellectual objections serve as little more than a smoke screen.

The real problem isn't lack of evidence, but moral stubbornness. Some folks would rather doubt than repent and change their lifestyle. "Men loved darkness instead of light because their deeds were evil" (John 3:19). And some would rather doubt than acknowledge a supreme being. For some, who live outwardly "moral" lives, the problem isn't so much a matter of doing obviously evil deeds as it is an unwillingness to submit themselves to God's authority. Remember, even someone like Saul of Tarsus needed the forgiveness found only in Christ, even though he had been a man who appeared moral on the outside (see Galatians 1:14 and Philippians 3:3-6). Likewise, Cornelius was a man who prayed and gave generously to help those in need, but this proud soldier still needed to submit himself to the Lord and accept the gospel (Acts 10:1-48).

Perhaps most frightening is the doubt of *complacency*—the "divided heart" of a person who remains uncommitted and apathetic—so comfortable with the status quo, he tries to live in the no-man's-land between godliness and worldliness. Curiously, the word from which we derive our word *apathy* (Greek *apeitheia,* which means "indifference" or "without feeling") is usually translated "disobedience" in the New Testament (Romans 11:30-32; Ephesians 2:2; 5:6; Hebrews 4:6-11). If we don't believe deeply, it's easy to drift into apathy; and apathy leads to disobedience. But Jesus finds lukewarmness nauseating (Revelation 3:16). "No one can serve two masters," the Lord said (Matthew 6:24).

At least Matt cares deeply about his faith. His discomfort with doubt drives him to search for the truth. And remember, God "rewards those who earnestly seek him" (Hebrews 11:6).

HOW TO HELP A DOUBTER

The Bible says, "Be merciful to those who doubt" (Jude 22). So how can we help friends like Matt whose honest questions never seem to ease up? Here are some suggestions.

Handling "Faith Stress"

1. *Be willing to intervene.* Some of our friends will find relief simply by being able to talk about their questions without receiving instant condemna-

FAITH'S FOUNDATION

Everybody faces sticky questions that are difficult to resolve. If you have no foundation in faith, when you wonder about spiritual things, you'll simply run into more questions. On the other hand, if you place your faith in God and his Word, you may still ask many of the same questions; but you'll have a solid foundation to guide you and God's power to support you as you wrestle with these troublesome issues.

$$\frac{?????????}{?????????} = \text{CONFUSION} \qquad \frac{?????????}{\substack{?????????\\ \textbf{FAITH}}} = \text{GROWTH}$$

Without faith, your questions just lead to greater confusion

But with faith in God undergirding your life, questions can lead to spiritual growth

tion and rejection. As Matt reported with a grin, "One of my Christian friends—a professor whose real name, by the way, is Dr. Wise!—helped me a great deal simply by saying, 'Let's talk about your doubts.'"

2. Be careful about your own attitude. It's good to approach any kind of spiritual intervention with the humble caution the apostle Paul prescribed in Galatians 6:1, 2: "Brothers, if someone is caught in a sin, you who are spiritual should restore him gently. But watch yourself, or you also may be tempted."

Matt urges, "Don't make outrageous claims. Admit the limits of your own knowledge. Approach other people with an attitude of humility and honesty."

3. Provide assistance in identifying the kind and cause of the doubt. This can help believers who struggle with false guilt because of their questions.

After all, what we sometimes label as sinful doubt is actually just "faith under stress." Everybody faces questions that are hard to answer. If you have no faith, the questions leave you even more confused. But Christians face questions with our feet firmly planted on a foundation of faith, which grows as we continue the learning process of discipleship.

Sometimes, as Os Guinness notes, "Instead of speaking clearly, faith is stammering with fright or choked with pain. But such doubt is still faith stammering, faith stumbling, faith being strangled. Whatever pressure it is under and however strange it sounds, it's not unbelief—at least, not until it gives up and turns back or goes over to the other side."[5] It's important to distinguish between willful disbelief and faith undergoing the painful process of growth.

Potential Remedies

Remember the different kinds of doubt described earlier in this chapter? Let's revisit them, and this time offer a potential remedy for each one.

If the problem is *lack of information,* lend your doubtful friend a book (perhaps this one!), bring him with you to a small group, meet with him for coffee and help him find the information he needs. Teach him "with great patience and careful instruction" (2 Timothy 4:2). Matt says, "God used the Scriptures to convince me. Faith comes by hearing, after all." As someone has said, "Feed your faith and your doubts will starve to death."

If the problem is *perplexity,* pray that God will give your friend wisdom. Our heavenly Father delights to answer our requests for wisdom with a resounding "yes" (James 1:5)!

If the problem is *weariness,* help your friend obtain the kind of rest that will nurture his soul—a spiritual retreat, a vacation, or even just a good night's sleep can help. Before sending Elijah back into the fray, God made sure he was fed and refreshed by hours of sleep (1 Kings 19:5-9).

If the problem is *inadequacy,* nothing works better than the kind of healthy encouragement a person can receive in the fellowship of other believers (1 Thessalonians 5:14). Invite your friend to attend church or a small group with you. If he's already a Christian, help him discover his spiritual gifts so he can find a place of satisfying ministry in the body of Christ.

People who have been *disillusioned* need us to patiently regain their trust. Over time, our consistent example and steady love will earn their respect as they observe our efforts to do what is right both to them and to God (2 Corinthians 8:21).

When stubborn *unbelief* causes a friend to reject all evidence for faith, we need to prayerfully engage in spiritual warfare, asking God to break down Satan's strongholds (2 Corinthians 10:3-5).

If the problem is *unsubmissiveness,* we need to tactfully but firmly confront the moral issues that lie behind our friend's intellectual objections. This requires courage and careful discernment. Jude tells us to "be merciful to those who doubt," but he also says there are others who need to be snatched "from the fire" (Jude 22, 23). James dared to confront some double-minded friends with these bold words: "Come near to God and he will come near to you. Wash your hands, you sinners, and purify your hearts, you double-minded" (James 4:8).

Finally, those afflicted by the doubt of *complacency* need encouragement to commit themselves firmly and wholeheartedly to the Lord. As Joshua put it, "Choose for yourselves this day whom you will serve. . . . But as for me and my household, we will serve the Lord" (Joshua 24:15). On Mount Carmel, Elijah challenged the people, "How long will you waver between two opinions? If the Lord is God, follow him; but if Baal is God, follow him" (1 Kings 18:21). The old hymn by Charlotte Elliott says it this way: "Just as I am, though tossed about, with many a conflict, many a doubt; Fightings and fears within, without, O Lamb of God, I come, I come."

Do you have a friend who struggles with doubt? Reach out to him or her in love. Are you a doubter asking honest questions? God wants you to come to him just as you are.

Matt says, "I began to confront the sin of my own pride. One definition of sin, after all, is trying to be independent of God. I realized I was trying to construct a bridge to God simply through my own intellect, without his even being involved at all.

"As simple as it sounds, I found help with my doubts when I admitted that I couldn't resolve them on my own. I was stirred by the gospel when I thought about Jesus, and how even he had a time when he asked, 'My God, my God, why have you forsaken me?'

"Think about it," Matt adds softly. "Jesus even took our confusion to the cross with him."

QUESTIONS FOR PERSONAL REFLECTION

1. What has been your most troubling doubt about the Christian faith? Have you resolved it satisfactorily? If so, how? If not, why not?

2. Can you think of a friend or neighbor who struggles with one of the eight kinds of doubt described in this chapter (lack of information, perplexity, weariness, inadequacy, disillusionment, unbelief, unsubmissiveness, or complacency)? What could you do to help him or her resolve this doubt?

3. Do you find it natural to talk openly with other people about your faith questions? Why, or why not?

RESOURCES FOR FURTHER STUDY

Alister E. McGrath, *The Sunnier Side of Doubt* (Zondervan, 1990).

Os Guinness, *God in the Dark* (Crossway Books, 1996).

FOOTNOTES

[1]Bertrand Russell, I *Believe* (Allen & Unwin, 1969), p. 116.

[2]Os Guinness, *God in the Dark* (Crossway Books, 1996), p. 23. Used by permission.

[3]C. S. Lewis, *Mere Christianity* (Macmillan, 1952), p. 123.

[4]Guinness, p. 148. Used by permission.

[5]Guinness, *In Two Minds: The Dilemma of Doubt and How to Resolve It* (InterVarsity, 1976), p. 224.

CHAPTER 8

BEV: WHY DID GOD LET THIS HAPPEN TO ME?

After twenty-six years as a flight attendant for United Airlines, Bev knows the routine well. A forty-five-year-old single mom, she leaves home before 5:00 A.M., hoping her boys (ages fourteen and sixteen) will wake up in time for school. Most of the time, they do; but nevertheless, they're on her mind as she begins her commute to Chicago's O'Hare International Airport.

The sun is just beginning to come up as Bev boards the early-morning flight to Phoenix. While the pilot navigates his way through three hours in the air, she navigates a cart through the DC-10's narrow aisle, serving croissants and coffee to her share of the plane's sleepy passengers. Along with the roar of the engines, other familiar sounds fill the air: "Ladies and gentlemen, we're experiencing some turbulence. Please stay in your seat with your seat belt fastened."

She notices the anxiety on the face of a little girl. The child is what airline personnel call a "UM"—an unaccompanied minor—traveling alone to see her dad in Arizona. Bev smiles and chats with the child. But she doesn't like the sound of those words. *Alone. Dad. Turbulence.*

What Does a Fourteen-Year-Old Understand?

"When I was a little girl, I was proud of my dad," Bev muses. "He was a physician at McNeal Memorial Hospital, where he organized and led the department of physical therapy. People would come from Europe so Dad could treat them."

Bev recalls a little European girl who'd been told she could never walk again. "I don't remember what was wrong with her, but my dad worked with her a lot. She could hardly crawl at first. Dad had me come to the hospital on weekends to play with her, and he gave me directions that when I threw the ball, I couldn't go get it—I had to make *her* go get it. I'd put her on a tricycle and push her through the halls of the hospital, while she kept her feet on the pedals to exercise her legs.

"Dad used to throw both of us into the swimming pool," Bev laughs. And she remembers how her young friend progressed.

"In a short period of time, the girl not only started to walk; she could run and play ball with me. My dad was a good doctor. He never said 'no' to anybody. Besides working at the hospital, he'd make house calls and go to people's homes because they couldn't get to him."

One night, Bev's mom and dad decided to go out for dinner with some friends. They'd planned a scavenger hunt—a fun way to spend an autumn evening. Bev's dad took her to the house where she was to baby-sit for the children of one of the couples involved in the scavenger hunt. Playing with the children, she waved goodbye as her dad drove away in his olive green Buick Electra.

It was the last time Bev ever saw her dad alive. He died that night from a massive heart attack. He was forty-one. She was fourteen.

"I've always felt that I was cheated," Bev laments. "He died before I got to know him. Why was he taken from me?"

She received very little assistance with her questions because her mother felt the same way. "Mom had no one to help her, and she asked for no help. It was kind of tough for all of us for a while."

The family decided not to take Bev to the funeral. It would upset her, her grandmother reasoned. Why make her cry even more? And anyway, what does a fourteen-year-old understand about tragedy and death?

Bev understood enough to hurt deeply—and enough to question the love of a God some call Father but who, it seemed, wasn't willing for her to have a dad nearby during her teen years.

"Why Did You Take Him Away?"

In the aftermath of her dad's death, Bev's friends and relatives tried to offer words of comfort, but there was something hollow about it all.

She and her brother had attended Sunday school when they were little—she remembers "the big statues and the big cathedrals"—but her parents didn't attend themselves.

"God was never mentioned, except sometimes during the holidays when someone would say a prayer," she recalls.

"I memorized some of the prayers I learned in Sunday school but never understood what I was saying," Bev admits. "I was mainly worried about whether or not one of the nuns was going to slap me on the back of my hand with a ruler. It never dawned on me that I could have a relationship with God."

When she became a teenager, her parents told her it was her choice whether she'd go to church or not. She chose not to go.

She often felt that something was missing. But all she really felt toward God was anger. And she wondered, "Why did you take my dad away from me, God—right when I needed him most?"

Trying to Fill the Void

"After my dad died, I was home alone when one of my boyfriend's buddies rang the doorbell at 6:00 in the morning. He said he was too drunk to drive home, and he wanted to come in and lie down on the living room couch for a while. Something in my heart said 'Don't let him in,' but I said 'OK' and opened the door, then went back to bed. A few minutes later, he came into my bedroom and raped me. I didn't report it. It was the first of four times I was sexually attacked—in part, I think, because I kept putting myself into dangerous situations. I thought that sex—even sex with someone I didn't know or care about—at least was a way to feel loved."

Still angry with a God she didn't know and didn't trust, Bev graduated from high school and began using drugs to fill the void—especially marijuana. "Pot would relax me and make me feel like a part of the crowd," she says. "I took uppers and speed; but then I had to drink to come down, so I was drunk a lot of the time."

At age twenty-nine, Bev married a man she met while double-dating with two other friends. She and her husband frequently used drugs together. But after having two babies, Bev determined to quit. "I knew that if I was going to keep my life together and raise two kids, I couldn't do it while I was on drugs," she says. With help from a rehab program and an employees' assistance program at work, Bev has stayed drug-free for the last thirteen years.

But her husband never quit. They stayed married for sixteen years, but after he went through four different treatment centers in unsuccessful attempts to get off drugs, the couple finally divorced two years ago. She has custody of the boys. Through it all, she was able to keep her job with the airline—but finances are tight, and Bev worries about her teenage boys when she flies off to Phoenix.

And she wonders, "If there is a God, why does he let so many bad things happen in a person's life? If he really cares, why doesn't he do something to fill that empty spot in a person's soul?"

Single parents often have to navigate their way through a lot of turbulence, but Bev has faced more than most. And today, she's got another plane to catch.

RESPONDING TO BEV

WHY DID GOD LET THIS HAPPEN TO ME?

What can you say to someone like Bev? Does she need your pity? She's been through a lot: the sudden death of her physician father, repeated sexual abuse, a prolonged bout with drug and alcohol abuse, a failed marriage.

Should you tell her you admire her? After all, despite her problems she has managed to hold down a job and stay drug-free for thirteen years. She's devoted to her teenage sons. And at least she's honest enough to ask, "Why did God let my dad die right when I needed him most?"

Should you tell her that you know how she feels? Her questions, after all, aren't unusual. Who hasn't wondered about life's unfairness? Who hasn't had to overcome some hurts from the past? Who hasn't wondered why bad things happen? Yet you have to admit, Bev has indeed faced more "turbulence" than most.

Unless you're an experienced counselor, you might feel stymied when a friend comes to you with honest questions like Bev's. While you and I may not be able to offer the kind of in-depth counseling that can untangle the knots from a person's past, there are some ways we can help. Faith in God plays a vital role in emotional healing, and ordinary believers can make a big difference if we're willing to come alongside friends like Bev who need us to respectfully, gently give the reason for our hope (1 Peter 3:15).

COUNTERPRODUCTIVE APPROACHES

First let me point out four counterproductive approaches—some unhelpful things we should *not* do or say.

1. Avoiding

When a person expresses anger toward God, we may not want to get involved. Why befriend someone like Bev who carries a lot of baggage from the past? Who needs another high-maintenance relationship?

I'm glad Jesus didn't take that approach. He didn't stay in an ivory tower in Heaven so he could avoid tough situations and difficult people. He came to earth as Immanuel, "God with us." He touched lepers. He dined with well-known sinners. He mingled with rough-cut carpenters, fishermen, and soldiers. He pursued a life-changing conversation with a Samaritan woman whose checkered past included five husbands and whose present included a live-in companion.

Avoid people like Bev? Not if we're going to follow in Jesus' footsteps.

2. Minimizing

Some Christians are quick to downplay life's unfairness. They deal with life's heartaches stoically, with a stiff upper lip. They treat people like Bev as if they are whiners and complainers.

Others adopt an over-simplified approach that dismisses the problem of evil with theological platitudes. "That's OK, everything works together for good." "Just pray and you'll feel better."

Still others attempt to minimize suffering through an indifferent attitude that says, "Yeah, well, life is tough all over. I could tell you about some problems of my own!"

But we shouldn't downplay Bev's pain when she asks, "Where was God when my dad died? Why did he allow me to be raped?" On a deeper level, philosophers speak of something they call a *theodicy*—a reasonable explanation of how God can be just even though he allows evil to exist in the world. People ask different versions of Bev's question every day in hospital rooms and funeral homes, at accident scenes and grave sites, through hushed conversations in doctors' offices and silent doubts in their own minds.

As someone has said, "It's a problem as old as the first tear and as recent as the latest news." Every day, people face the frustrating realization that something or someone they valued is irretrievably gone, irreversibly lost. Health fails. A plane crashes. A factory lays off workers. A young mom comes home to find her husband gone. A baby dies. A tornado devastates a town. With one wrong turn of the steering wheel, a teenager leaves behind dozens of grieving family and friends.

We want to know why. If God is powerful and loving, why doesn't he intervene?

Don't minimize a question this important.

3. Blaming

Another counterproductive technique is blaming. We could call this the "sin and suffer syndrome."

"No wonder you've had problems in your life," a hard-liner might say to Bev. "What do you expect? You brought it on yourself by ignoring God, using drugs, violating God's standards of sexual purity, and marrying unwisely."

Now, there is a kernel of truth in this point of view. The Bible teaches, "Do not be deceived: God cannot be mocked. A man reaps what he sows"

(Galatians 6:7). Much human suffering results from our own foolish choices, and we have no one to blame but ourselves. As Proverbs 19:3 points out, "A man's own folly ruins his life, yet his heart rages against the Lord." We shouldn't blame God for problems of our own making.

But not all suffering can be explained as the direct consequence of our own personal sin. Jesus never sinned, but he suffered intensely. Job was a blameless and upright man who "feared God and shunned evil" (Job 1:1), yet he endured one hardship after another. When Jesus came upon a man who'd been blind since birth, the disciples tried to find someone to blame. They asked, "Rabbi, who sinned, this man or his parents, that he was born blind?" And Jesus responded, "Neither this man nor his parents sinned, . . . but this happened so that the work of God might be displayed in his life" (John 9:2, 3).

Some of life's sorrows result from our own sinful misuse of God-given freedom; some from the sins of others; some from the direct attacks of Satan; some from natural laws God has ordained to operate in our world. All human suffering is traceable to Adam and Eve's disobedience in the Garden of Eden that introduced sin to the world. The result? Physical death for all of humanity and a world "subjected to frustration," in "bondage to decay," and "groaning as in the pains of childbirth" (Genesis 3; Romans 8:18-22).

Car accidents, heart attacks, and emotional anguish should come as no surprise in this sin-tarnished world that the Bible describes with unvarnished realism. That's why Jesus stated so honestly, "In this world you will have trouble" (John 16:33). It's why 1 Peter 4:12 bluntly warns, "Dear friends, do not be surprised at the painful trial you are suffering, as though something strange were happening to you." As someone has said, to be surprised by suffering is to be surprised that something Jesus predicted has actually come true! Bad things happen routinely enough that you can't always pin the blame on any specific sin a person has committed.[1]

Surely no one would argue that Bev's dad died when she was fourteen to punish her for something bad she had done.

4. Pitying

Pitying doesn't help much either. Pity dismisses the wounded questioner with a condescending pat on the head, but genuine concern offers a hand to help. Pity says "I feel bad for you" while walking away, but empathy says "I'll try to understand what you're going through" and sticks around.

Bev doesn't want anyone's pity. Misguided pity is what caused her grandmother and other relatives to advise that she not even attend her dad's funeral. "It would upset her more," they reasoned.

But we shouldn't short-circuit grief. The grief process is part of our God-given emotional equipment for dealing with loss in a loss-prone world.

There's a big difference between godly compassion and shallow pity. When Jesus encountered a grieving widow on her way to bury her only son, "his heart went out to her" (Luke 7:13). At the tomb of his friend Lazarus, "Jesus wept" (John 11:35). He not only cared enough to weep, but also to stick around and intervene, bringing hope to his grieving friends.

God calls us to do more than feel sorry for others; he calls us to "be kind and compassionate to one another" and to "live a life of love, just as Christ loved us and gave himself up for us as a fragrant offering and sacrifice to God" (Ephesians 4:32; 5:2).

Christians must be honest: disappointments and griefs like Bev's are an all-too-common fact of life. But we do not "grieve like the rest of men, who have no hope" (1 Thessalonians 4:13). Our hope in Christ makes all the difference when we confront life's injustices.

CONSTRUCTIVE APPROACHES

What are some better ways to handle the honest questions of those who feel angry with God? A beginning point is to acknowledge that anger itself can be an expression of faith. You can't be angry with someone who doesn't exist! To feel angry with God is to admit, at least, that he is there. In their book, *Trusting God Again*, Glandion Carney and William Long analyze the suffering of Job. They point out that "Job was angry principally because he did believe, deep down, that God is a just and good God and that therefore what happened to him was unjust and should be rectified."[2]

Let's revisit Bev and consider where her spiritual journey has taken her since she first verbalized her angry questions toward God. Her story has a happier ending than you might imagine. About two years ago, Bev became a Christian.

Here are some things that helped her.

Help Your Friend Discover the Fatherly Love of God

Just as a child doesn't understand everything his parents say and do, sometimes God's ways appear bewildering to us. Deuteronomy 29:29 says, "The secret things belong to the Lord our God, but the things revealed belong to us and to our children forever, that we may follow all the words of this law." In other words, there are mysteries ("secret things") we can't understand about God and about life. But God has revealed much that we *can* understand and obey—enough to keep us busy for a lifetime. Bev's heart still aches because of her dad's death, but as she's become better acquainted with the Bible, she's learned to trust the fathomless love of God who is a "father to the fatherless" (Psalm 68:5).

Bev says, "I was raised to think lightning was going to strike me down if I sinned or did wrong. Well, I did sin and I did a lot wrong, so how could God love me?

"But now I realize God loves everybody—not only me, the victim who was raped. He also loves the guys who raped me. It was hard for me to understand that. But now I realize that you can do something wrong, and God still loves you. He does want you to be accountable for what you did wrong, though, and learn from it."

When she became a Christian, Bev says, "I let go. I told God, 'Now you take care of things.' I didn't say it in anger like I'd done over the years. Before, I'd say to God, 'You take care of my bills.' Then I wouldn't pay my bills and my house would go into foreclosure! Now I realize that that's not what it's all about. I still have to write the checks, but God is going to help put it all together. And since I've let go and told God, 'You do it,' he has."

"I still have trouble understanding the Bible," Bev admits. "Mark (my minister) suggested that I read children's Bibles, and that's what I read now. I go to church, but I also go to Sunday school with the second, third, and fourth graders. I'm one of the assistants. I help the kids get to know one another. Then when the teaching part of the class starts, some of the adult helpers leave, but I stay there to listen to the stories and learn what the kids are learning. I'll say, 'Boy, I didn't know that! Jesus was on a boat, and there was a big storm, and everyone was all upset, and Jesus said, "Where's your faith?"'

"The kids laugh at me," Bev chuckles, "because they've heard these stories before!"

If you've been a Christian for a long time, you may find it hard to relate to Bev's newfound excitement about God's love. But don't forget: the heart of the gospel—the ultimate answer to the problem of evil—rests in the work of Jesus Christ. As author Philip Yancey has asked, "Where is God when it hurts?" Right here with us, that's where.

Why did so many bad things happen to Bev? I don't know. But I do know this: God isn't aloof, detached, and unaffected by our sorrows. Christ shows that he is a *vulnerable* ("woundable," from the Latin *vulnus*) God who takes our pain upon himself. Yet God isn't powerless either. Through his resurrection, Christ gives us "living hope" (1 Peter 1:3).

"I still have trouble when people talk about God's anger—probably because of my childhood experiences," Bev acknowledges. "I'm learning to trust God, but I still feel uncomfortable when I think about the disappointments I've experienced in my life."

Introduce Your Friend to the Healthy Fellowship of God's People

When Jesus died on the cross, every part of his body suffered. His back was torn by the scourging. His head bled from the crown of thorns. His mouth was parched from thirst. His side was ripped open by a spear. His hands and feet were pierced by the nails. All the muscles, bones, and nerves in his body were affected. Inwardly, his emotions endured wrenching pain as he bore our sins and cried out in agony, "My God, my God, why have you forsaken me?" Jesus' entire body suffered on the cross.

Similarly, when one part of Jesus' spiritual body (the church) suffers, "every part suffers with it" (1 Corinthians 12:26). Hard questions, sudden deaths, bitter suffering—all grow more intense when we face them alone. And all grow more bearable when we find ourselves surrounded by a community of caring believers. People who grieve painful losses often find comfort and growth when they're able to open up and talk about their experiences with others.

Several years ago, Professor Tom Lawson of Kentucky Christian College suffered through the sudden death of his first wife. Reflecting on what brought him comfort, Lawson writes:

"God comforts us in our suffering (through the presence of the Holy Spirit and through the love of other people) so that we can provide that same comfort to others (2 Corinthians 1:3-7). The parents who lost an infant find themselves drawn to the young couple in the church whose baby just died. The man who was laid off last year finds himself having coffee with a member of his Sunday school class whose business went under.

"'Why?' is less awkward when you remember your own moments of grief, confusion, and pain. You just reach up and brush aside your own tears, hold out your arms, and offer your friends a shoulder to cry on. And more often than not you find your own tears wetting their shoulders, even as their tears touch yours.

"It is that image, even more than faces bright with smiles, that demonstrates the power and presence of the Holy Spirit in the life of the church. People with hurts of their own reach out to others who are hurting, and both find the presence of God. . . . Here questions are laid aside, human pride dissolves, and all the masks fall away. Here, if we would only open our hearts to see, is the very presence of the Spirit of God in our midst."[3]

How did Bev come to know the Lord? A new neighbor, Susan, moved in across the street from Bev's house. Susan was looking for a church.

"When she talked about church or about God, I was really interested," Bev says. "But I'd make up an excuse and say, 'I need to go to the store, so I don't have time to talk.' Susan picked up on the fact that I was curious, but afraid.

"One day she invited me to a barbecue sponsored by her church. I said, 'No, I don't want to go to church.' But she knew that I didn't have much money, and she said, 'Just come and get a free hamburger.' So I went, and at that picnic, many people came up and talked with me. They weren't walking around singing hymns and doing whatever I thought religious people did.

SOME PRACTICAL LESSONS FROM THE BOOK OF JOB

When pondering the question, "Why does God allow bad things to happen?" no book offers more profound insights than the Old Testament's book of Job. Bob Russell, senior minister at Southeast Christian Church in Louisville, wrote an article based on the book of Job called "When Life Isn't Fair," in which he identified these five principles:

1. Human suffering is not easy to explain. Don't always try.

2. Being good does not exempt us from calamity. Don't expect it to.

3. God is not the author of most suffering, so don't blame him.

4. Genuine faith does not require immediate answers, but anticipates ultimate justice. Don't doubt.

5. God's blessings are promised to those who persevere. Don't quit.[4]

They were laughing, eating hamburgers, playing volleyball. And there were so many children—happy, laughing children.

"Susan said, 'Maybe you'd like to meet Mark.' Well, I didn't know that you could call your priest—your minister, or whatever—by his first name! That was unheard of where I came from! It sounded disrespectful. But I did meet with him, and that's where it all started."

It hasn't been easy for everyone around her to adjust to Bev's new outlook on life.

"I fear for my boys," she confesses. "I didn't raise them with the Lord at all. It's hard for them as teenagers. They'll be listening to music with bad words in it. I let them listen to songs like those last year, and then this year, I'm saying, 'Please, guys, you can't listen to that.' It's hard, but they respect me.

"One day before I accepted the Lord, I was at church and Mark was talking in his sermon about procrastination. I realized that I was waiting for everything in my life to be perfect—and all my questions answered—before I'd be baptized. Well, I realized I shouldn't put it off anymore. I came home from church, got my two kids out of bed, dragged them back over to the church, and I was baptized. My sons were proud of me! They were clueless about what I was doing, but they could see my joy.

"My ex-husband is excited for me, too, and I'm hoping that somehow I'll be able to bring him into a relationship with God. That's the only thing that can pull him out of the hole he's in.

"I want my mother to accept the Lord too, and let her anger go. It's been thirty years since my dad passed away, and she's still angry with God. But she loves talking about Christ on the phone when I call her, so the seed has been planted there. I hope she can let go of that anger and accept Christ before she passes on."

Encourage Your Friend to Focus on Christ

In *The Problem of Pain*, C. S. Lewis wrote that pain is God's "megaphone to rouse a deaf world."[5] In other words, life's hurts compel us to think about the devastating consequences of sin and our need for God's grace. Whatever else we can say about the tragic death of Bev's forty-one-year-old father, it reminds us of the brevity of life and the need to prepare ourselves for eternity. "Why, you do not even know what will happen tomorrow. What is your life? You are a mist that appears for a little while and then vanishes" (James 4:14).

Hard questions like Bev's cannot find resolution in philosophical arguments alone, but in the One who came to earth and confronted the problem of evil in person.

There is no adequate answer to the problem of evil apart from Jesus Christ. Jesus' suffering on the cross shows the depths of God's love, and his resurrection underscores the reality of God's power. If we complain that "bad things happen to good people," we need to remember that the worst thing happened to the *best* of people, the Son of God himself.

Dave Stone, preaching associate at Southeast Christian Church in Louisville, Kentucky, tells the following story about his colleague Ross Brodfuehrer:

"The day before his son Chris died in a tragic automobile accident, Ross wrote an article for the church paper. He wrote, 'Faith is trusting the Father, staying true to him when the road is hard and the road is easy; when you don't understand and when you understand all too well; when the bottom drops out and when the sky opens up; when the disease is incurable and when the recovery is miraculous; when a loved one is buried and when a new one is born. If you don't trust when uncertain, then you don't trust. Fair-weather faith is not faith at all. Real faith hopes when it is hopeless and trusts when it is impossible. Real faith looks at the cross and knows that no situation in which God takes part is really without remedy. Faith knows that God can make a resurrection out of any corpse, and that the word *hopeless* is not in the Divine's dictionary.' Later, Ross said, 'When I wrote that, I had no idea that I would be the one reading it. Those reminders . . . have really helped me.'"[6]

Give It a Try

What would Bev say to someone else who struggles with anger toward God?

"Go to church even if you don't believe in anything. Walk through the door. Let the people who are standing there come up and say 'hi' and give you a hug. They don't care where you've been or what you've done. They're not going to hurt you. They're excited that you're there.

"That's what I did. And I discovered that God is more loving, more caring, than I'd ever imagined.

"You don't have anything to lose. Just give it a try."

QUESTIONS FOR PERSONAL REFLECTION

1. What spiritual disappointments have you experienced in your life? Have you ever felt angry with God? Why? How did you handle those feelings?

2. What biblical truths have given you comfort in times of tragedy or pain? What Scriptures have you found most helpful in comforting others?

RESOURCES FOR FURTHER STUDY

Philip Yancey, *Disappointment With God* (Zondervan, 1988) and *Where Is God When It Hurts?* (Zondervan, 1977).

Glandion Carney and William Long, *Trusting God Again* (InterVarsity, 1995).

FOOTNOTES

[1] dealt more fully with the problem of suffering in my earlier book on First and Second Peter, *Faith Under Fire* (Standard, 1997), pp. 82-95.

[2] Glandion Carney and William Long, *Trusting God Again* (InterVarsity, 1995), p. 95.

[3] Tom Lawson, "How Could God Let This Happen?" *The Lookout*, December 8, 1996. Used by permission.

[4] Bob Russell, "When Life Isn't Fair," *Christian Standard*, June 14, 1981. Used by permission.

[5] C. S. Lewis, *The Problem of Pain* (Macmillan, 1962), p. 93.

[6] Dave Stone, "Mary Trusted When Uncertain," a sermon preached at Southeast Christian Church, Louisville, Kentucky, December 28, 1997. Used by permission.

CHAPTER 9

WHAT IS FAITH, ANYWAY?

If you've been trying to take the truth next door recently, you may have noticed: Many postmodern people are uncertain not only about *what to believe*. Many of them are confused about *what it means to believe at all*.

Few words in the English language are used more frequently, and misunderstood more often, than the word *faith*. If I invite you to come to my home for dinner tomorrow night, and you say, "I'll definitely be there," I know I'd better clean the house and put some food in the oven. But if you say, *"I believe* I can come," I'm uncertain. Will you show up for dinner, or won't you? In our culture, faith often carries a strong connotation of uncertainty and doubt.

Let's pause for a moment and clear up some common misconceptions about faith.

Is Faith Illogical?

Many postmodernists assume that faith is completely irrational, with no basis in fact.

This isn't a new idea. Tertullian, one of the early church fathers who died about A.D. 200, argued that faith and reason are incompatible. "What has

Athens to do with Jerusalem?" he asked. In other words, why try to blend human reason with faith in God? Twentieth-century writer H. L. Mencken said, "Faith may be defined as an illogical belief in the occurrence of the improbable." R. W. Bradford, a secular humanist, wrote that faith is "willful belief in the absence of evidence." And the noted theologian and philosopher, TV character Archie Bunker, spoke for many people when he blustered, "Faith is believing something so ridiculous that no one in his right mind would believe it's true!"

Thoughtful Christians, however, not only want *to believe;* we also want *reasons to believe.* Surely the Lord doesn't want us to be gullible (and believe anything), nor does he want us to be cynical (and believe nothing). The right balance is to "test everything" and "hold on to the good" (1 Thessalonians 5:21). As Clark Pinnock wrote in *Set Forth Your Case,* "The heart cannot delight in what the mind rejects as false. . . . The gospel makes sense, not non-sense."[1]

I enjoy reading the comics in the daily newspaper, and when I lived in New York, I always took time to read a little one-line feature called "Today's Chuckle" that New York *Newsday* included in its comics section. One day's "chuckle" read, "Faith is the quality which allows us to believe what we know to be ridiculous." I like to laugh, but I didn't see anything funny about that statement. Irritated, I wrote a letter to the editor which *Newsday* published in its entirety. Here's what I wrote:

> Pardon me, but someone's bias is showing! I am sure many of your readers shared my dismay upon reading "Today's Chuckle" in the June 30 edition of *Newsday,* which stated, "Faith is the quality which allows us to believe what we know to be ridiculous." In my opinion, that statement is neither humorous nor accurate. It is not humorous, for it belittles people of all faiths. Nor is it accurate, for many of us have found faith to be a sensible, reasonable alternative to unbelief. My Christian faith is based upon historical evidence, not wishful thinking or religious absurdities. Furthermore, countless individuals have found strength, hope, and inner peace through faith. Such faith is not ridiculous and certainly not just something to chuckle about.

A Biblical Understanding of Faith

We need to insist on a more biblical definition of faith. Nowhere does the Bible define faith as an irrational, absurd leap in the dark. Quite to the contrary, faith means we rely on God and his promises enough to leap into the light. It is a confident loyalty that makes us "sure of what we hope for and certain of what we do not see" (Hebrews 11:1).

Mindless Christianity is not biblical Christianity. The foundational rule of the Old Testament stated, "Love the Lord your God with all your heart and with all your soul and with all your strength" (Deuteronomy 6:5). In other words, God deserves a wholehearted allegiance that includes every part of our inner selves. Lest we miss the point, Jesus called this commandment "the most important" precept in all of God's law—but he also added, love God . . . "with all your *mind*" (Mark 12:30, emphasis added). Jesus deliberately emphasized the way his disciples must love God thoughtfully, using our minds—our intellects—to honor the Lord. This hardly sounds like irrational faith!

Romans 10:17 says that faith comes by hearing the Word. John's Gospel was written so that those who read it will find convincing evidence that persuades them to believe in Jesus (John 20:30, 31). Christian faith is not illogical; it means accepting the testimony of the biblical witnesses who wrote the facts about what they saw and heard. "Faith is not believing what you know to be absurd. It is trusting what on excellent testimony appears to be true."[2]

In his book, *Prepare to Answer,* Rubel Shelley divides beliefs into several categories:

1. There are *"credulous* beliefs," supported by little or no evidence. Only gullible people would accept them. For example, "John F. Kennedy is still alive."

2. There are *"shallow* beliefs," based on weak evidence and influenced heavily by one's own personal desires or wishes. For example, "My favorite team, the Cincinnati Reds, will win the World Series this year."

3. There are *"mistaken* beliefs," in which well-intentioned people simply get the facts wrong. I used to believe Venezuela was on the southwestern side of South America—until I went there and discovered it's actually located on the northern-most coast of the continent!

4. But there also are *"substantive* beliefs" undergirded by solid evidence so strong it's unlikely you would ever change your mind about them. Without any fear of contradiction, I believe the Cincinnati Reds won the World Series in 1990. I also believe that a real historical figure named Saul

of Tarsus persecuted Christians in the first century, then was converted into a committed believer and apostle who traveled the world as a missionary for the faith he previously opposed. These are substantive beliefs, with a wide range of evidence to support them.[3]

When Christians talk about faith, we're not arguing for credulous, shallow, or mistaken beliefs. Our convictions are substantive beliefs, supported by a wide range of credible evidence.

Three Components of Faith

Students of the Bible find that biblical faith involves three main components: understanding, assent, and trust.

No human being possesses a complete and exhaustive *understanding* of all truth; only God does. But we can grow in our discernment and learn the will of God; in fact, God wants us to do so. (See Colossians 1:9, 10; 2 Peter 1:3-9.) While we cannot fully comprehend all the infinite meaning of Christ's death on the cross, even a child can grasp the basic idea that God loves us and Jesus died to save us from our sins. Proverbs 14:15 warns, "A simple man believes anything, but a prudent man gives thought to his steps." God wants us to exercise prudence. It's legitimate to ask honest questions about the Bible like, "Do you understand what you're reading?" (See Acts 8:30.)

Faith also involves *assent*—a mental willingness to affirm or agree with a fact, based on the sufficiency of the evidence. I have never been to Hawaii, but I believe its climate is warm and pleasant. I've never been to the Arctic Circle, but I'm quite sure it's cold there. Other credible witnesses have visited these places, so I trust their testimony. Likewise, I have not seen God with my own eyes, but I believe that he exists (Hebrews 11:6), and I affirm that Jesus rose from the dead (Romans 10:9), because of the credible testimony of those who saw him alive.

But faith not only means understanding and assent. It also includes *trust*, which is a decision of the will—a voluntary choice to place oneself or one's property into the hands of a trustworthy person. You exercise trust every time you pay a mechanic to fix your car, leave your children with a baby-sitter, fly in a commercial airliner, or allow a barber to change your appearance with a few swift snips of the scissors.

Saving faith involves more than mere intellectual assent or lip service to God's existence. Even the demons believe that God exists, but they tremble in the face of coming judgment because they have never trusted God enough to surrender their will to him (James 2:19).[4]

Trust is a reasonable act; but to be honest, it's the part of faith that often looks irrational to an unbeliever. If you don't know my wife, you might not understand why I trust her to be faithful to me and why I don't worry that she will overspend when she goes shopping with our credit card. Likewise, if you don't know the Lord, you may not understand why Christians tithe, pray, give, serve, and trust God even when our circumstances seem to contradict God's wisdom and goodness.

Properly understood, faith isn't irrational or illogical. It's a reasonable alternative to unbelief.

Is Faith Completely Subjective?

Another common misconception about faith—especially in a postmodern culture—is that it's completely a subjective, personal matter with no connection to objective reality.

Subjective feelings refer to perceptions of reality as experienced by the individual—the "inside of me" kind of feelings that vary from one person to another.

TEN BIBLICAL FACTS
ABOUT FAITH

1. Faith is supposed to be a way of life for God's people. "We live by faith" (Habakkuk 2:4; 2 Corinthians 5:7; Galatians 3:11).

2. Faith comes by hearing God's Word (Romans 10:17; 1 Peter 1:25).

3. Faith means trusting in God's promises even when we can't see any tangible proof (John 20:29; 2 Corinthians 4:18; Hebrews 11:1-3, 27; 1 Peter 1:8).

4. Faith is grounded in the testimony of credible eyewitnesses who *did* see tangible proof (John 20:30, 31; 2 Peter 1:16).

5. Faith is an active expression of reliance on God, not merely a passive state. "Faith without deeds is dead" (Hebrews 11; James 2:24-26).

6. Faith in God leads to obedience. If we call Jesus "Lord," we'll want to do what he says (Luke 6:46; John 14:15; Romans 1:5; 16:26).

7. Faith stabilizes us in difficult times. "It is by faith you stand firm" (2 Corinthians 1:24; 1 Peter 1:6-10; Revelation 14:12).

8. Faith is forward-looking. It doesn't demand immediate results, but looks ahead to the ultimate realization of God's promises (2 Corinthians 4:13, 14).

9. Faith is an indispensable ingredient in our relationship with God. "Without faith it is impossible to please God" (Hebrews 11:6).

10. Faith is more powerful than many people realize. "This is the victory that has overcome the world, even our faith" (1 John 5:4).

I like to watch football games; my wife doesn't. She enjoys walking through antique and craft stores; I don't. It's hard for either of us to understand the other's point of view about these different interests.

Objective facts, on the other hand, refer to realities that exist independent of any reflections or feelings—the "outside of me" kind of truth that others can perceive and verify regardless of personal biases. My wife doesn't have to like football to agree that the ball is made of pigskin or leather and the field is one hundred yards long. I don't have to enjoy shopping in craft stores to agree that the items there appear to be colorful, creative—and over-priced. (Whoops, my subjective biases are showing!)

Candy and I were married on August 31, 1975. That fact is objectively true. You could verify it by viewing a marriage license on file in a government office in Bay Shore, New York. You could interview some of the people who attended the ceremony. We could even show you some fading photos taken at our wedding. The wedding rings we wear, the three children we have raised together, the bank accounts we share, even our joint income tax returns, all bear objective testimony to the reality that Candy and I are husband and wife.

Subjectively, I have many feelings for Candy. I appreciate her kindness and hard work. (She's a nurse who works nights in the maternity ward of a local hospital.) I like the way she looks, the way she cooks, and the way she tolerates the time I spend writing books! Our marriage thrives when we express romantic love toward one another. But even on those days when we don't feel so great about each other—and let's be honest, every married couple does have those days!—nothing can change the objective truth that we stood before witnesses on August 31, 1975, and committed ourselves to be husband and wife.

Likewise, Christian faith involves both objective facts and subjective feelings. Jesus Christ lived in real history. An article in *U.S. News & World Report* stated, ". . . the fact that Jesus . . . was executed in Roman-occupied Palestine is one part of the Passion story that modern historians believe is well corroborated by extra-biblical sources. The Roman historian Tacitus, for example, writing in A.D. 110 of the persecution of Christians under the emperor Nero, refers to followers of 'Christ, whom the procurator Pontius Pilate had executed in the reign of Tiberius.'" The article continues, "Striking corroboration of the type of crucifixion that is described in the Gospels was discovered in 1968 at an excavation site near Mount Scopus, just northeast of Jerusalem. Three tombs were found at the side, one of them containing the remains of a man who had been crucified between A.D. 7 and 70. The man's feet had been nailed together at the heels, his forearms had nail wounds and the bones of his lower legs had been broken—wounds that are entirely consistent with the description in John's Gospel of the crucifixion of Jesus and the two thieves."[5]

Jesus died on a wooden cross so real you could have gotten a splinter from it. He rose from the dead, leaving behind an empty tomb and neatly folded grave clothes examined by eyewitnesses (John 20:1-9). Curiously, a slab of stone was found in Nazareth, the childhood home of Jesus, by archaeologists in 1878. It contains an inscription known as the Nazareth Decree issued by the Roman emperor Claudius, who ruled from A.D. 41 to 54. The emperor decreed that no graves should be disturbed or bodies removed from them, and anyone violating the rule shall "be sentenced to capital punishment on the charge of violation of sepulcher." This seems like a pretty harsh punishment for disturbing graves! Professor Norman Geisler observes, "A likely explanation is that Claudius, having heard of the Christian doctrine of Resurrection . . . decided not to let any such report surface again. . . . This is early testimony to the strong and persistent belief that Jesus rose from the dead."[6]

Christians contend that these biblical events really happened. They are objective realities, regardless of how anyone feels about them. We worship a God who is really there, who exists regardless of how we feel about him.

Now, our subjective reactions to all of this may vary. As a Christian, I feel a deep sense of gratitude to God for what he's done for me. I want to honor, worship, and obey him because I've learned to trust him. My relationship with Christ is personal and precious to me, and sometimes during moments of quiet reflection or corporate worship I find myself almost overwhelmed by love for the Son of God who died for me. But my faith is not based simply on what I feel in my heart. It's rooted in objective facts and historical truths that are real regardless of how I react to them.

IS FAITH JUST FOR SUPER-SAINTS?

Another common but flawed view of faith is that it's only for "religious people." "So you're involved in church? Good for you," some folks nod. "That's fine if you're into that kind of thing—but me, I'm not a religious person," they say, while edging away from the conversation.

THE CIRCLE OF FAITH

Faith in God operates on both an objective and subjective level. Christ and his Word provide not only the solid foundation on which we build (1 Corinthians 3:10, 11; 15:1-3; Ephesians 2:19-22), but also the faith-stretching goals toward which we aspire (Ephesians 3:20, 21).

The study of apologetics and Christian evidences shows that our faith is grounded in objective truths that merit our understanding and assent. Because our faith rests on facts, we can explain why we believe and give logical reasons for our hope (1 Peter 3:15).

But faith also requires trusting God even when we can't fully understand and explain his ways. This is the more subjective realm of faith, in which we pray to our heavenly Father and rely on his providence to work all things together for the good of those who love him (Proverbs 3:5, 6; Romans 8:28).

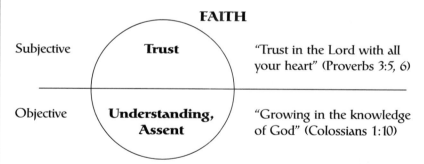

FAITH

Subjective — **Trust** — "Trust in the Lord with all your heart" (Proverbs 3:5, 6)

Objective — **Understanding, Assent** — "Growing in the knowledge of God" (Colossians 1:10)

To grow more mature in Christ, we need to develop all three components of our faith: understanding, assent, and trust. If we neglect Bible study, we'll weaken the objective part of our faith; and if we neglect prayer and Christian service, we'll weaken the realm of trust. God's instruction to a growing Christian? Be "rooted and built up in him, strengthened in the faith as you were taught, and overflowing with thankfulness" (Colossians 2:7).

But wait a minute. Christian faith isn't merely a "religion," but a way of life. God calls us to *live* by faith. In other words, faith affects everything we do. We shouldn't compartmentalize our personalities as if people were bookstores with different sections marked, "Health," "Social Life," "Work," "Family," "Finances," and "Religion."

Faith isn't for super saints. The fact is, everyone lives by faith in something or someone. All history is based on faith. We haven't met George Washington, Christopher Columbus, or Alexander the Great in person, but we believe they existed because we know certain things they did and said. Daily life requires faith. If you eat in a restaurant, you trust a cook you probably will never see—and depend on him not to poison your food. If you fly in an airplane, you place your life in the hands of a pilot you probably will never see—and trust in the overwhelming probability that the pilot is sober, he is properly trained, and he will not try any crazy stunts with you on board! If you don't believe in the Lord, that doesn't mean you have no faith, but a misplaced faith. Instead of believing in God, some place their faith in their own thought processes or the conclusions of their peers. Others risk their eternal future on hazardous assertions like, "I don't believe in an afterlife," or "I don't believe in Hell." But, there's a lot at stake. What if these faith statements are wrong? Everyone exercises faith. The question is, Who or what is the object of your faith?

God takes ordinary people, and by the power of his Holy Spirit working through the Word, he transforms us into holy people—not "super saints," but real people indwelled by his powerful Spirit. (See Romans 8:9-11; 1 Corinthians 1:2; and Philippians 1:1.)

BUT ISN'T SINCERITY ALL THAT MATTERS?

Still another popular misconception about faith is that sincerity alone determines the validity of one's beliefs. Many well-intentioned people insist, "It doesn't matter what you believe as long as you're sincere."

Now, of course it's important to be sincere about our faith. In fact, Jesus reserved some of his harshest words for the hypocrites of his day who devalued the truth by their insincerity and phoniness. But sincerity isn't the only issue that matters.

According to one study, eighty-seven percent of American adults say they "believe in the resurrection of Christ," but thirty-nine percent believe Jesus "did not return bodily from death."[7] Such confusing, selective beliefs reflect the vague spirituality, the "faith in faith," which is in vogue today. But the Bible often refers to *"the* faith"—a clear, discernible body of biblical beliefs or teachings. Jude says to "contend for the faith that was once for all entrusted to the saints" (Jude 3). Paul says there is "one Lord, one faith, one baptism" (Ephesians 4:5). He devoted his life to the task of keeping and spreading "the faith" (1 Timothy 4:1-6; 2 Timothy 4:7). We must be sincere—but there's more to faith than sincerity alone.

No matter how sincerely I believe my Toyota Tercel will win the Indianapolis 500, I'm mistaken. No matter how earnestly I think that I could jump from the top of the Empire State Building without harming myself, I'll die if I try it. It's possible to be completely sincere, yet also be completely wrong. Would you place your health in the hands of a medical doctor who prescribes the wrong medicine even if "he means well"? Would you submit to surgery under the shaky hands of a surgeon who sincerely cares about her patients but lacks the skill to operate successfully? If you worked as a chef in a restaurant, would you keep your job very long if the food always tasted terrible even though you "sincerely cared about your customers"?

In biblical times, the Jews were "zealous for God," but their zeal was "not based on knowledge" (Romans 10:2). Before Saul of Tarsus became a Christian, he opposed Christianity so earnestly that he persecuted the church and tried to destroy it (Galatians 1:13), but later he admitted that he had been acting "in ignorance and unbelief" (1 Timothy 1:13). Sincerity isn't all that matters.

An Examined Faith

As cultural analyst Os Guinness has said, "Christianity invites people to an examined faith. . . . The pale brand of modern faith which lapses into 'easy believism' has little in common with the virile attitude of understanding plus commitment which is the biblical notion of faith."[8] This is not to imply that faith can be reduced to mere intellectual concepts and rational assertions. As Guinness points out, "Christianity is second to none in the place it gives to reason, but it is also second to none in keeping reason in its place."[9]

Christian faith makes good sense. That's why we need to keep taking it next door. Christ is accessible to anyone who will hear his invitation and approach his Word with an open mind. "Whoever is thirsty, let him come; and whoever wishes, let him take the free gift of the water of life" (Revelation 22:17).

QUESTIONS FOR PERSONAL REFLECTION

1. How would *you* define faith?

2. Which component of faith has been the most difficult for you to grasp—understanding, assent, or trust? Why?

3. Read Hebrews 11 in light of the following questions:
   a. What are some facts believers affirm as true? (See especially vv. 3 and 6.)
   b. This chapter mentions several people who lived by faith. Which of these people do you relate to most? Why?
   c. Verses 29 through 35a mention people who won great victories by faith. On the other hand, verses 35b through 38 mention others who endured terrible suffering by faith. Both kinds of people were "commended for their faith" (v. 39). Why do you think both groups are included in this chapter? Which group do you identify with more—the group that won great victories, or the group that suffered? Why?

RESOURCES FOR FURTHER STUDY

Francis Schaeffer, *The God Who Is There* (InterVarsity, 1968).

Winfried Corduan, *Reasonable Faith* (Broadman & Holman, 1993).

FOOTNOTES

[1]Clark H. Pinnock, *Set Forth Your Case* (Moody, 1967), p. 13.
[2]Pinnock, p. 73.

[3]Rubel Shelley, *Prepare to Answer* (21st Century Christian, 1990), pp. 18-20.

[4]For this analysis of the three components of faith I am indebted to Dr. Jack Cottrell and his Christian Apologetics course at Cincinnati Bible Seminary. Cottrell has since expanded his explanation as follows:

> Prerequisite of faith: understanding
>
> Faith per se: assent (believing *that* . . .) and
>   trust (believing *in* or *on* . . .)
>
> Result of faith: obedience

[5]"The Crucifixion," *U.S. News & World Report*, April 16, 1990, p. 50.

[6]Norman Geisler and Ron Brooks, *When Skeptics Ask: A Handbook on Christian Evidences* (Victor Books, 1990), p. 206.

[7]Russell Shorto, "Belief by the Numbers," *The New York Times Magazine*, December 7, 1997, p. 61.

[8]Os Guinness, *In Two Minds: The Dilemma of Doubt and How to Resolve It* (InterVarsity, 1976), pp. 103, 104.

[9]Guinness, p. 253.

CHAPTER 10

YOSHI: WHAT ABOUT MY FAMILY TRADITIONS?

The port city of Niigata is located on the west coast of Japan, across the Sea of Japan from Russia and China. It was my first visit to Japan, so as my plane made its final approach, I gazed out the window with fascination at the bright green rice paddies laid out in symmetrical designs in the valleys below.

Yoshi Kobyashi and his daughter, Emiko (one of my former students), greeted me at the airport with an Asian-style bow and an American-style handshake. Briefly, I savored the pleasant realization that friendship can transcend cultural barriers even when I'm half a world from home.

Ceremonies Without Commitment

Yoshi (pronounced "YO-she") has been married for thirty-four years to his wife Etsuko ("Et-SU-ko"). He worked at Niigata city hall for more than forty years before retiring, and now works as director of a day care service center for the elderly, people with disabilities, and children. He and his wife have two sons: one who works at Niigata's city music hall, and another who is a music instructor in Tokyo. Emiko

("EM-e-ko") lives at home and works as an English instructor. She and her mother are Christians; the other members of the family are not.

I knew some things about the country already, of course, but I enjoyed hearing a native of Japan tell a "gai-jin" (foreigner) about his local customs. "Since our country is surrounded by sea, we are able to eat fresh fish all the time," Yoshi explains. "We eat some of it raw—that's sushi. And rice is our daily food."

I had a lot to learn about Japanese culture, including some important facts not mentioned in the travel guides. For example, after about a week in Japan, I noticed that I hardly ever saw a church building or a cross anywhere we went. (Quite a contrast, I should note, with The Republic of Korea, where I was amazed by the number of growing churches filled with eager Christians praying and worshiping God.)

"Our family religion is traditional," Yoshi says. "Our culture has been influenced by other countries like China and India through many years. There are Buddhist temples and castles here built hundreds of years ago.

"We have two different altars at home. One is a Buddhist altar which comforts our ancestors' spirits. Also there is a Shinto altar which is believed to offer protection of our home. Although," Yoshi quickly adds, "I don't have personal faith in any gods."

"I hope you understand what he is saying," his daughter Emiko interjects. "His point of view about religion is rather complex, yet it seems many people in Japan feel the same way. Many refer to themselves as Buddhists, but they don't necessarily have faith in it. Religious rituals are performed on ceremonial occasions, but often are not a matter of individual faith.

"For example, it's common for people to ask a Buddhist

monk to perform a funeral, whether they have faith in Buddha or not."

Emiko has spent enough time in the United States to offer another observation: "I think Japanese Buddhists are like some Americans who go to church twice a year for Easter and Christmas. Whether they actually believe in Jesus' resurrection or not, it's a common practice to do."

At Least It Feels Familiar

"I was raised in a culture surrounded by temples and shrines. They are so natural to me," Yoshi continues. "Even though I don't have strong feelings toward them, they are still familiar to me. Many Japanese go to those places to receive their blessings of good luck on occasions like New Year's Day, or when they get married, when they have new-born babies, or even when they get new cars. Those places don't ask us for strong commitment. They don't train people to learn more about Buddhism or Shintoism, unless some-one really wants to know.

"Basically everyone is welcomed. I think that is how they make money," he notes matter-of-factly. "They charge money for prayers, and people offer money for their luck."

"However, the Christian church is different," says Yoshi. "I feel uncomfortable there, because the difference between Christians and non-Christians seems big. And the idea of Hell is unacceptable to me. If I don't follow the Christian God, why must I go to Hell?

"I don't know about Christian theology, and I don't know the Bible," he admits. "But this is what I am feeling toward Christians."

WHAT ABOUT MY FAMILY TRADITIONS?

Remember the classic musical, *Fiddler on the Roof?* It begins with the Jewish father, Tevye, singing enthusiastically about the value of tradition. While Tevye's Jewish culture is worlds apart from Yoshi's Japanese culture, at root they both have a lot in common—and to an extent, they both have a point.

While most Americans don't have Buddhist or Shinto altars in our homes, we can understand how it feels to be comfortable with traditions. After all, we have plenty of our own—from fireworks on the Fourth of July to parades on New Year's Day, from chocolate Valentine's hearts to flowers for Mom on Mother's Day.

In my family, my wife and three children and I customarily hold hands around the dinner table and pray before we eat. We enjoy holiday customs, too: going to Grandpa and Grandma's farm for Thanksgiving, putting the same old ornaments on the Christmas tree every year.

Even though we often don't give much thought to the way certain customs originated, we follow them anyway. We celebrate birthdays by blowing out candles on a cake and singing an off-key rendition of "Happy Birthday to You." At weddings, the bride and groom place rings on their left hands, and the bride tosses her bouquet over her shoulder. Why? Who knows?

Churches have traditions too. Before preaching in Korea, I was advised to remove my shoes. It was a bit uncomfortable standing behind the pulpit on a small cushion in my sock feet, but I was humbled by this simple reminder that I was standing on holy ground as I proclaimed the Word of God. Many things our American culture associates with Christian faith are matters of tradition, not biblical requirements: from steeples to hymnals, from the style of music we sing to the way we celebrate Christ's birth on December 25.

Traditions can be valuable. They can link us with past generations of believers—their wisdom, their celebrations, their love for God. Like the roots of a healthy plant, they can give us stability in changing times. They remind us that we are part of a great heritage of faith. They nurture our sense of history and connect us with the church through the ages.

But there's another side to the story. Before answering Yoshi's questions, let's examine our own cultural biases and take a look at what the Bible says about the problem with religious tradition.

THE PROBLEM WITH TRADITION

Jesus lived in a Jewish culture saturated with tradition. His words recorded in Mark 7 help us identify five problems with religious tradition.

1. Traditions can cause us to *overemphasize the unimportant.*

Some of the Pharisees and teachers of the law saw that Jesus' disciples were eating their food with "unclean" hands. The issue wasn't a matter of hygiene; it was a matter of ceremony. Before every meal, the Pharisees went through an elaborate hand-washing ritual, pouring water over their hands in certain prescribed ways to symbolically rinse away any impurities from sin.

As Mark puts it, "The Pharisees and all the Jews do not eat unless they give their hands a ceremonial washing, holding to the tradition of the elders. When they come from the marketplace they do not eat unless they wash. And they observe many other traditions, such as the washing of cups, pitchers and kettles" (Mark 7:3, 4). When Jesus' disciples ignored these ceremonial washings, their critics considered it more than bad manners; they considered it sin. Now, God's law did prescribe certain washings to be performed by the priests (Exodus 40:30-32, for example). But the Pharisees had added an encyclopedic pile of regulations to what the Scripture required, and they pressured others to follow their rules—which in many cases were more detailed and difficult to keep than the actual laws of God. In fact, some of the Jews adhered so stubbornly to their hand-washing tradition that one Pharisee, imprisoned by the Romans, nearly died of thirst because when his captors gave him water to drink he used it for ceremonial washing instead of drinking it![1]

Elsewhere Jesus warned that strict adherence to human tradition can result in overemphasizing minor matters and overlooking the major ones. "Woe to you, teachers of the law and Pharisees, you hypocrites!" His eyes must have flashed indignantly as he spoke. "You give a tenth of your spices—mint, dill and cummin. But you have neglected the more important matters of the law—justice, mercy and faithfulness. You should have practiced the latter, without neglecting the former. You blind guides! You strain out a gnat but swallow a camel" (Matthew 23:23, 24).

Religious tradition can deceive us into emphasizing things that really aren't important in the eyes of God. We can end up assuming that our relationship with God is mainly about food, clothing, religious objects we wear as jewelry or use to decorate our homes, or even a certain kind of music. But "the kingdom of God is not a matter of eating and drinking, but of righteousness, peace and joy in the Holy Spirit" (Romans 14:17).

2. Another problem is, traditions can cause us to make *inaccurate, self-righteous judgments of ourselves and others.*

A few verses earlier, Mark informs us that the disciples were so busy assisting crowds of needy people, they barely had time to eat at all, let alone observe all the Pharisees' hand-washing traditions (Mark 6:30, 31)! But the critical traditionalists didn't see the good the disciples were doing and the stress they were enduring; they only saw what was lacking. Confronting Jesus, they demanded, "Why don't your disciples live according to the tradition of the elders instead of eating their food with 'unclean' hands?" (Mark 7:5). If these critics were upset now, I wonder what they thought when Jesus fed five thousand men, plus women and children? All those people were out in the countryside where there weren't any ceremonial water pots to use. But they were hungry, and Jesus fed them even though they had to eat with unwashed hands.

These critics were the same guys, remember, who prayed boastfully on street corners and blew trumpets to announce they were giving their offerings (Matthew 6:1-5). "They have received their reward in full," Jesus wryly pointed out. In other words, if they want the applause of their peers, they'll get it—but nothing more. By contrast, our heavenly Father rewards the humble, the meek, the sincere—like the tax collector who cried out earnestly, "God, have mercy on me, a sinner." As Jesus said, "Everyone who exalts himself will be humbled, and he who humbles himself will be exalted" (Luke 18:13, 14).

Religious rules sound impressive: "Do not handle! Do not taste! Do not touch!" But while "such regulations indeed have an appearance of wisdom,

AN EMPTY WAY OF LIFE

First Peter 1:18 makes an important point when it says, "For you know it was not with perishable things such as silver or gold that you were redeemed from the empty way of life handed down to you from your forefathers."

Even though our forefathers cherished certain traditions, even though they meant well, and even though we may hold strong emotional ties to our ancestors' points of view, we have to be honest and admit: tradition alone can't satisfy our souls, cure our guilty consciences, or give us hope. To accomplish these goals, we need "the precious blood of Christ, a lamb without blemish or defect" (1 Peter 1:19).

with their self-imposed worship, their false humility and their harsh treatment of the body," the fact is "they are based on human commands and teachings" and "they lack any value in restraining sensual indulgence" (Colossians 2:20-23).

By the way, prideful attitudes can be found in non-traditionalists just as much as in traditionalists. Since the Bible doesn't tell us what kind of clothes we must wear to worship, it's just as wrong to judge those who dress up as it is to judge those who dress down. I've known Christians who criticize any new idea because "we've never done it that way before," and I've known Christians who irrationally refuse to do anything traditional. (Wouldn't many debates in the church fade away if we surrendered our pride and humbly sought to approach God with sincerity and reverence?)

3. Here's another problem: tradition often results in *shallow, heartless worship.*

Jesus told the traditionalists, "Isaiah was right when he prophesied about you hypocrites; as it is written: 'These people honor me with their lips, but their hearts are far from me. They worship me in vain; their teachings are but rules taught by men'" (Mark 7:6, 7). If our hearts are wrong, it's not enough just to say the right words, sing the right songs (whether from a

hymnal or an overhead projector), or vainly mouth the words of a memorized prayer.

Most traditions start with good intentions. But they can easily degenerate into meaningless habits where we merely go through the motions. If
Jesus were preaching to us, would he point out some contradictions between
the words of our lips and the conditions of our hearts? Do we sing, "It Is
Well With My Soul," while inwardly we're so stressed out we can hardly
think about God at all? Do we sing, "Nothing Is Too Difficult for Thee,"
while privately doubting God can solve our problems? Do we sing, "We Are
One in the Spirit," while harboring resentment in our hearts toward other
Christians? Do we sing, "Have Thine Own Way, Lord," then leave church to
do things our own way?

4. Another problem? Traditions *distract attention from the genuine commands of God.* "You have let go of the commands of God and are holding
on to the traditions of men," Jesus insisted (Mark 7:8). He gave as an example what some were doing with the Jewish practice of "Corban" (a gift
devoted to God). Instead of using some of their savings or property to help
their parents, some of Jesus' contemporaries were telling their parents basically, "Sorry, we can't help you because we've devoted our belongings to
God." By neglecting their parents, Jesus told them, "you nullify the word of
God by your tradition that you have handed down" (Mark 7:9-13). No
doubt, someone like Yoshi sincerely wants to honor his parents and other
ancestors. But we need to honor our parents in a way that pleases God, who
created our families, not in a way that offends him.

5. A fifth problem with tradition is this: it *emphasizes outward ceremonies rather than inward realities.*

Yoshi's daughter Emiko makes a good point. Is there really much difference between Japanese Buddhists and many American "Christians" who "go
to church twice a year for Easter and Christmas" even though they don't
actually believe in Jesus' resurrection? Isn't it sad when someone assumes it's
enough merely to claim the family's religious tradition without any personal
commitment? When someone depends on an infant baptism, a confirmation
ceremony, or a name written on a church membership list to make him
right with God?

Jesus made it clear that one's relationship with God requires an inward
commitment, and that sin is a matter of the heart as well as one's actions.

"Listen to me, everyone, and understand this," he said. "Nothing outside a man can make him 'unclean' by going into him. Rather, it is what comes out of a man that makes him 'unclean'" (Mark 7:14, 15).

Traditions can be helpful, but only if we recognize them for what they are, keep them flexible, and submit them to the authority of God and his Word. "See to it that no one takes you captive through hollow and deceptive philosophy, which depends on human tradition and the basic principles of this world rather than on Christ" (Colossians 2:8).

WHAT CAN WE SAY TO YOSHI?

Cross-cultural communication is never easy, even if you were simply ordering dinner in an unfamiliar ethnic restaurant. It's even more difficult when you're trying to communicate about matters of eternal truth. Conveying the gospel to someone like Yoshi won't be easy. (Just ask missionaries who have spent their lives serving the Lord in a challenging place like Japan.)

Nevertheless, let me offer the following suggestions.

Be Patient

We must never limit what God can do, but the fact is, most of the time, someone like Yoshi will not be won to Christ quickly. His heart, surrounded by layers of resistance and cultural conditioning, will not easily comprehend and accept the good news of Christ.

With him (as with an increasing number of people in American culture today), our evangelistic method must involve much more than a one-shot approach. It will probably require a patient, painstaking effort to build trust and communicate God's love over a lengthy period of time.

Jesus' parables of the sower, the growing seed, and the mustard seed (Mark 4:1-20, 26-32) suggest that our job is to sow the seed of the gospel in faith, then prayerfully join hands with others—perhaps over a period of many years—who will water the seed and eventually reap the harvest. Sometimes we sow seed and never see results, but if we're planting the true Word of God in others' hearts, we can be confident it will sprout and grow even when we don't know how (Mark 4:27). (See also John 4:34-38 and 1 Corinthians 3:5-9.)

The great missionary William Carey labored in India for seven years before baptizing his first Indian convert, then he stayed for thirty-three more years and enjoyed great success—but only after patiently laying the groundwork for cross-cultural evangelism in a difficult mission field.

Be Curious

Ask questions. Listen carefully. You may want to read up on your friend's religion so you can talk intelligently with him about it. At the least, your own life will be enriched as you learn more about your friend's beliefs and culture. And sometimes the conversation will help you build bridges for the gospel.

Here are some of the questions I asked Yoshi: "Do you see any difference in your daughter since she became a Christian? Do you ever wish you had some of the hope and joy you see in her? How do you feel about the way the Buddhist priests make money from people? Does it ever bother you to go through the motions of religious ceremonies even though you don't believe in their power or the gods they represent? Deep in your heart, have you ever longed to know God personally? Have you ever wondered if the Christians really are right? If you could know for sure that you'd go to Heaven when you die, wouldn't you want that assurance?"

Be Clear

While we should always handle ourselves with gentleness and respect, there are some points we must make, clearly and without compromise, whether we're talking with someone like Yoshi or anyone else.

• Christianity *isn't about a place; it's about a person (Jesus Christ)*. We don't just call people to worship at shrines and temples. We call them to worship the Son of God who comes near to us wherever we are.

• Christianity *isn't about luck; it's about faith*. We aren't trying to manipulate spiritual powers for our own benefit. We want to be loyal to the Father in Heaven who cares for us and has revealed how we can live the abundant life.

WHAT CAN WE SAY
ABOUT HELL?

It's hard to think of a subject that makes people squirm more than this one does. According to a recent survey, about ninety percent of Americans say they believe in Heaven, but fewer (seventy-three percent) believe in Hell—and only six percent think that they'll personally go to Hell.[3] The Christian message of "salvation" and "eternal life" loses much of its urgent appeal if there's nothing to be saved from!

No matter how uncomfortable it makes us, however, if we believe the Bible we can't avoid the doctrine of Hell. Jesus had a lot to say about it (Matthew 13:42, 50; 25:41; Mark 9:43-48; Luke 13:23-28; 16:23-28; John 5:28, 29). So did Paul (2 Thessalonians 1:6-9), Peter (2 Peter 3:7), Jude (vv. 5-7, 13-15), and John (Revelation 20:10-15). The reality of Hell motivates us to live holy lives (Matthew 10:28), prods us to proclaim the gospel, and increases our appreciation for Christ, who rescued us from the punishment we deserve (Romans 5:8-10). Curiously enough, the New Testament (which says so much about God's gracious gift of salvation) tells us far more than the Old Testament does about Hell.

What other lines of argument show that it's reasonable to believe in the reality of Hell?

1. Justice requires it. "Human experience has universally taught the concept that when you break a rule, you ought to be punished," says Dr. Johnny Pressley of Cincinnati Bible Seminary, who teaches a course on the Doctrine of Hell. "In every culture and every age, parents have punished their children for disobeying their authority. Societies have established laws and ways to enforce those laws. If you believe there's a Creator who has created us, and thus has authority over us, it's not unreasonable to say that this Creator has some expectations, and if we violate them, he will punish us just as we punish those who are under our authority."

Dr. Pressley goes on to say, "Here's another analogy from common human experience: The punishment for a crime is often conditioned upon the greatness of the offense. If a neighbor shoots my dog or cat, I can get legal recourse, but we would never execute someone for that. If he shoots my son or daughter, the killer will pay a greater penalty. But if he shoots the President of the United States, we call it assassination and deal with it as a much more serious matter—because the greater the person who is offended, the greater we think the penalty ought to be. Apply this to God, and you can see how the penalty ought to increase by proportion. How high a penalty should someone pay for offending an infinite God?"

2. God's authority as Creator harmonizes with it. "If you build something, you can tear it back down if you wish," Pressley points out. "If you paint a picture and you don't want anyone to see it, you don't have to show it to anybody. It's yours. Nobody can tell you what you can and can't do with your creation. A person may feel like, 'This is the way things ought to be; God shouldn't give us rules, and if he does, he shouldn't punish or send anyone to Hell.' But it's illogical for us to say that the Creator must do what we're thinking and feeling. Rather, we should be asking God, 'What is it you want us to do?'"

3. God's work as Redeemer underscores the reality of Hell. "Any effort on our part to minimize the punishment of sinners will also at the same time minimize the pain of Calvary," Pressley continues. "If God never truly punishes sin, then there's no way to account for the horrible suffering Jesus endured on the cross. You can't minimize Hell without minimizing the atonement that keeps us from going there."

• Christianity *isn't just about what your ancestors believe; it's about what you believe.* We should respect our elders and maintain a sense of spiritual history (Leviticus 19:32; Deuteronomy 6:20-25), but ultimately each of us must give an account of ourselves to God (Ezekiel 18:20-32; Romans 2:1-16; 2 Corinthians 5:10).

• Christianity *isn't about loyalty to one's ethnic group; it's about God's love for all people.* The Bible isn't just about "the Christian God." It's about God, who created all things, who rules over all the universe, and sent his Son to give his life so that "whoever believes in him shall not perish but have eternal life" (John 3:16). Jesus told his followers to make disciples "of all nations" or ethnic groups (Matthew 28:19). Heaven will include a great multitude "from every nation, tribe, people and language" (Revelation 7:9).[2]

4. It's not surprising that sinners would try to deny the reality of Hell. Pressley notes that "In every culture, when someone has a guilty conscience he tries to rationalize, justify, defend, and do whatever he can to get out of any guilt and any penalty. We're always hopeful that we won't get caught; then if we get caught, we hope we won't be punished. We try to get a good lawyer, and hope the jury will set us free. And when it comes to God, we hope there isn't a day of judgment, a day of accounting—so we're always open to any suggestion that will give us a way past a God who judges. Guilty, sinful people have an inherent fear of facing God as judge. The devil holds us in slavery to our fear of death (Hebrews 2:14, 15). So the devil can offer dozens of deceptions and we'll grab them."

5. God's grace offers hope. What about the heathen who have not heard of Christ? "God's grace has already been broader in our lives than we would have imagined, so we don't know how far his grace will go with others," Pressley adds. "What we know is, the Scripture clearly teaches that we must be saved through Jesus Christ (Acts 4:12). We know there's a Great Commission that tells us to go to all the world—everyone needs to hear the name of Jesus. Romans 3:23 says that all have sinned. So I view the world as lost, but I don't put the world in Hell. I let God the judge do so based on both his justice and his grace, trusting him to do what is appropriate. I preach more of a plan of salvation than a word of condemnation."

• Christianity *isn't about money; it's about a relationship with God.* Jesus' disciples should see money as a blessing from God to be used sincerely, wisely, and generously, with proper stewardship (Matthew 6:1-4; Luke 6:38; 12:32-34; 16:10-13). God is pleased with our generosity, but he cannot be bribed or manipulated. We don't earn Brownie points in Heaven by donating money to religious causes. Christians give willingly out of love for the one who first loved us (2 Corinthians 9:6-15; 1 John 3:16-18; 4:19).

• Christianity *isn't about leaving people out; it's about bringing them in.* Yoshi feels uncomfortable because there seems to be a big difference between Christians and non-Christians. Is this because Christians leave him out when he attends their meetings with his daughter? Or is it because the offense of the cross is confronting Yoshi's heart (1 Corinthians 1:18-25)? The road to eternal life is indeed narrow (Matthew 7:13, 14), but it's wide enough that Yoshi can walk on it if he chooses to. Christ's invitation is open to him just as much as anyone else. If he feels like an outsider, he doesn't have to remain one.

• Christianity *isn't about condemning people to Hell; it's about saving them from it.* "For God did not send his Son into the world to condemn the world, but to save the world through him. Whoever believes in him is not condemned, but whoever does not believe stands condemned already because he has not believed in the name of God's one and only Son" (John 3:17, 18).

Be Persistent

Yoshi opened the door to further discussion when he acknowledged, "I don't know about Christian theology, and I don't know the Bible." This presents a natural opportunity for a Christian to say, "Would you like to know more? If so, I'll be glad to continue meeting with you to study and discuss these matters."

Someone did that for another man I met in Japan. A few years before, he had bravely become a Christian despite strong opposition from his family. When I asked what made the difference for him, he pointed to a missionary and said, "Bill studied with me the evidence for Jesus' resurrection. I decided that if Jesus rose from the dead, I needed to follow him even if that didn't go along with my country's traditions."

QUESTIONS FOR PERSONAL REFLECTION:

1. What traditions do you observe? How do they *help* your walk with God? Are there some ways these traditions *hinder* your walk with God?

2. What are some cultural obstacles that make it difficult to reach out to a person like Yoshi?

RESOURCES FOR FURTHER STUDY:

George W. Braswell, *Understanding World Religions* (Broadman & Holman, 1994).

Eddie Gibbs, *In Name Only: Tackling the Problem of Nominal Christianity* (Victor, 1994).

FOOTNOTES

[1]William Barclay, *Mark* (Westminster, 1975), p. 165.

[2]It could be argued that every ethnic group contributes something positive to our overall understanding of what it means for human beings to be created in the image of God. Perhaps that's why "the glory and honor of the nations" will be brought into Heaven (Revelation 21:26). At the same time, there may be unique temptations in every culture (materialism, intellectual pride, sensuality, self-sufficiency, or superstition) that make it vulnerable to the devil's wiles. Once institutionalized by decades or centuries of tradition, do these customs harden into strongholds of Satan's power?

[3]Russell Shorto, "Belief by the Numbers," *The New York Times Magazine*, December 7, 1997, p. 61.

CHAPTER 11

TOM AND DANIELLE: WHY SO MANY PHONY CHRISTIANS?

Tiny but trendy. Crowded in the summer, deserted in the winter. Vacation getaway for presidents and movie stars. And a good place to ask some honest questions.

Ten miles wide and twenty miles long, Martha's Vineyard is a foggy ferry ride from the coast of mainland Massachusetts. Only about ten thousand residents live on the island year-round, but during the height of the summer tourist season, one hundred thousand visitors crowd its beaches and wander the quaint, sandy streets of its six small towns. Each town has its own personality, the locals say— one is upscale and another is blue-collar, while still another is home mainly to Native Americans.

"Everything is geared toward tourists," Tom laughs. "I can walk downtown and buy T-shirts anytime I want, but Heaven help me if I need to buy something my family needs, like a baby's crib!"

And baby cribs are no small concern to Tom and his wife, Danielle. Their multi-racial family includes six children ranging in age from two to fifteen, all adopted—two originally from New York, one from Rhode Island, one from Jamaica

(West Indies), and two more from Texas.

Tom and Danielle's house—a tall colonial "saltbox" typical of New England—lies right at the geographic center of the island. Tom and three of his friends built the house themselves. Not that he was ever trained as a carpenter. A jack-of-all-trades, Tom earned college degrees in business and law. Today, he serves as administrator for the Martha's Vineyard Commission. Previously, he worked for several years as the island's transportation planner—no small task in a place where ferryboats serve as the population's lifeline.

Along with her responsibilities as a mom, Danielle has developed her own home-based business. She makes and markets baby slings moms and dads can use to carry their little ones. Her workspace at home is filled with colored fabrics in traditional or ethnic prints, including kente cloth (a colorful African design).

"She's had a lot of experience carrying babies," her husband grins.

And a lot of experience with some hard questions about God.

Why Don't They Act Like Christians?

Tom and Danielle believe deeply in God, and they became Christians several years ago. But they remember vividly how, in their pre-Christian days, it bothered them to see so much phoniness in many professed Christians. They wondered, "Why do so many church services seem out of touch with real life? And why do so many churchgoers seem to play religious games instead of doing what the Bible says followers of Jesus should do?"

"When I was young, I faithfully went to classes at the Catholic church," Danielle reflects, "and I had a lot of questions—but I couldn't get any answers. I was told to be quiet, so I gave up asking questions. I kept a relationship with God in terms of prayer, but I had no concept of who Jesus was, and no real personal relationship with God. By the time Tom and I got together, I had become jaded about Christianity. In college, I grew cynical about the need to know God at all."

"It doesn't help," she adds, "when so many people who call themselves Christians don't act like they really believe it."

Budgets, Bazaars, and Bingo

Tom's story is similar. "I had been an altar boy in the Episcopal church as a seven-, eight-, and nine-year-old. But then the local congregation closed due to financial problems and church politics, and our family never went back to church. I figured there was nothing real about the church, because it was so important to our family one year, and the next year it had no impact on our lives whatsoever.

"During my teen years, I didn't see any relevance or reality to the church at all outside of a social club that you joined if you wanted to. Later, I began studying the Bible on my own and became very excited about what I was reading. It made sense to me that Jesus was the Son of God.

"But then," Tom adds with a note of frustration, "I had a hard time finding a church that practices what the Scripture requires."

"When I read Scripture, it talks about people who were joyful. They would do things like praying all night for Simon Peter when he was in prison. I'd go into a church looking for real belief in Jesus and real worship. Instead, people would stand up and sit down and kneel, and say the same words over and over like they're supposed to—but there didn't seem to be any heart in it at all.

"It was different from what I was reading in Scripture

that the church should be. Jesus said to feed the hungry and clothe the naked, and all I saw churches doing was worrying about budgets, flea markets, bazaars, bingo games, and casino nights. It just didn't make sense to me. What I saw Scripture requiring was not what I saw in any churches around me. I thought, 'Am I demanding too much of the church, or does it just not exist in the real world?'"

True Love for Jesus

Tom and Danielle's island home is accessible from the mainland only by plane or by ferry. It's easy to feel isolated, especially during the cold winter months when the tourists are gone.

But Tom has a lot of company when he voices the honest question that began troubling him years ago: "Where can I find a church," he remembers asking, "where people truly love Jesus, and don't just get wrapped up in the social club and the institution?"

RESPONDING TO TOM AND DANIELLE

WHY SO MANY PHONY CHRISTIANS?

As a longtime baseball fan, I felt disappointed when Bob Engel was arrested one spring day soon after the start of the 1990 season.

A National League umpire for years, Engel was charged with shoplifting 4,180 baseball cards from a retail store in Bakersfield, California. A security officer at the store told police that he caught Engel (who was fifty-six years old at the time) putting seven boxes of cards, valued at about $144, into a brown paper bag.[1]

I was disappointed to think that an experienced umpire would do something like that. It's common when an umpire calls a base runner out for trying to steal; but it's altogether unacceptable if the umpire himself gets caught stealing! He's supposed to be the good guy, the authority figure, the one you have to respect even when you boo him. He's supposed to enforce the rules, not break them. As I read the allegations in the sports page, I felt like saying, "No, Bob, don't do that! Don't let us down. We're counting on you to do the right thing!" It's disillusioning when someone who knows the rules fails to live by them.

A worker in the medical profession wrote to Dear Abby (Abigail Van Buren) to ask for advice in dealing with a cranky coworker who constantly cursed and complained about the patients and the working conditions at her job. The writer, who signed her letter "Up to Here," was especially bothered by her coworker's claim to be a faithful Christian. She wrote: "Her conversations are peppered with 'the Lord this' and 'the Lord that.' I have great difficulty understanding the inconsistencies between her professed faith and her actions. Although I am not an active member of my church, I wouldn't treat a dog the way this pious churchgoer treats people. . . . In my experience, those who thump their Bibles the loudest would benefit more by being thumped by them."[2]

PHONINESS IS NOTHING NEW

Hypocrisy. Phoniness. Lack of authenticity. Problems like these have plagued God's people for centuries.

Hundreds of years before Christ, the prophet Jeremiah warned God's people, "Do not trust in deceptive words and say, 'This is the temple of the Lord, the temple of the Lord, the temple of the Lord!'"—as if merely showing up at the place of worship and repeating pious-sounding words over and over would make everything OK with God. Instead, God wanted the people to change their ways, to treat others justly, and to quit following other gods. "Will you steal and murder, commit adultery and perjury . . . and follow other gods," the Lord asked, ". . . and then come and stand before me in this house which bears my Name, and say, 'We are safe'—safe to do all these detestable things?" (Jeremiah 7:4-10).

It's sad when people who claim to know God gossip, cheat, lie, and hurt others just as much as others do who don't claim to know the Lord at all. The late Carl Ketcherside wrote that in the early church, Christians "claimed to love each other and talked about Jesus; now they claim to love Jesus and talk about each other. In those days all exerted an effort to exhort; now all must be exhorted to exert an effort."[3] Whatever else you can say about our current culture, one thing's for sure: our friends and neighbors can sniff out a phony a mile away. People like Tom and Danielle are turned off when professed Christians simply play religious games.

Maybe that's why the New Testament warns in such direct terms about the dangers of an inconsistent life. James wrote, "With the tongue we praise our Lord and Father, and with it we curse men, who have been made in God's likeness. . . . My brothers, this should not be" (James 3:9, 10). The apostle Peter said to rid ourselves of all kinds of hypocrisy (1 Peter 2:1). Paul wrote that Christians must "put off falsehood and speak truthfully" (Ephesians 4:25). In other words, be real!

Inconsistent Lifestyles = Ineffective Evangelism

I read about some business owners in Utah who joined with the tourist bureau to urge residents of the state to spend their vacation dollars at home. A grocery store chain sponsored a photo contest. The theme? "Travel Utah First." The grand prize? A trip to Hawaii.[4] Sometimes Christians appear equally inconsistent.

The apostle Paul said to "fight the good fight of faith," but we also need to fight the good fight of *fake*. Sadly, the history of the church is filled with stories about people who failed to live consistent lifestyles of righteousness and faith. Popes have insisted on celibacy for their priests, but sired children out of wedlock. Preachers have used their pulpits to denounce sexual immorality while secretly practicing the very sins they condemned. Worshipers who sang, "Praise the Lord" a few moments ago at church yell "Same to you, fella," as another driver cuts them off in traffic during the drive home. Parents send their children to Sunday school, but in everyday life at home they never pray, never talk about God, and never discuss spiritual issues. Christians divide from other believers over minor matters of opinion. Nasty splits tarnish churches' reputations for years.

JESUS' EXPOSÈ OF HYPOCRISY

Jesus reserved some of his most scathing rebukes for the religious leaders of his day—the Pharisees and Scribes who were experts in the law. The Lord's exposé of hypocrisy in Matthew 23:1-39 makes painful but worthwhile reading, because it paints a vivid portrait of religious phoniness. Here are some of the lessons we find there:

1. Hypocrites do not practice what they preach (v. 3).

2. Hypocrites place heavy demands on others which they are unwilling to shoulder themselves (v. 4).

3. Hypocrites emphasize appearance rather than substance—"everything they do is done for men to see" (v. 5).

4. Hypocrites are preoccupied with recognition and status symbols. They want to impress others and receive public honors like sitting in the right seats and being called by impressive titles (vv. 6-12).

5. Hypocrites hinder others from entering the kingdom of God (vv. 13-15).

6. Hypocrites highlight little things that others might notice, but overlook the big things (like justice, mercy, and faithfulness) that matter most in God's eyes (vv. 16-24).

7. Hypocrites look good on the outside, but are corrupt on the inside (vv. 25-28).

8. Hypocrites bring harm to those who are truly trying to do God's will (vv. 29-36).

9. And yet, despite all their flaws, hypocrites are still the objects of Jesus' caring love. He's willing to embrace and help them, but first they must be willing to receive him (vv. 37-39).

Obviously, not everyone who claims to be a Christian really is following Christ. Jesus compared the kingdom of Heaven to a field where weeds take root among the wheat, and both kinds of plants grow together until the harvest (the final judgment) when God separates his true followers from the false followers (Matthew 13:24-30, 36-43).

Not long ago, while standing in an airport check-in line, I noticed a woman ahead of me holding two large boxes she wanted to carry onto the plane with her. When the attendant at the check-in counter informed her that the boxes were too big to carry onto the plane, the woman flew into a rage. While the rest of us looked on, she argued loudly and angrily until the airline employee finally called in her supervisor, who verified that indeed, the two boxes were too large to qualify as carry-ons.

When the situation was finally resolved, I was the next passenger to approach the counter. I told the flustered-looking attendant, "It must be hard to stay calm when someone makes a scene like that."

And she replied, "Yes, and do you know what was in those two boxes? Bibles! You'd think that someone carrying two boxes of Bibles wouldn't act like that, wouldn't you?"

Chagrined, I told her, "Ma'am, I'm sorry you were treated that way. Not everyone who believes the Bible acts like that." No wonder so many people think the church is full of hypocrites. No wonder so many ask, as Tom put it, "Where can I find a church where people truly love Jesus?"

HOW CAN WE RESPOND TO THIS QUESTION?

We have to be honest. We can't deny that Christians often act inconsistently. Jesus rebuked the religious leaders of his day for being like "whitewashed tombs, which look beautiful on the outside but on the inside are full of dead men's bones and everything unclean" (Matthew 23:27). Let's not apply yet another layer of whitewash.

As professor R. C. Sproul explains, Christians tend to make one of two mistakes. One mistake is to take the law of God and reduce its demands through "cheap grace." (In other words, we're tempted to adopt an "I'm OK, you're OK" easy-believism that waters down what God expects of us.) The other mistake, Sproul says, is to acknowledge that God's standards are high, but simply pretend that we are living at a higher level than we actually have attained. Either way, we're not being true to God, true to God's standards, or even true to ourselves.[5]

Nevertheless, there are some helpful things we can say when a friend accuses the church of phoniness.

Clarify What Hypocrisy Means

The Greek word *hupokrites* referred to an actor—a performer in the theater who wore a mask or played the part of another person. Hypocrisy is playacting or pretending—claiming to believe something is true, but acting in a way that contradicts our stated beliefs. Notice: by this definition, Christians are not the only ones sometimes guilty of hypocrisy.

An Earth Summit held in Rio de Janeiro, Brazil, brought together dignitaries from all over the world to discuss environmental problems. A noble goal, right? But delegates arrived for their meetings in gas-guzzling luxury cars; and throughout the conference, trash cans overflowed with throwaway plates, aluminum cans, and plastic utensils. Altogether, more than two hundred copy machines produced roughly a million photocopies per day. As Manuel de Soto, a Brazilian garbage collector, swept up streamers, wrappers, and soda cups near a pavilion on waste management, he grumbled, "These greenies have nice speeches, but in practice, they're pigs."[6]

A hypocrite is not simply someone who makes mistakes. A hypocrite is someone whose actions belie his professed beliefs. Christians aren't unique in their struggle with this, but we do need to guard against it, for it distorts the truth and gives ammunition to opponents of the gospel.

My guess is, a large percentage of Christians at least recognize and struggle against their own hypocrisy. As R. C. Sproul points out, many of a sincere minister's sermons "are born out of the minister's own personal struggles. The minister is required to preach about the holiness of God and perfect obedience when he himself is not perfectly obedient. To preach at a higher level than you perform is not hypocrisy. To claim a higher level of performance than you have attained is hypocrisy."[7]

Clarify What Salvation Means

It's odd that Christians would be accused of hypocrisy, for everyone who accepts salvation is by open admission, a sinner! We have accepted the painful reality that "all have sinned and fall short of the glory of God" (Romans 3:23). We agree with the apostle John who wrote, "If we claim to be without sin, we deceive ourselves and the truth is not in us" (1 John 1:8).

During a debate, Abraham Lincoln's opponent kept referring to him as "two-faced." Finally Lincoln responded, "Ladies and gentlemen, I ask you, if I were two-faced, would I be wearing this one?" If Christians were really two-faced, would we openly admit that we are sinners?

The church is not a club for perfect people. It's a hospital where the wounded find forgiveness and grace. According to the New Testament, part of becoming a Christian is to turn from sin in earnest, genuine repentance. We accept the humbling fact that we've done wrong, and we acknowledge the even more humbling fact that we can't make things right with God through our own human effort. Instead, we can be saved only through the undeserved kindness of God expressed to us through the sacrificial death of his Son Jesus Christ. "It is by grace you have been saved" (Ephesians 2:8-10).

When as repentant sinners we believe in Jesus Christ and are baptized into him (Acts 2:38; Galatians 3:27), we are not declaring to the world that we are now graduates of the Ain't-I-Perfect School of Theology; we're like newborn babies, dependent on our heavenly Father, eager to learn and grow in his grace. Christians trust in God's blessed assurance that "if we confess our sins, he is faithful and just and will forgive us our sins and purify us from all unrighteousness" (1 John 1:9).

Clarify What Holy Living Means

Nevertheless, while we must be honest about our imperfections, the Christian life also requires that we make a realistic attempt to grow in godliness with the help of the Holy Spirit. Our walk speaks louder than our talk. Even a Christian as great as the apostle Paul was willing to admit that he had not already been made perfect, but he was determined to press on toward the goal God had put before him (Philippians 3:12-14). That's why he told Christians, "continue to work out your salvation with fear and trembling" (Philippians 2:12).

TWO ASPECTS OF HOLINESS

For the Christian, holiness (or what theologians call *sanctification*) is both a state and a process. When we accept Christ as Savior, we become "holy people"—distinct, pure, and set apart in a special state of holiness in God's eyes—not because of our own merits but because we are in Christ (1 Peter 2:9).

And as soon as we are saved, we enter a process of holiness in which the Holy Spirit helps us grow more and more like Christ. Thus, Peter could call Christians "a holy nation" while also urging, "be holy in all you do" (1 Peter 2:9, 1:15). Or as another biblical author puts it, "by one sacrifice he [God] has made perfect forever those who are being made holy" (Hebrews 10:14).

As we grow in godliness, our outward actions and inner character should correspond more and more to the holiness of our perfect Savior (2 Peter 1:5-11). But during this growth process, we still make plenty of mistakes.

Tom eventually came to understand this after he and Danielle became Christians themselves. "As I've grown and matured," Tom says, "I've become more willing to point the finger at me and not at others—which makes it a lot easier to overlook the faults of others. When I was a young Christian, I was more legalistic than I am now—but back then, I wouldn't have seen myself as a legalistic person at all. As I've had some low times in my own walk with Christ, and I've realized what a sinful person I am, it has become easier for me to overlook the minor faults of other Christians. I've become more willing to help instead of criticize."

Clarify What Personal Responsibility Means

What would have been helpful to Tom and Danielle during their times of doubt? "I can tell you my answer straight out," Tom immediately responds. "Be a real person. Don't quote me chapter and verse, don't give me the pat answers they taught you in theology school, don't throw three points at me, don't tell me what I'm doing wrong and the 'right' way to do it. Be normal. Be real. Laugh with me. Cry with me. Explain how you messed up in the same way. Talk me through it."

Danielle adds, "I had to learn some things the hard way. Before I accepted Christ, I saw that the Bible said to honor your father and mother and things would go well with you. I had no relationship with my father at all—we weren't even speaking to one another. But I decided to give the Bible's way a try. And as I began to show honor to my father, things improved a lot between us. I learned that you don't have to be afraid of God. He's up to the challenge. His way really does work."

"It's also important to challenge ourselves," says Tom, "and ask why we're saying certain things or rebelling against certain things. A lot of our pushing God away and pushing the church away is deeper than just saying what's wrong with 'them.' Maybe the real issue is how I feel about myself and not how I feel about the church. There needs to be some healthy self-examination as well."

Even if the church were full of hypocrites, that still wouldn't excuse each of us from our own personal accountability to God.

Clarify What the Church Means

What is the church really about? This is a crucial question. Our goal is far more than just winning people to a flawed human institution. We're helping people find the Lord who will add them to the body of Christ and bring them into intimate connection with other believers who are likewise saved by grace.

As Rubel Shelley writes in his book, *Prepare to Answer,* "My role as a 'Christian apologist' . . . does not obligate me to defend any particular expression of Christian faith within a certain denomination or sect. . . . Neither am I committed to defend the wicked things that people have done in the name of Christianity through the centuries—whether the Spanish Inquisition or a personal sin in my life. The truth or falsity of Christian faith is a separate issue from the faithfulness or unfaithfulness of its adherents in practicing it."[8]

If Goldilocks had been searching for a church instead of porridge, she would have learned that some congregations seem too hard, some too soft, some too hot, some too cold. Where could she find a church that was just right?

How about this one? It was a church built on the foundation of Christ as Lord and Savior. A church that proclaimed the good news and joyfully baptized those who believed. A church where young and old met together consistently for prayer, fellowship, teaching, and Communion. A church where people loved each other, met one another's needs, and worshiped together in unity. A church that grew spontaneously—not because of elaborate programs, but because of a Holy Spirit-engendered genuineness that no one could deny or quench. That is the kind of church we see in Acts 2:36-47. Even though we may not reproduce it perfectly, can't we strive to be that kind of church today?

We're Not Perfect, But We Know Someone Who Is

The bottom line? If you identify some inconsistency in the life of any Christian, you haven't destroyed the credibility of the gospel. Christians aren't all just a bunch of phonies—but even if we were, the fact remains that the head of our church is no hypocrite. Jesus Christ never sinned, never lied, never pretended to be something he is not.

We are imperfect followers of a perfect Lord. No matter how closely you look at him, you'll never find anything phony about Jesus Christ.

QUESTIONS FOR PERSONAL REFLECTION

1. Have you ever felt disappointed by a Christian whose actions were inconsistent with what he or she claimed to believe? How did you deal with your disappointment?

2. Has anyone ever accused you of being a hypocrite? If so, do you think the accusation was valid? Why, or why not?

3. How can we enthusiastically invite people to consider being part of a church we know is imperfect?

RESOURCES FOR FURTHER STUDY

Charles Colson with Ellen Santilli Vaughn, *The Body* (Word, 1996).

LeRoy Lawson, *The New Testament Church Then and Now* (Standard, 1981).

R. C. Sproul, *Reason to Believe* (Zondervan, 1982).

FOOTNOTES

[1] *The Cincinnati Enquirer,* April 25, 1990.

[2] *The Cincinnati Enquirer,* March 29, 1990.

[3] W. Carl Ketcherside, *The Royal Priesthood* (Mission Messenger, 1956), p. 2.

[4] *The Summit,* October, 1997, p. 4.

[5] R. C. Sproul, *Objections Answered* videotaped lecture (Ligonier Ministries, 1982).

[6] *The Cincinnati Enquirer,* June 10, 1992.

[7] R. C. Sproul, *Reason to Believe* (Zondervan, 1982), pp. 82, 83.

[8] Rubel Shelley, *Prepare to Answer* (Baker, 1990), p. 17.

CHAPTER 12

TRUTH, FREEDOM, AND TOLERANCE

Do you ever find it hard to tell the truth? When I was growing up, my parents always expected me to be honest. So when a baseball crashed through the dining room window, I told them the truth: "My *brother* threw it!"

My parents said, "Don't jump on the bed." But one day my brothers and I were horsing around, wrestling on the bed, and all three of us crash-landed onto the bed at the same time and split the old wooden bed frame right down the side. My dad was so angry with us—he was still mad later that week when we got into our cars and drove back to college! Sometimes it's hard to face the truth.

I decided to conduct my own informal survey. I passed out pieces of paper to people and asked them to complete the sentence, "It's hard to tell the truth . . ." I also asked them to list their age and whether they were male or female. Nearly two hundred people responded, ranging from age four to age seventy-nine. Some of their responses were amusing:

"It's hard to tell the truth . . .

. . . when you return from a fishing trip." (Male, age forty-nine)

. . . when someone asks your age and weight." (Female, age forty-nine— *presumably*, age forty-nine!)

. . . when your mouth is full." (Male, age five)

Other responses were quite insightful:

"It's hard to tell the truth . . .

. . . when you want to fit in." (Female, age thirteen)

. . . when you don't know what the truth is." (Male, age twenty-two)

. . . when people are going to laugh at me." (Female, age nine)

. . . when the truth isn't the answer people want to hear." (Male, age nineteen)

. . . when my family members don't agree with my Christianity." (Female, age seventy)

Sometimes it's hard to tell the truth. But if there's anything our world needs today, it's truth. And more important, our creator wants us to tell the truth. David wrote that God desires truth in our inmost being (Psalm 51:6). At least eighty times in the Gospels Jesus said, "I tell you the truth" (or as the *King James Version* puts it, "Verily, verily, I say unto thee"). Jesus rebuked the religious leaders who devalued the truth by their hypocrisy. But to those who believed in him, he said, "If you hold to my teaching, you are really my disciples. Then you will know the truth, and the truth will set you free" (John 8:31, 32).

WHAT DO WE KNOW ABOUT TRUTH?

If we're going to take the truth next door, we need to grasp some basic facts about truth itself.

The Truth Is Real

Truth does in fact exist, for Jesus says we can know it. There was a time in America when hardly anyone would have disputed that. Where I grew up, right and wrong were pretty clear-cut. My high school colors were black and white! (Really!) People didn't always agree, but they generally assumed that truth was real and you could know it.

But today, our culture has sacrificed truth on the altar of tolerance. As someone has put it, in the old days, at least we knew when we were getting off track; but nowadays, many are saying there never was a track in the first place. It's like erasing the lines on the court and taking down the goal, then trying to play basketball. It's like removing the steering wheel, the speedometer, and the brake pedal, then trying to drive a car.

There's a lot at stake for our families, churches, and nation if we give up the concept of truth. In fact, this is an area of intense spiritual warfare; for as Jesus pointed out, when the devil lies, "he speaks his native language" (John 8:44). But as the song, "A Mighty Fortress Is Our God," reminds us, "Though this world with devils filled may threaten to undo us, we shall not fear for God hath willed his truth to triumph through us."

The Truth Is Written

God has made his truth known through Scripture. When my wife, Candy, was studying to be a registered nurse, she took a class on medical ethics where the teacher said that in most situations there are no certain truths, no right and wrong answers. Funny—they didn't say that in Candy's chemistry class, or microbiology, or anatomy and physiology. In those classes, the professors were very *picky* about truth! They made her memorize countless facts about medicines and hospital procedures. They insisted she learn the truth about bones, blood, organs, and nerves. Why? Because a patient's well-being is at stake.

But the same God who designed our physical bodies also has revealed what's right and wrong and how the spiritual body of Christ (the church) should function. The first verse of the Bible tells the truth: "In the beginning God created the heavens and the earth" (Genesis 1:1). The last verse of the Bible tells the truth: "The grace of the Lord Jesus be with God's people. Amen" (Revelation 22:21). Everything in between tells us the truth. "All Scripture is God-breathed" (2 Timothy 3:16).

The Bible is factual, not imaginary. Authentic, not fake. Genuine, not pretend. Real, not make-believe. It's not full of myths, legends, fairy tales, and pie-in-the-sky foolishness. The truth is written.

The Truth Is Revealed in Jesus

The introduction to the TV show, "The X Files," says "The truth is out there." But the Bible insists that the truth has come here. In person. In Jesus.

At Jesus' trial Pilate asked, "What is truth?" All he had to do was look more closely at the one standing quietly in front of him.

Life magazine ran a Christmas issue (December, 1994) with a picture of Jesus on the cover next to the question, "Who Was He?" An article inside quoted a variety of views. Some said Jesus never existed. Others saw him as a well-meaning but misguided teacher, a radical feminist, or a tragic victim of circumstances. But it seems to me that the magazine's cover answered its own question. Who was Jesus? Who is he? "Life!" In our postmodern age, as in any age, Jesus doesn't need to be reinvented, reinterpreted, or reimagined. He needs to be received as Savior and respected as Lord, before he returns in glory!

Truth isn't a riddle, it's the answer. It isn't a mystery, it's a message. It isn't confusion, it's the solution. It isn't just a philosophy, it's a Person.

The Truth Sets Us Free

Jesus' original listeners didn't understand what he meant when he said, "The truth will set you free." They began arguing with him, saying, "We are Abraham's descendants" who have "never been slaves of anyone." But freedom-stealers like the Pharisees didn't really understand spiritual liberty. They used their version of "truth" to enslave people. They loaded heavy burdens on people's shoulders. Mark Twain was right when he said, "Loyalty to petrified opinion never yet broke a chain or freed a human soul."

Let me pause here and ask some pointed questions of my Christian readers. How well do we actually understand and experience spiritual freedom? Many times, "freedom" isn't the first word that comes to a Christian's mind to describe the way he or she feels from day to day. Are you the parent of a prodigal son or daughter who is breaking your heart? Are you a burned-out servant of God who feels like you don't have any more to give? Have you tried unsuccessfully to break a bad habit? Are you hanging on to some old grudges and hurts?

The truth will set us free—but notice, Jesus put an important condition on this promise: "If we hold to his teaching." When we hold to Jesus' teaching about grace and forgiveness, he can set us free from a guilty conscience and free from bitterness against others. When we hold to his teachings about his own lordship, we're free from trying to live up to everyone else's expectations. When we imitate the way he treated Samaritans and centurions, we can be free from racism and prejudice that keep God's people apart. When we heed his teachings about moral purity, we'll find freedom from sexual diseases and addictions that weaken bodies, poison minds, and ruin families. When we take to heart his prayer for unity, we'll be set free from sectarianism that divides and distracts the church. And when we put into practice what he taught about prayer, he will free us from trying to do ministry in our own human strength alone.

Christians disagree profoundly with the philosophy espoused by Hindu teacher Krishnamurti, who said, "One should neither have followers nor should one follow someone. The moment you follow someone, you cease to follow Truth. . . . Truth is in everyone. No man from outside yourself can make you free."[1] The Bible offers a completely different perspective. We find true freedom only by following Jesus. We need the power of his Holy Spirit to truly be free (see Romans 8:1-11).

But there's another important point to notice.

The Truth Hurts

When I conducted my informal survey, by far the most common response was, "It's hard to tell the truth when it will hurt someone's feelings."

Some of Jesus' teachings sound remarkably unpopular today: *We are sinners. Hell is real. We're accountable to God. Jesus is the only way to salvation.* Truths like those can be painful to hear, and painful to say. That's why we need to follow the example of Jesus who was "full of *grace* and truth" (John 1:14).

"The message of the cross [that is, Jesus' death, burial, and resurrection] is foolishness to those who are perishing," the apostle Paul wrote (1 Corinthians 1:18). Many people today find it offensive if we talk about sin and salvation on God's terms. We can't change the truth of the cross, even if some find it offensive. But we need to make sure the offense doesn't come from our own attitude. If people hear our message and turn away, we need to make sure they do so because of the offense of the cross, not merely because we were rude or overbearing, or that we refused to listen to them and love them. The truth does hurt; but let's not infect the wound with a poisonous attitude.

Grace and truth—that's the right combination. Grace isn't just a mushy feel-goodism; and truth isn't a ball and chain. Truth is the hand God uses to guide us; grace is the hand he uses to pick us up when we fall. Truth is the Good Shepherd's rod of correction; grace is the green pasture where he makes us lie down.

INFATUATED WITH TOLERANCE

One of my former students, Michael Tolle, related the following true story about something that happened in a class he took at a local university. Michael happened to be assigned to a discussion group led by a man who was selected as the university's "professor of the year."

"After asking all the members of the group to introduce themselves," Michael says, "the professor told about two scientists who were debating whether the sun revolved around the earth or the earth revolved around the sun. They disagreed about the issue so they decided to settle it by watching the sun rise together. So the next morning the two men met at a park bench and watched the sun rise together. And as the sun finished breaking off the horizon, both men looked at each other and simultaneously shouted, '*See!?!*'"

Michael continues, "The professor explained that the point of the illustration was to get all members of the discussion group to recognize that we can all look at the same thing and see something different based on our individual points of view—and that we should be open to everyone's opinion.

"But I saw another side to that illustration, so I raised my hand. I told the professor, 'I understand that there were different viewpoints. But the fact is, the guy who thought the earth revolved around the sun was *right!*'

Right on, Michael! In a confused world where more and more people "call evil good and good evil, put darkness for light and light for darkness," and "put bitter for sweet and sweet for bitter" (see Isaiah 5:20), facts are still facts, and some things are just plain right!

Not Every Option Is a Good One

In a culture suffering from a severe case of truth decay, tolerance has become the cardinal virtue. And most people seem to define tolerance something like this: "accepting everyone's viewpoints as equally valid." But while we can respect a person's right to hold a personal opinion, this does not mean every opinion actually corresponds to reality.

Give me one hundred dollars and send me to the local supermarket, and I'm free to purchase a wide variety of items. But not everything I can purchase possesses equal nutritional value if I decide to eat it. I could use my hundred dollars to purchase ten gallons of premium ice cream, or fifty pounds of broccoli. I could also, I suppose, buy a hundred dollars worth of rat poison. I'm free to purchase whatever I want, but some things are good for me; others are not. Similarly, as an American citizen I enjoy great freedom to believe and practice whatever faith I choose; and our nation presents a wide variety of religious options. But that doesn't mean every religious option is equally healthy to my soul.

As Christian writer Paul Copan explains in his helpful book, "*True for You But Not for Me,*" "Contrary to popular definitions, true tolerance means 'putting up with error'—not 'being accepting of all views.' We don't tolerate what we enjoy or approve of—like chocolate or Bach's music. By definition, what we tolerate is what we disapprove of or what we believe to be false and erroneous." And, as Copan continues, "if disagreement didn't exist, then tolerance would be unnecessary."[2]

Copan recommends that if someone accuses you of being intolerant, you should first ask him to clarify what he means by "intolerant." "If by 'tolerance' the person means 'accepting all views as true,'" Copan says, "then you can say, 'You don't accept my view as true. Are you being intolerant?'"[3]

The Power of Persuasion

In a recent speech, Senator Dan Coats explained that tolerance has two different extremes: permissiveness and persecution. Some see it as permissiveness—standing for nothing and falling for everything; allowing, endorsing, and encouraging any behavior at all, including those that are destructive to individuals and to society. Non-Christians often assume that Christians are at the other extreme—so intolerant that we persecute anyone who disagrees with us and try to force them to accept our position. But, Coats argues, there is a middle ground: persuasion. We realize we can't force people to accept God's standards. But we believe the truth has the power to change minds and hearts, and then actions will follow.[4]

Perhaps the current infatuation with tolerance is really just a somewhat distorted expression of our human longing for God's grace. Undeserving, we long to be accepted (by God and by others) in spite of our imperfections. And the good news is, God offers sufficient grace—unfathomable grace, grace greater than all our sins. But he does so in harmony with his truth, not at the expense of it.

How odd that Christians would be considered intolerant. Jesus was criticized for being the friend of tax collectors and sinners. No one else is so merciful, so loving, so compassionate. But Jesus doesn't say, "Go, it isn't sin anymore." He says, "Go and sin no more." He doesn't just "tolerate" us; he tells us the truth about who we are and what we have done. Then if we're willing to accept it, he forgives us, redeems us, washes us, saves us, and fills us with hope. All of this is possible because Christ did far more than merely "tolerate" wrong. He endured the penalty of Hell for us when he died on the cross for our sins. Once we're persuaded that this good news is true, we can't stop talking about God's amazing grace.

When God's truth becomes a fire in our bones, a light in our eyes, a path for our feet, a treasure in our hearts, and a consistent message others hear from our lips and read from our lives, then our faith will be contagious.

And the truth will set us free.

QUESTIONS FOR PERSONAL REFLECTION:

1. Do you agree that the concept of "truth" has lost its force in our current culture? Can you cite specific symptoms of this trend in today's news?

2. Is it possible to tell the truth consistently without appearing judgmental or harsh?

RESOURCES FOR FURTHER READING:

Josh McDowell, *The New Tolerance* (Tyndale House, 1998).

Paul Copan, *"True for You But Not for Me"* (Bethany House, 1998).

FOOTNOTES

[1] Madhu Bazaz Wangu, "Hinduism: World Religions," *Facts on File 1991*, p. 120.

[2] Paul Copan, *"True for You But Not for Me"* (Bethany House, 1998), p. 35.

[3] Copan, p. 37.

[4] Quoted by Steve Singleton in "The Challenges College Students Face on Secular Campuses," *Does God Exist?* (May/June 1998), p. 17.

TO WHOM SHALL WE GO?

I'm writing this chapter on the day after Christmas. I have to admit, this isn't my favorite day of the year—the day after the big day. You know the feeling, don't you?

Shreds of wrapping paper from yesterday's gifts still clutter the floor. The refrigerator overflows with leftovers from two weeks of heavy eating, and I'm not sure the fudge I ate for breakfast counts as one of the basic food groups.

But now the big day is over. Soon the poinsettias will begin to wilt. Around the neighborhood, dried-up Christmas trees will be placed by the curb for sanitation workers to carry away. The parking lot at the mall that looked so refreshingly quiet and deserted yesterday will be crowded with cars this morning. Cheerful carols on the radio will give way to the whine of the daily news.

Even when we manage to stretch the holidays into a six-week affair, the fun is soon over and life returns to normal.

My twenty-one-year-old son made an interesting observation a couple of nights ago as we observed a family tradition by munching homemade pizza together on Christmas Eve. "What if Heaven is a bit like Christmas?"

Good question. And here's another: "What if the reason people put so much emphasis on Christmas and other holidays is that they're really long-ing for what only Heaven can give them?"

Doesn't every human heart long for Heaven? Think of the best Christmas you ever enjoyed: delicious food, satisfying conversation, beautiful music, soul-stirring worship, peaceful rest. Heaven will have all of that and more. And it will contain none of the bad things that make us dread the holidays: family conflicts, loneliness, emptiness because we miss loved ones, anxiety over what the new year will hold.

At their best, earthly holidays are only a pale reflection of the never-ending celebration awaiting us in Heaven. As C. S. Lewis pointed out, "Our Father refreshes us on the journey with some pleasant inns, but will not encourage us to mistake them for home."[1]

Before closing this book filled with honest questions, you and I must dare to ask ourselves one more. It goes something like this: "What makes my own life meaningful? What gives me a reason to get up in the morning and face each new year and each new day with a spring in my step and hope in my heart?"

Looking in the Wrong Places

Almost three thousand years ago, a deep-thinking individual dared to ask honest questions like those, and he wrote them down. Ecclesiastes may be one of the most important parts of the Bible for any of us trying to com-municate with postmodern people. This ancient book asks honest questions everyone wonders about. And, as someone has said, "It asks the questions the rest of the Bible answers."

King Solomon begins the book with a depressing conclusion: "Meaningless! Meaningless! . . . Utterly meaningless! Everything is meaning-less" (Ecclesiastes 1:2). It's actually the Hebrew word *abel*, which other trans-lations render as "emptiness" or "vanity." Like the man named Abel whom we meet in the book of Genesis, whose life was cut short by his angry brother Cain, *abel* means "short-lived" or "transient," like a breath, or a puff of air. Life, Solomon points out, seems brief, empty, pointless. It's like chas-ing after the wind, trying to grasp air in your hand.

Can **education** fill the void? Solomon decided to find out. He devoted himself to study. According to 1 Kings 4:32-34, he became a world-renowned expert on literature (he wrote three thousand proverbs), music (he composed one thousand and five songs), botany (he described plant life, from cedar trees to hyssop plants that grow out of walls), and biology (he taught about animals, birds, reptiles, and fish). But education alone isn't the key to a satisfying life. While it's good to learn all we can, in the process, we're likely to discover many problems we can't solve on our own. "What is twisted cannot be straightened; what is lacking cannot be counted. . . . the more knowledge, the more grief" (Ecclesiastes 1:15, 18).

So, maybe **pleasure** can satisfy one's soul. Solomon says, "I tried cheering myself with wine, and embracing folly" (Ecclesiastes 2:3). In other words, he made a deliberate choice to become an expert at fooling around, making small talk, making people laugh. But even if you're the life of the party, you still have to figure out what to do when the party's over. A vacation, a holiday, a fun evening with friends—it soon ends. What then? Just surviving from one weekend to the next? Solomon experimented with all kinds of pleasure. But "that also proved to be meaningless," he eventually had to admit (Ecclesiastes 2:1).

What about **possessions**? Solomon tried that route too. He built houses, vineyards, gardens, and tree-lined parks for himself. His palace took thirteen years to build, had rooms paneled with sweet-smelling cedar, and was half the length of a football field (1 Kings 7:1-12). In a day when clean water wasn't readily available, he "made reservoirs to water groves of flourishing trees" (Ecclesiastes 2:6). He owned servants to take care of his property, vast herds to provide plenty of good-tasting meat, choirs of singers to entertain him with music, a "bank account" overflowing with silver and gold, and plenty of women to meet his sexual desires (Ecclesiastes 2:4-9). "I denied myself nothing my eyes desired; I refused my heart no pleasure," he says (Ecclesiastes 2:10). But all the things money could buy still left him saying "everything was meaningless, a chasing after the wind; nothing was gained under the sun" (Ecclesiastes 2:11).

So, maybe **work** is the answer. Immerse yourself in your career. Set high goals, achieve all you can, make a name for yourself in your chosen profession. Solomon did that too. In fact, his wealth and wisdom earned him a world-wide reputation. But he soon discovered that work alone can't fill the void in a person's soul. When work is your god, your mind won't be at rest when you lie down to sleep at night; and besides, eventually you'll retire or die and leave everything you've worked for into the hands of somebody else who didn't work for it. "This too is meaningless," sighs Solomon. His conclusion? "I hated life" (Ecclesiastes 2:17-26).

John Lennon's widow, Yoko Ono, once wrote a little poem called "Lighting Piece" that simply says, "Light a match and watch it till it goes out." Is that what life is like? Brief, transient, meaningless, quickly gone? Is it simply a game of Trivial Pursuit in which we work and laugh and try to squeeze out a bit of joy before we grow old and die?

Several years ago, a fourteen-year-old boy named Jason Lehman wrote the following poem, which was published in Abigail Van Buren's "Dear Abby" column:

PRESENT TENSE

It was spring,
But it was summer I wanted,
The warm days,
And the great outdoors.

It was summer,
But it was fall I wanted,
The colorful leaves,
And the cool, dry air.

It was fall,
But it was winter I wanted,
The beautiful snow,
And the joy of the holiday season.

It was winter,
But it was spring I wanted,
The warmth,
And the blossoming of nature.

I was a child,
But it was adulthood I wanted,
The freedom,
And the respect.

I was twenty,
But it was thirty I wanted,
To be mature,
And sophisticated.

I was middle-aged,
But it was twenty I wanted,
The youth,
And the free spirit.

I was retired,
But it was middle age I wanted,
The presence of mind,
Without limitations.

My life was over.
But I never got what I wanted.[2]

Looking in the Right Place

My friend Jim Bird asked questions like the ones Solomon asked.

"Church was not a part of my life as a young man," Jim says. "I didn't know Jesus Christ as Savior or Lord. So I spent the better part of my life trying to fill the emptiness in me."

He married and fathered a son, but found that his relationships with his family didn't fill the void in his soul.

A hard-driving entrepreneur in the real estate and construction business, Jim was a self-made millionaire by age twenty-six. His family bought fine houses, took European vacations, and drove big cars.

"Eventually I decided I was being selfish," Jim admits. "I needed to devote my time and energy to the people of my community." He did so much community service, eventually he received an award recognizing him as one of the Outstanding Young Men in the Commonwealth of Kentucky (an honor he shared with corecipient United States Senator Mitch McConnell).

When Jim's friend the governor created a new Bureau of Public Properties, he asked Jim to head it up. "I had seven hundred employees, a near billion dollar budget, and I was twenty-nine years old," Jim recalls.

But soon afterward, Jim entered a decade he says can only be described as "desperate and futile."

"Nothing had filled that emptiness in me," he remembers. "I began buying personal things at a frantic pace. I was making repeated trips to Las Vegas and gambling tens of thousands of dollars. With partners I bought four banks. We built shopping centers, eleven hundred homes, a lumber yard, a panel plant. We were racing thoroughbred race horses all over the East coast. All in a desperate attempt to fill that emptiness."

Jim became addicted to alcohol and drugs. He was in the winner's circle for the 1985 Kentucky Derby, and attended a party filled with dignitaries. "I know this because people told me," Jim says, "But I don't remember doing it. I experienced frequent blackouts."

Finally he entered a treatment center, and with the Lord's help, he hasn't taken a drink or another mind-altering drug since. One day, as a last resort, he went to the inaugural meeting of a support group called H.O.P.E. (He Offers Peace Everlasting) sponsored by Southland Christian Church in Lexington.

"I began the process of surrendering my life and my will to Jesus Christ," he continues. "I didn't consider myself worthy to enter the sanctuary of a church. But when we walked into Southland Christian Church, we were greeted with warm smiles, open arms, and loving hearts. They accepted us right where we were, and I'll be eternally grateful."

Jim and his wife had finally found the one thing that could fill the void. Groups of mature Christians shepherded and taught them.

"I'm not going to suggest to you that my life was easy," he points out. "One word to describe it is *tumultuous* when we first accepted Christ. It wasn't easy."

Tumultuous, but also victorious as Jim and his wife continued to grow in the Lord. Ultimately Jim dismantled his business. Today he says, "The money's gone, but I'm rich in the things that matter! I'm a child of the King!"

His preacher, Wayne Smith, befriended and discipled him. Eventually Jim went to Bible college—he was an "A" student in classes I taught—and in time, he became a preacher himself. Today Jim Bird serves as senior minister of Broadway Christian Church in Lexington, Kentucky. His life is a testimony to the saving, transforming power of God.

He says, "The church is no longer just a hospital for sinners; it is a M.A.S.H. unit on the front lines where the bruised and the bleeding can come in and be attended to by the Great Physician. At Broadway, we consider ourselves 'Physician's Assistants.'"[3]

To Whom Shall We Go?

Solomon eventually learned what life is all about. Reflecting on what he learned from his long quest, he advised young people, "Be happy . . . while you are young, and let your heart give you joy in the days of your youth. . . . But know that for all these things God will bring you to judgment. . . . Remember your Creator in the days of your youth, before the days of trouble come. . . . Fear God and keep his commandments, for this is the whole duty of man" (Ecclesiastes 11:9; 12:1, 13). Or to put it another way, life's most worthwhile goal is the quest to love the Lord our God with all our heart, soul, mind, and strength.

On the day after Jesus fed more than five thousand people, many of his disciples grumbled when Jesus said, "I am the bread of life"—the spiritual nutrition a person needs to live forever. This was a hard teaching to understand and accept, so "from this time many of his disciples turned back and no longer followed him" (John 6:48, 66). But Jesus had been spending extra time teaching twelve of his disciples. Turning to them, Jesus asked a poignant question: "You do not want to leave too, do you?"

Simon Peter spoke for the rest of the group. He answered, "Lord, to whom shall we go? You have the words of eternal life. We believe and know that you are the Holy One of God" (John 6:68).

Peter was right. In the final analysis, the question isn't, *Where* shall we go? The question is, To *whom*? Only the resurrected Lord Jesus can fill us with living hope (1 Peter 1:3). Only he can give us life "to the full" (John 10:10) so that others will ask us the reason for the hope overflowing from our hearts (1 Peter 3:15).

What will it be like to experience eternal joy? Think of it this way. Remember how you felt when you were a child, looking forward to Christmas morning? Remember the fun of opening the gifts and celebrating with your family? Do you enjoy looking back on pleasant memories like those? Joyful experiences take one of three forms: looking forward to an important event that will happen in the future, participating in something significant in the present, and looking back with satisfaction on something good that happened in the past. Only an eternal God could combine all three kinds of joy—*future anticipation*, *present participation*, and *past recollection*—into one never-ending experience of heavenly joy.

Maybe Heaven will be a bit like Christmas after all. No, it will be far more. It won't be the least bit boring—just sitting around on a cloud strumming a harp. I think it will be more like this:

A person who likes to build things having all the time and materials he could ever need to construct great masterpieces.

A person who likes to read and learn having time to consume every book she'd ever want to read.

A person who enjoys athletics being able to run and jump without getting tired.

A person who likes to travel having unlimited opportunities to explore the vast array of God's "new heaven and new earth."

A person who enjoys music having unlimited opportunity to compose and perform beautiful songs of praise to God.

A person whose dreams and aspirations have been frustrated here on earth finding deep, unending fulfillment at last.

A person who has been misunderstood or belittled by others here on earth finding himself enveloped at last in God's abiding love.

A person who was blind on earth, now with wide-open eyes beholding the glorious colors and splendors of Heaven.

A person who was paralyzed or lame on earth, now leaping with joy and never growing weary.

A person who was lonely now enjoying sweet, untainted fellowship with dear old saints who served the Lord for years, and little children whose lives were snuffed out prematurely, and faithful servants of God who believed God's promises even when others around them succumbed to sin and doubt.

A person who has asked hard questions, never felt completely content with the answers he received, yet trusted God anyway, finally experiencing a satisfied mind.

And all of us who've been saved by grace, worshiping the all-wise Lord who deserves all praise.

Until then, let's follow the example of the shepherds who first heard "good news of great joy" from angels in the fields near Bethlehem. After the angels were gone, the shepherds left the manger where they viewed the Christ child and "spread the word concerning what had been told them about this child, and all who heard it were amazed" (Luke 2:17, 18).

People are asking honest questions. They're searching for the joy and hope Christ alone can give.

Spread the word.

FOOTNOTES

[1]C. S. Lewis, *The Problem of Pain* (Macmillan, 1962), p. 115.

[2]This poem by Jason Lehman first appeared in "Dear Abby," February 14, 1989, a syndicated column copyrighted by the Universal Press Syndicate.

[3]Jim Bird presented his full testimony at a main session of the North American Christian Convention in St. Louis, Missouri, on June 26, 1998. Audio tapes of his message are available from Christian Audio Tapes (1-888-228-2737). His story is used by permission.

APPENDIX 1

MORE QUESTIONS
FROM PAT

In chapter five, I introduced my readers to a woman named Pat who asked some tough questions about God. Pat and I have continued to correspond about her questions via e-mail, and the interchange has been lively and mind-stretching. Some of her questions challenge the very core of what Christians believe.

As part of my earlier response to her questions about God, I told Pat about what I sometimes call "the Jesus argument for the existence of God." Basically, my point is that Christians do not believe in a vague, faceless deity (what Pat called the "Big Fuzzy White Thing"); we believe in God, who made himself known in person, in real history, through Jesus Christ.

The Ultimate Question

To me, the ultimate question in regard to the existence of God is simply, **"Who is Jesus Christ?"** If Jesus is who he claimed to be, then we not only know that God *exists;* we also know what God is *like.* "Anyone who has seen me has seen the Father," Jesus insisted (John 14:9). Jesus focused attention on this issue at a crucial moment in his ministry when he asked his disciples, "Who do you say I am?" (Matthew 16:15).

Daring to drag Pat with me into some deep waters, I explained to her that I like the "Jesus argument" because to me, it incorporates in capsule form the best of the various arguments history has offered for the existence of God.

For example, the Moral Argument argues that there must be a God, for he is the source of a universal moral law—an inborn "sense of ought"—we find within ourselves.[1] *Christ is morality personified.* Not only did his teachings capture both the letter and the spirit of the moral law; he also lived it, embodied it, and perfectly fulfilled it.

The Cosmological Argument points to the principle of cause and effect and argues that God is the first cause (or uncaused cause), the source of all created things.[2] *Christ is the first cause personified.* "Without him nothing was made that has been made" (John 1:3)."By him all things were created" (Colossians 1:16).

The Teleological Argument points to the many evidences of design and order in the universe and insists that God is the divine architect or designer who made all things to fulfill the purpose of his perfect will.[3] *Christ is purpose and order personified.* He "works out everything in conformity with the purpose of his will" (Ephesians 1:11).

The so-called Intuitional Argument says there's something inside the heart of every human being that instinctively longs for God. *Christ came in person to fill the void.* "In him was life, and that life was the light of men" (John 1:4).

Jesus: Christianity's Central Figure

Pat still wanted to pose some other questions about Jesus. With characteristic frankness, she prefaced her queries with an apology ("Hey, if the tone sounds testy in spots, forgive me, OK?"). Then she laid out the following questions, which I'm including here along with the answers I gave her.

Pat: The "saving" aspect of Jesus never made sense to me. I've always believed he existed and that he was a great teacher and a very good example, but I still can't swallow the saving, for the following reasons:

1. It feels dishonorable to me. I don't think it's right when

someone takes the rap for someone else—and the person he took the rap for usually doesn't learn anything from it.

2. It also feels a little like blackmail, or bribery—like saying, "If you're nice to me, you don't get punished."

3. It seems to remove accountability from individuals for their actions.

According to my sister (who is now a Christian), the only thing that gets you into Heaven is Jesus. I'd like to run the following scenario by you:

A. Scumbag person who has been mean all his life, repents, "gets Jesus" near the end, and gets into Heaven.

B. Person who has been truly good all his life, tried to be nice, generous, etc., doesn't "get Jesus," and doesn't get in.

I have trouble believing that person A finds greater favor in the eyes of God than person B. This also means that there is little incentive to behave oneself during the majority of one's life, since you obtain a "get out of jail free" card at a later date. In the words of Homer Simpson, "I'll repent on my deathbed."

My response:

You raise a number of important issues here. First, I agree with you on some things about Jesus: 1. He did indeed live on earth, as extensive historical evidence demonstrates. 2. He was indeed a great teacher, whose teachings amazed people then and still do now. 3. He did indeed set a very good example.

However, Jesus must have been more than merely a good teacher and a good example, because the main focuses of his teaching concerned *his own identity as the Son of God* and *his saving work on the cross*. He didn't just say, "I've come to teach you a better way to live; follow my example." He said, "I am the way and the truth and the life. No one comes to the Father except through me" (John 14:6). He summarized his life's purpose by saying, "For even the Son of Man [Jesus' favorite title for himself] did not come to be served, but to serve, and to give his life as a ransom for many" (Mark 10:45), and "the Son of Man came to seek and to save what was lost" (Luke 19:10).

He could not have been a good moral teacher if he was wrong about the central facts of his message. As Josh McDowell has pointed out, he's either a *liar* who knowingly misled people, a *lunatic* who meant well but misled people nonetheless, or the *Lord* who was indeed who he claimed to be. To me, the most reasonable alternative is to conclude he's really the Lord.

Now, about the "saving" aspect of Christ's work. It seems to me that you've underestimated the seriousness of our sin problem. Even the "person who has been truly good all his life," who's tried to be "nice" and "generous," still doesn't deserve to go to Heaven. As my friend, theology professor Dr. Jack Cottrell, often points out, "Being 'good enough' isn't good enough." We're all in bigger trouble than you seem to assume, for even the best of us has fouled up big time. Comparing one person's righteous acts to another's is like saying, "Let's all jump into the Pacific Ocean in San Francisco and see who can swim to Hawaii first." Some of us might make it several miles; others only a few hundred yards; I would sink like a rock. But none of us would make it to Hawaii by swimming under our own strength. We need a boat or a plane to take us there. Likewise, we need a perfect Savior to take us to Heaven; we can't get there by our own strength, no matter how "good" we appear to be.

It also seems to me you've missed the whole idea of God's grace, which is at the core of the Christian gospel. If we got what we truly deserve, we'd all end up in Hell, for we've all done wrong and fallen short of God's perfect standards (Romans 3:23). You're right: In a sense, it *isn't* fair for someone else to "take the rap" for others who have done wrong. It's *more* than fair; it's grace. Why should Jesus, who never sinned, be willing to take the rap for us and endure unspeakable suffering on the cross because of our offenses? That's the marvel of God's love and mercy.

This introduces a new and powerful incentive "to behave oneself during the majority of one's life." Instead of doing the right thing in a fearful, futile, guilt-ridden effort to please a demanding Lawgiver, we're free to serve out of love and gratitude because he's forgiven and accepted us.

And by the way, Homer Simpson is treading on dangerous ground. Not everybody gets a chance to repent on his deathbed. It's hazardous to put off accepting Christ, since none of us know exactly when we'll die. And there's no reason to wait. "Now is the time of God's favor, now is the day of salvation" (2 Corinthians 6:2).

Pat: True or false section. God creates me imperfect, lands me in a lifetime guaranteed to test the imperfections of even the strongest person, then can't stand to look at me because I'm imperfect. Then tells me that he won't have anything to do with me unless I love his Son. This same Son he killed so that I don't have to pay the price for my actions—those same actions that I did because I am imperfect (and was created that way!). He also never gave me the choice whether I wanted to do the time myself or have Jesus killed for me instead. If I could have picked, I would have spared Jesus. What happens to us "unsaved" who feel they should pay the price for their own actions themselves?

My response:

Wait a minute. God didn't "create you imperfect." Where did you get that idea? "Everything created by God is good," the Bible says (1 Timothy 4:4). In the first chapter of the Bible, it says "God saw all that he had made, and it was very good" (Genesis 1:31). We've all sinned—but it isn't God's fault we've chosen to do wrong. "When tempted, no one should say, 'God is tempting me.' For God cannot be tempted by evil, nor does he tempt anyone; but each one is tempted when, by his own evil desire, he is dragged away and enticed" (James 1:13, 14).

Yes, the entire world is pretty messed up. But it's a dilemma we've brought upon ourselves through our own foolish choices. Even humanist author Margaret Laws Smith pointed out, "Collectively we are much more like two-year-olds in a petrol store with a box of matches than we are like gods or even responsible adults."[4] There's no way we can fix things without God's help. Occasionally we hear about a coal-mining tragedy in which some miners end up trapped in a collapsed mine. They dug the hole themselves; but once the roof caves in, they can't dig their own way out. They might remove a few stones, but they won't be saved without a rescue effort from outside. Likewise, we've dug ourselves into our own problems, and when life caves in around us, we need a Savior from outside the cave to dig us out. That's exactly what Jesus came to do.

No, God didn't let us decide whether or not he should send Christ to be our Savior. He took the initiative out of love. But he still gives us the freedom to decide whether we will accept Christ personally or not. He doesn't force himself on us. To use a couple of biblical analogies, he "stands at the door and knocks," waiting for us to open the door. He offers us "living water," but he won't force us to drink.

And Pat, if Hell is real (as the Bible says), then none of us would logically choose to "do the time ourselves"! That's the genius of God's grace and love. Christ "bore our sins in his body" when he died on the cross (1 Peter 2:24). He took the pain he didn't deserve (death) so we could receive a gift we don't deserve (eternal life). Salvation can't be reduced to raw mathematical terms, but there's definitely a divine logic to it. Dr. Cottrell puts it this way: "An infinite Being (God) suffering a finite death is equivalent to a finite being (one of us) suffering an infinite death (in Hell)."

Pat: Devils. If God created everything, why did he create Satan? And if he's all-powerful, why doesn't he just nuke Satan and get it over with? For myself this is a rhetorical question, since I don't believe in Satan (mostly just in human stupidity, which usually looks identical), but I'd still like your take on it. My view from the peanut gallery: To blame all bad actions on a devil externalizes our own dark side and removes our personal responsibility for those nasty actions. "The devil made me do it" is no excuse.

My response:

You're right: "The devil made me do it" is no excuse. We're personally responsible for our actions. But the Bible does portray Satan as a real personality. (For example, Jesus conversed with him—see Matthew 4:1-11.) The devil is a formidable enemy of God's people, but his spiritual power is not equivalent to God's (Ephesians 6:10-13; James 4:7; 1 Peter 5:8, 9; 1 John 4:4).

Based on his track record described in the Bible, it's clear that Satan tempts people to sin, twists the truth, and even pretends to be "an angel of light" (Genesis 3:1-6; 2 Corinthians 11:14).

To be honest, assigning all this world's "bad stuff" to mere "human stupidity" strikes me as naive. There's a ton of genuine evil out there. The Holocaust wasn't just stupid; it was evil. So are child abuse, sexual perversion, and cruelty of all kinds. Evil is real; it's deadly. It's the opposite of the healthy life God wants for us; in fact, it's "live" spelled backwards!

Why did God create Satan? For the same reason, I suppose, that all other free will beings, angelic and human, were created: to experience the joy that comes from serving and worshiping God. But Satan misused his will and rebelled against God.

Why doesn't God "just nuke Satan and get it over with"? It's only a matter of time. Jesus came the first time "to destroy the devil's work" and "destroy him who holds the power of death—that is, the devil" (1 John 3:8; Hebrews 2:14). When he comes back the next time, it'll be all over for Satan—and "nuking" is a pretty accurate way to describe what will happen to him (Revelation 20:10).

Pat: Jesus is said to be the only Son of God. But I've also been told that we are all children of God. Since the term "children" incorporates sons, then it follows that he's not the only one. Is this just a semantic argument, or is there really an inconsistency here?

My response:

It's not just semantics, but there's no inconsistency. In one sense, we're all children of God by virtue of creation. Paul told the Athenians, "We are God's offspring" (Acts 17:29). But sin disrupted the relationship God desires to have with us, so we need to be "born again," or to use a different analogy, "adopted" back into God's spiritual family (John 3:1-5; Romans 8:15-17; Galatians 4:1-7). There's a special sense in which we become God's children when we accept Christ as our Savior and are baptized into him. This is something we must decide for ourselves, not something others can decide for us (John 1:12, 13; Galatians 3:26-28).

Jesus is God's "only begotten" Son. Since he is divine, he bears a unique relationship to the Father that none of us possess (John 1:14; 3:16). But since he also came to earth as a real human being, he understands our humanity; and he's even willing to call us "brothers" (Hebrews 2:9-18).

Pat: Any ideas on what Jesus was doing in those missing years of his life?

My response:

By "missing years" I presume you're talking about the years before Jesus' public ministry, which the Bible says he began when he was thirty years old (Luke 3:23). Actually, the Bible does tell us several facts about his early years, and many of the details are recorded in the Gospel of Luke, a book widely respected for its historical accuracy.

We know Jesus was born in Bethlehem and was "consecrated to the Lord" in Jerusalem as a baby in accordance with Old Testament law (Luke 2:1-38; see also Exodus 13:2, 12). After traveling to Egypt for a while to escape from King Herod's violence (Matthew 2:13-23), Joseph and Mary brought Jesus back to their hometown of Nazareth, a village in Galilee. There Jesus grew up, we presume, much like other Jewish boys in his day. Luke simply records, "And the child grew and became strong; he was filled with wisdom, and the grace of God was upon him" (Luke 2:40).

At age twelve he traveled with his parents to Jerusalem for the Passover feast, and later "they found him in the temple courts, sitting among the teachers, listening to them and asking them questions." The Bible adds, "Everyone who heard him was amazed at his understanding and his answers." When Mary questioned him, his response says a lot: "Didn't you know I had to be in my Father's house?" (Luke 2:46-48). He was only twelve, but he was already quite aware of where he belonged, who his real Father was, and what his priorities were.

It might seem strange that the Bible bypasses the next eighteen years and picks up the story of Jesus' life when he was baptized at age thirty. But there's another key verse that summarizes Jesus' "missing years." Luke 2:52 says, "Jesus grew in wisdom and stature, and in favor with God and men." Those years might appear to be "missing" from our perspective, but there was nothing missing from Jesus! He was the perfectly balanced individual, complete in every aspect of his life.

He grew in wisdom. Jesus obeyed his parents while he grew up (Luke 2:51), and Joseph and Mary were godly people of faith and integrity. During his ministry, Jesus frequently quoted Scripture, and applied it to life in a fresh, memorable way that amazed his first-century listeners and still impresses us two thousand years later. How did he spend his "missing" years? Studying, thinking, and observing, it seems to me.

He grew in stature. His physical body developed as ours do—from the soft skin and tiny limbs of vulnerable childhood to the tanned, muscular physique of a full-grown man. Jesus wasn't a wimp. Having grown up in a carpenter's home, it's not surprising he would be physically strong. How did he spend his "missing" years? Working, walking, and building, it seems to me.

He grew in favor (literally, in grace) with God. He prayed a lot during his ministry (see Mark 1:35 and Luke 5:16, for example), so it's reasonable to conclude he developed this habit during his youth. No doubt he also spent a lot of time pondering his mission and the way God's grace related to real people with real problems. How did he spend his "missing" years? Praying, meditating, maintaining a deep relationship with the heavenly Father, it seems to me.

He grew in favor with men. Jesus wasn't a hermit. During his ministry he attended dinner parties, preached to throngs of thousands, and met one-on-one with powerful individuals like Nicodemus. How did he spend his "missing" years? Listening, rubbing shoulders with friends and neighbors, interacting with others in social settings, it seems to me.

Non-canonical books (those not included in the Christian Scriptures) devote chapter after chapter to fanciful stories about Jesus' "childhood miracles" in a futile attempt to "fill in the gaps" of silence in the genuine Scriptures. But to me, the restraint exercised by the biblical authors is a testimony to the Bible's truthfulness and inspiration. Years ago St. Bonaventure had this to say about the relative quietness of Jesus' first thirty years: "His doing nothing wonderful was itself a kind of wonder. . . . As there was power in his actions, so is there power in his silence."

The bottom line? Jesus did far too many things for anyone to write them all down. The Bible itself acknowledges this. "Jesus did many other things as well," John says in his Gospel. But what is written is sufficient to convince us that Jesus is the Christ, the Son of God; and by believing, we can have life in his name (John 20:30, 31; 21:25).

FOOTNOTES

¹See C. S. Lewis, *Mere Christianity* (Macmillan, 1952), pp. 17-39.

²See Norman Geisler, *Christian Apologetics* (Baker, 1976), pp. 237-259.

³See Batsell Barrett Baxter, *I Believe Because* (Baker, 1971), pp. 59-73.

⁴Quoted by Denis Alexander in *Beyond Science* (Lion Publishing, 1972), pp. 42, 43.

SOME BIBLICAL QUESTIONS AND ANSWERS

God: "Where are you?"

Adam: "I heard you in the garden, and I was afraid because I was naked; so I hid." (Genesis 3:9, 10)

Abraham: "Will a son be born to a man a hundred years old? Will Sarah bear a child at the age of ninety?"

God: "Your wife Sarah will bear you a son, and you will call him Isaac." (Genesis 17:17-19)

Moses: "Who am I, that I should go to Pharaoh and bring the Israelites out of Egypt?"

God: "I will be with you." (Exodus 3:11, 12)

Elkanah: "Hannah, why are you weeping? . . . Why are you down-hearted?"

Hannah: "I am a woman who is deeply troubled. . . . I was pouring out my soul to the Lord." (1 Samuel 1:8, 15)

Nathan: "Why did you despise the word of the Lord by doing what is evil in his eyes?"

David: "I have sinned against the Lord." (2 Samuel 12:9, 13)

King Xerxes: "What is your request? Even up to half the kingdom, it will be granted."

Queen Esther: "Grant me my life—this is my petition. And spare my people—this is my request." (Esther 7:2, 3)

God: "Have you considered my servant Job? There is no one on earth like him."

Satan: "Skin for skin! . . . A man will give all he has for his life." (Job 2:3, 4)

God: "Whom shall I send? And who will go for us?"

Isaiah: "Here am I. Send me!" (Isaiah 6:8)

Peter: "Lord, how many times shall I forgive my brother when he sins against me? Up to seven times?"

Jesus: "I tell you, not seven times, but seventy-seven times." (Matthew 18:21, 22)

A lawyer from the Pharisees: "Teacher, which is the greatest commandment in the Law?"

Jesus: "Love the Lord your God with all your heart and with all your soul and with all your mind." (Matthew 22:36, 37)

Nicodemus: "How can a man be born when he is old?"

Jesus: "I tell you the truth, no one can enter the kingdom of God unless he is born of water and the Spirit." (John 3:4, 5)

Apostles: "Lord, are you at this time going to restore the kingdom to Israel?"

Jesus: "It is not for you to know the times or dates the Father has set by his own authority." (Acts 1:6, 7)

People gathered for the Day of Pentecost: "Brothers, what shall we do?"

Peter: "Repent and be baptized, every one of you, in the name of Jesus Christ for the forgiveness of your sins. And you will receive the gift of the Holy Spirit." (Acts 2:37, 38)

Philip: "Do you understand what you are reading?"

Ethiopian: "How can I . . . unless someone explains it to me?" (Acts 8:30, 31)

Jailer in Philippi: "Sirs, what must I do to be saved?"

Paul and Silas: "Believe in the Lord Jesus, and you will be saved—you and your household." (Acts 16:30, 31)

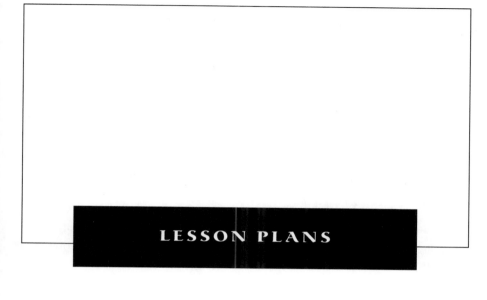

LESSON PLANS

The following eight lesson plans have been designed for group study based on the material in this book. Each lesson plan is divided into two sections:

Plan A *contains suggestions for leading a discussion group for seekers who are not yet Christians but who are willing to dialogue about faith.*

Plan B *contains suggestions for a Sunday school class or believers' small group whose members are interested in learning how to reach postmodern people for Christ.*

Group leaders should feel free to pick and choose from both plans and use whatever ideas or activities you think will work best with the people in your group. The lesson plans contain discussion starters that focus on three basic areas: **Relate** (to help group members build community), **Reflect** (to promote open sharing of ideas about the lesson topic and biblical passages), and **Respond** (to encourage personal application of the material).

Make sure there are Bibles available for every member of the group. Decide other practical details in advance (or let the group decide at their first meeting). How long will the meetings last? (The discussion questions can be adapted for sessions lasting from forty-five to ninety minutes.) Will you serve refreshments? If so, who will provide them? How will you handle child care (if necessary)? How will you handle group dynamics (giving everyone a fair

HOW CAN YOU GET A
SEEKER GROUP STARTED?

Here are some steps my wife and I took when we started a group.

* Pray for God's guidance.

* Determine a time and place to meet. (Our church's campus minister and his wife volunteered to let us meet in the living room of their house on Wednesday evenings.)

* Write down a list of friends you've met at work, school, or social settings who might like to be part of a group like this one. Perhaps your minister or another church leader can suggest people you could invite.

* Contact each person and explain what the group is going to be about. My wife and I obtained addresses of several people who had visited our church during recent weeks. We phoned several of them, sent letters to others, and approached others in person.

Whatever method you use, remember to be completely up-front about your purpose. Tell your friends that you're starting a discussion group that will meet for eight weeks to talk frankly about issues of faith. Give them a copy of *Searching for Hope* and invite them to come discuss the questions in the book with others who are interested in topics like these.

chance to present his or her ideas, preventing one or two people from dominating the group)?

The eight lesson plans include:

1. QUESTIONS PEOPLE ASK . . . based on chapters one and two, "Questions People Ask" and "Communicating Our Faith to 21st-Century People" (see pages 19 through 42).

2. IS THE BIBLE REALLY TRUE? . . . based on chapter three and the story of Ben (see pages 43 through 62).

3. WHERE DOES FAITH FIT IN THE REAL WORLD? . . . based on chapter four and the story of Cathy (see pages 63 through 78).

4. WHO IS GOD, ANYWAY? . . . based on chapter five and the story of Pat (see pages 79 through 96).

5. WHAT ABOUT DOUBTERS LIKE ME? . . . based on chapter seven and the story of Matt (see pages 107 through 122).

6. WHY DID GOD LET THIS HAPPEN TO ME? . . . based on chapter eight and the story of Bev (see pages 123 through 138).

7. WHAT ABOUT MY FAMILY TRADITIONS? . . . based on chapter ten and the story of Yoshi (see pages 153 through 168).

8. WHY SO MANY PHONY CHRISTIANS? . . . based on chapter eleven and the story of Tom and Danielle (see pages 169 through 182).

L E S S O N   1

QUESTIONS PEOPLE ASK

PLAN A (SEEKERS)

Relate

1. Let's get acquainted. Each of you can introduce yourself to the group by mentioning your name plus one of the following:
   a. What you're usually doing most days at 11:00 A.M. (and why, and where).
   b. What you're usually doing most nights at 11:00 P.M. (and why, and where).

2. Let's talk about this group. Why did you accept the invitation to come?
   a. Curiosity . . . I've never been to a group exactly like this one before and it sounded interesting.
   b. Enthusiasm . . . I've been to other discussion groups like this one, and I like the healthy interchange of ideas.
   c. Pressure . . . my friend _____ twisted my arm and refused to take no for an answer!
   d. Growth . . . I'm wanting to grow as a person and find answers to some of my questions about faith.
   e. Other:

3. How should this group operate? The discussion material is designed for groups that plan to meet a total of eight times. Shall we do this weekly, or according to some other schedule? How long should our meetings last?

Reflect

1. Our spiritual journeys.

- What was your exposure to spiritual things *when you were a child*? Were your parents people of faith? What church or religious group influenced you? Did you learn about God and the Bible in Sunday school? What were your impressions, either good or bad?

- How would you describe your attitude about spiritual things *now*?
   a. Mild curiosity . . . I think spiritual issues are important, but I'm not looking to be converted to anything.
   b. Strong interest . . . I think spiritual issues are important, and I'm eager to grow in my personal faith.
   c. Disillusioned . . . I've been burned by my past religious involvement, so I tend to be pretty cautious about making any commitments.
   d. Doubtful . . . I'm not sure there's much spiritual truth to be known.
   e. Other:

2. Read and react briefly to the following verses from the Bible:
   a. Matthew 7:7, 8 . . . Jesus encouraged his disciples to "ask," "seek," and "knock." When you think about your own spiritual growth, what are you seeking right now?

b. Hebrews 11:6 . . . How does God "reward" those who seek him earnestly?

c. Matthew 22:34-40 . . . What do you think was the motivation of the person who asked this question of Jesus? Do you like Jesus' answer? Why, or why not?

3. If you could ask Jesus one key question, what would it be?

4. OPTION: If time allows, read and discuss Luke 15:11-32. What is the main point of this story? Which character do you identify with most in the story? Why?

Respond

1. Make sure each member of the group receives a copy of the small book, *Searching for Hope: Seven Honest Questions*. Before the next meeting, each person should read the chapter about Ben called, "Is the Bible Really True?" and come prepared to discuss Ben's question. Make available copies of *Taking Truth Next Door* for any group members who want to dig deeper into the issues raised in the smaller book.

2. Close with prayer by the group leader.

PLAN B (BELIEVERS)

Relate

1. Let's get acquainted. Each of you can introduce yourself by telling your name plus one of the following:
   a. Your favorite restaurant or favorite home-cooked meal.
   b. Your favorite way to spend a Sunday afternoon.

2. When you were growing up, did you ever ask questions about your faith? What was the main question you asked? Did you ever resolve it? If so, how?

3. What person(s) led you to Christ? What did they do that was especially helpful to you?

Reflect

1. Read each of these passages from the Bible and answer the following questions about each one:

   What question was asked of Jesus? Did the questioner(s) seem sincere, or insincere? What was Jesus' response? Do you think Jesus' answer satisfied the person(s) who questioned him?
   Matthew 22:15-22
   Mark 10:17-22
   John 3:1-10
   John 9:1-3
   John 18:33-38

2. Read Acts 17:2, 3, 17; 18:4, 19, and 19:8. Discuss:
   a. The apostle Paul often "reasoned" with others about the gospel. Have you ever done this?
   b. What is the hardest question anyone ever asked you about God, the Bible, or the church? What did you say in response? Did your answer satisfy your questioner?

3. Jesus' disciples Peter and John said, "We cannot help speaking about what we have seen and heard" (Acts 4:20). How do you feel about defending or sharing your faith?
   a. Excited and eager
   b. Fearful and unprepared
   c. Frustrated and anxious
   d. Other:

4. What changes—positive or negative—have you observed in our culture during the last ten years? Do you think these changes affect the way Christians need to communicate the good news of Christ today? If so, how? If not, why not?

Respond

1. Do you think most Christians today really want to "Take Truth Next Door"? What hinders us from doing so?

2. Read aloud 1 Peter 3:15. Which part of this verse do you need to apply in your life during the coming week?
   a. Set apart Christ as Lord in my heart.
   b. Prepare myself to give answers to others who ask about my faith.
   c. Set a better example in my daily life so others will want to ask me about my faith.
   d. Defend my faith with greater gentleness and respect.

3. Make sure each member of the group has a copy of *Taking Truth Next Door* and at least two or three copies of the smaller book, *Searching for Hope,* to share with friends. Before the next meeting, each person should read chapter three in *Taking Truth Next Door* and come prepared to talk about Ben's question, "Is the Bible Really True?"

   Each member of the group should also begin to prayerfully identify at least one friend with whom to share a copy of the small book, *Searching for Hope.*

4. Close with prayer led by a member of the group.

IS THE BIBLE REALLY TRUE?

PLAN A (SEEKERS)

Relate

1. "My Favorite Book." Tell the group about one of the following (or more, if time allows):
   a. The best book you ever read (and why you enjoyed it).
   b. A book you loved reading when you were a child (and why you enjoyed it).
   c. A book other people enjoy, but you don't (and why you don't).

2. "My View of the Bible." Which of these statements best describes the way you think about the Bible?
   a. "I believe it is the written Word of God, and I trust that whatever it says is the truth."
   b. "I think it's a good book to read, but I'm not convinced it's the Word of God."
   c. "I've not read it enough to say one way or another."
   d. Other:

Reflect

1. What did you think about Ben's story in *Searching for Hope*?
   a. "I'm a lot like him, because . . ."
   b. "I'm quite different from him, because . . ."
   c. "When I read his story, I feel . . ."

2. The authors of the Bible make some bold claims about what they were writing. Read 1 Thessalonians 2:13; 2 Timothy 3:16, 17; and 2 Peter 1:20, 21. What did authors like the apostles Paul and Peter consider to be the significance of their written words? Do you find these claims easy to accept? Why, or why not?

3. The author of *Searching for Hope* suggests the following acrostic as a summary of some of the reasons Christians believe in the reliability of Scripture:

C laims . . . The authors repeatedly say they're communicating God's Word. While this claim alone doesn't prove the Bible is true, it shows that we aren't being true to the authors' intent if we hold that the Bible is nothing more than a human book.

H istorical accuracy . . . Archaeological evidence supports the accuracy of the Old and New Testaments.

R emarkable style . . . Many readers find that the Bible rings true because of its frankness and its spiritual power.

I ndestructibility . . . This two-thousand-year-old volume has survived through the centuries and still speaks to current issues with relevance and wisdom.

S cientific and prophetic accuracy . . . While some may assume that the Bible clashes with scientific facts, its message fits remarkably well with modern scientific discoveries; and fulfilled prophecies point to God's superintendence of the production of the Scriptures.

T otal unity . . . The writers of Scripture were a diverse group, but their books don't contradict one another.

(Note to group leader: refer to chapter three of this book, and especially the sidebar on page 54, so you can lead the group in discussing each point of the acrostic.)
- What do you think about each of these points?
- The above acrostic reminds us that Christ himself is the central character of the Bible. What was his view of Scripture? (See Luke 24:44–47 and John 17:17.) Why is this important?

4. Ben complains, "If you get ten different people to read the Bible, you might come out with ten different interpretations." But Christians believe God gave us the Bible so we can know and understand his will. What could help you understand more clearly and believe more strongly in the Bible's message?
   a. "A translation of the Bible that speaks my language."
   b. "A knowledgeable teacher who can explain what certain confusing passages mean."
   c. "Greater unity among Christians who read the same Book but come to different conclusions."
   d. Other:

Respond

Willing to try some homework? Before the next group meeting, select and read one of the following books of the Bible and come prepared to tell the group your reaction to it:

- The book of James. A short, practical book about Christian living. Estimated reading time: twenty to thirty minutes.
- The Gospel of Luke. A physician's description of the historical life of Jesus Christ. Estimated reading time: two hours.
- The Gospel of John. An eyewitness account of Jesus' life and teaching written by one of the twelve apostles. Estimated reading time: two hours.
- The book of Acts. An introduction to the history of the early Christian church. Estimated reading time: two hours.

Before your group's next meeting, read the chapter about Cathy in *Searching for Hope*. The chapter is entitled, "Does Faith Fit in the Real World?"

Close in prayer led by the group leader.

PLAN B (BELIEVERS)

Relate

1. Each member of the group should complete one of these statements (or more, if time allows):
   a. "My favorite book of the Bible is _____ because _____."
   b. "Without the Bible, my life would be different because _____ _____."
   c. "I believe the Bible is God's Word because _____ _____."

2. OPTION: *Bookmarks.* Give each group member a 3" x 5" card and a pencil. Each person has three minutes to write on the card a favorite Bible reference (for example, "John 3:16") and a sentence or two

explaining why this verse has been helpful to you. Insert the card into your Bible at the appropriate page and hand it to the person on your right. Take turns reading each person's favorite verse and words of explanation.

Reflect

1. What do you think of Ben's question? Have you ever met anyone like him?

2. What do you think is the main reason Ben doesn't believe the Bible?

3. Christians have many solid reasons to believe the Bible accurately conveys the truth of God in written form. Which one of the following evidences seems most impressive to you? Why? Which one seems least likely to convince a skeptic? Why?

The Bible's claims about itself (2 Timothy 3:16; 2 Peter 1:20, 21).
The Bible's historical reliability (see pages 48-50 of this book for examples).
The Bible's fulfilled prophecies (see pages 50-55 of this book for examples).
The Bible's scientific accuracy (see pages 55, 56 of this book for examples).
The Bible's influence on individual lives (Hebrews 4:12).

4. Read these Scripture passages: Matthew 4:4, 7, 10; 26:52-54; Luke 24:44-47; John 10:35; 17:17. Based on these verses, how would you summarize Jesus' view of Scripture? Why is this important?

5. On pages 57-59, the author lists seven basic principles of biblical interpretation. Which of these steps is most difficult for you to put into practice? Why? Can you suggest any other steps that you've found helpful?
   (1) Focus on what you CAN understand, not what you CAN'T.
   (2) Ask God to help you.
   (3) Study the Bible with an open mind.
   (4) Let the Bible speak for itself.
   (5) Use common sense.
   (6) Focus on the book's main theme.
   (7) Apply it to your life.

Respond

Tell the group about the person or persons you're planning to give a copy of *Searching for Hope*. If you've already given a copy to a friend, tell the group how it went. What reaction did you receive? What questions did you encounter?

Homework: Before the next time the group meets, each member should read chapter four and prepare to discuss Cathy's question, "Does Faith Fit in the Real World?"

Close by asking two volunteers to lead in prayer focused on two main topics:
- Pray a prayer of praise and thank God for revealing himself through the written Word. See Psalm 119:9-16 for ideas.
- Pray specifically for all the people who will be receiving copies of *Searching for Hope* from members of your group. Ask God to open doors for the gospel.

DOES FAITH FIT IN THE REAL WORLD?

PLAN A (SEEKERS)

Relate

1. Which of the following best describes your daily life?
   a. Zoo
   b. Peaceful lake
   c. Jungle
   d. Circus
   e. Chess match
   f. Boxing match
   g. Marathon race
   h. Demolition derby

2. *Pieces of the pie.* Give each person a blank piece of paper and a pencil. Each member of the group should draw a circular "pie chart" and divide it into the following categories to portray the amount of time the following activities require in your daily life:

   Work (or school)
   Sleeping
   Household tasks (cleaning, cooking, paying bills, etc.)
   Recreation (sports, TV, reading, etc.)
   Other (anything that's left after the other four items)

Show the rest of the group your pie chart and explain it. Then discuss:

- What do you *like* most about your regular routine? What do you *dislike* most about it? What would you change if you could? Why?
- Where does *faith* fit into your routine? Where do spiritual things fit in the "pie"?
   a. "Nowhere. I don't even think about my faith when I'm dealing with the 'real world.'"

b. "My faith occupies a small piece of the pie. I think about it when I pray or go to church."

c. "Everywhere. My faith is the filling of the pie. It affects everything I do."

d. Other:

3. OPTION: Did one or more members of the group accept the challenge offered at the end of the previous group meeting to read a New Testament book? If so, ask them to tell briefly about what they read, any new insights they gained, and any questions they wondered about.

Reflect

1. What do you think about Cathy's story? Do you empathize with her concerns? Why, or why not? Have you ever struggled to discover how your faith meshes with the rest of your life?

2. Cathy expressed her view of Christians as follows: "The way I looked at it, those people who went to church lived squeaky-clean lives, and I didn't. I lived a fast life, and they didn't. They didn't have fun, and they didn't know what was out in the world. They lived in closed, protected environments. . . . They were cloistered people, with no sense of reality."

Do you agree or disagree with Cathy's sentiments? Explain.

3. Do you ever think of faith in God as a crutch for weak people? Why, or why not? What other "crutches" do people lean on when they're weak? Do you have any "crutches" in your life?

4. Read a portion of Jesus' prayer for his followers recorded in John 17:13-23. How did Jesus intend for his disciples to relate to the "real world"?

5. Read the description of the early church recorded in Acts 4:32-35. How did these Christians integrate their faith with the "real world"? How did their actions fulfill the portion of Jesus' prayer recorded in John 17:13-23?

Respond

1. James 4:8 says, "Come near to God and he will come near to you." What is one way you could draw closer to God in your daily life?
   a. "I could think about him more while I'm at work."
   b. "I could pray more, and learn more about how to pray."
   c. "I could attend a worship service regularly at a local church."
   d. "I'm not ready to do any of these things, because . . ."
   e. Other:

2. Before your group's next meeting, read the chapter about Pat in *Searching for Hope*. The chapter is entitled, "Who Is God, Anyway?"

PLAN B (BELIEVERS)

Relate

1. *Word Association*. Give each person a blank piece of paper and a pencil. As the group leader reads each of the following words or phrases, members of the group should write down the first word each term brings to mind. After all the answers are recorded, the leader should read the list again and let everyone share his or her answers with the group.
   a. The place where you work
   b. Football game
   c. Hot fudge sundae
   d. Your desk at home
   e. School
   f. Your favorite thing to watch on TV
   g. Your car
   h. Bible study

2. *Definition*. Nowadays it's common to hear people talk about how tough it is to live in the "real world." In your opinion, what does this phrase mean? Does the "real world" include God, the Bible, and personal faith? If so, why do so many people find it hard to see how spiritual things fit in their daily lives?

3. OPTION: *Agree/Disagree*: "Faith in God is a crutch for the weak."

4. OPTION: *Bumper Stickers*. Have you ever seen those bumper stickers that say, "I'd rather be sailing" (fishing, bowling, etc.)? Give each member of the group or class a blank piece of paper. Pass around a box of crayons or different-colored marking pens. Each person has two minutes to design a "bumper sticker" by writing the following message and filling in the blank:

"I'd rather be _____."

After two minutes, have each person show and explain the completed bumper sticker to the rest of the group. Or better yet, shuffle the papers and let the group try to guess who wrote each one.

Reflect

1. What is your impression of Cathy?
   a. "I sympathize with her concerns. I've felt that way myself."
   b. "I feel frustrated with her because . . ."
   c. "I think it would have helped her if she could have . . ."
   d. Other:

2. Do you think some Christians are in fact out of touch with the "real world"? Why do you think this perception is so common among non-Christians?

3. Read Jeremiah 2:13.

- Do people today still dig "broken cisterns" in a vain attempt to satisfy their spiritual thirst? Name some "broken cisterns" you've been tempted to dig in your own life.

- How has God been "the spring of living water" for you?

4. Chapter four of this book identifies three assumptions many people make about living by faith (see pages 72-75):

   (1) "If you live by Christian values, you won't make it in the real world."

(2) "Christians believe in God mainly because he gives them comfort."

(3) "The Christian life is boring."

Read the apostle Paul's description of his ministry recorded in 2 Corinthians 1:3-11; 11:23-29, and Philippians 3:7-14.

In light of these passages, what might Paul say about the three "assumptions" above?

5. Read Jesus' challenge to his disciples recorded in Mark 8:34-38. In light of this passage, how should Christians respond to the accusation that people who live by faith are emotional weaklings?

Respond

1. By now each member of the group should be able to identify at least one specific person he or she is hoping to lead closer to Christ. Ask volunteers to tell the group about their progress as they continue to build relationships with their unchurched friends.

2. Homework: Before the next group meeting, each member should read chapter five and prepare to discuss Pat's question, "Who Is God, Anyway?" Also, each person should read Appendix One, "More Questions From Pat," found on pages 203-210.

3. As you close with prayer, thank God for the reality of his existence, the relevance of his Word, and the comfort of his presence in our times of need.

WHO IS GOD, ANYWAY?

PLAN A (SEEKERS)

Relate

Great Journeys. What is the best vacation you ever experienced? Where did you go? What did you do? What is your favorite part of a vacation— anticipating it for weeks in advance, the day it begins, the vacation itself, or the way you feel when it's over?

Spiritual Journeys. Right now, where would you place your relationship with God on a scale of zero to ten? Where was it five years ago?

0   1   2   3   4   5   6   7   8   9   10

Not sure God   Strong faith
even exists   in God

Reflect

1. In the chapter we're discussing this week, we meet a woman named Pat who makes some interesting statements about her faith. What's your initial reaction to her comments listed below?
   a. "I've been turned off to the words God and Jesus because of the bad things people have done while invoking those names."
   b. "What is the point of Jesus? Example? Teacher? Savior? Lunatic? None of the above?"
   c. "Some people see no value in a journey unless they reach a destination. I'm the opposite. I think the journey is often more interesting than the destination."

2. Do you believe in God? If so, why? If not, why not?

3. Even a person who is struggling to know God usually has some ideas about the kind of deity he or she *doesn't* believe in. What kind of god are you pretty sure you *don't* believe in? Why?

4. According to the Bible, God possesses a number of personal attributes:

Alive, and the giver of life (Matthew 16:16; John 1:4)
Spirituality and personality (John 4:24; Exodus 3:14)
All-knowing and all-powerful (Hebrews 4:13; Psalm 115:3)
Eternal and ever-present (Genesis 1:1; Jeremiah 23:23, 24)
Holy (Psalm 99:5; 1 Peter 1:15, 16)
Truthful and faithful (Titus 1:2; Hebrews 10:23)
Righteous and just (Psalm 52:1; Romans 2:6-11; 1 John 1:5)
Jealous and angry (Exodus 20:5; Romans 1:18; 2:5)
Loving and gracious (Romans 5:5; Ephesians 2:8-10)
Unchanging (James 1:17)

Are some of these characteristics relatively easy for you to understand and accept? Which ones seem most difficult to understand and accept? Why?

5. Let's take an honest look at the consequences of *disbelieving* in God. If the God of the Bible didn't exist, then what would that say about . . . ?
   • The significance of your own existence?
   • The logic and consistency of your own worldview?
   • Your hope for life after death?
   • How you might explain the origin of the universe and the complexity of life?

6. Christians believe that God personally visited our planet nearly two thousand years ago when Jesus Christ came to earth. What do you know about Jesus? What do the following selections from the Bible tell you about Jesus?

John 1:14, 18
John 20:30, 31
Colossians 2:9

Respond

1. The well-known English author C. S. Lewis wrote about Jesus, "Either this man was, and is, the Son of God, or else a madman or something worse. You can shut him up for a fool, you can spit at him and kill him as a demon; or you can fall at his feet and call him Lord and God. But let us not come with any patronising nonsense about his being a great human teacher. He has not left that open to us" (*Mere Christianity*, Macmillan, 1952, p. 56).

What is your reaction to Lewis's statement?

2. Are you interested in talking further with a Christian about how to develop your personal relationship with God through Jesus Christ?

3. Before the next meeting, read the chapter in *Searching for Hope* that deals with Matt's question, "What About Doubters Like Me?"

4. Close with prayer by the group leader.

PLAN B (BELIEVERS)

Relate

Giving Directions. Which of the following statements best describes you?
   a. "I'm usually too stubborn to ask for directions. I'd rather find my own way."
   b. "I'm terrible at finding my own way. If I had been Lewis & Clark's guide, they'd still be wandering somewhere in the Rocky Mountains!"
   c. "I'm willing to ask for directions, but they'd better be accurate!"
   d. "I avoid traveling to new places, so I never need directions."
   e. "I'd much rather ask directions than fumble around by myself."

Pointing Others to God. If someone were to ask you, "Why do you believe in God?" and you only had one minute to answer, what would you say?

Reflect

1. What are your impressions of Pat, the woman described in chapter five? Have you ever met anyone like her? What do you like about her? Do you think you'd enjoy talking about your faith with someone like her? Why, or why not?

2. The author of this book points out three basic reasons it makes sense to believe the God revealed in Scripture really exists:

   The universe requires a Creator (Genesis 1:1; Romans 1:18-20; Hebrews 11:3)
   Life requires a Designer (Psalm 139:13, 14)
   The Bible requires a Revealer (Deuteronomy 29:29; Ephesians 3:2-5)

   Which of these reasons do you think is most likely to help convince a skeptic about the reality of God? What reasons would you add to this list?

3. The author of this book says, "When you're talking about the existence of God, the ultimate question is simply 'Who is Jesus Christ?'" Do you agree with this statement? Why, or why not? How did Jesus demonstrate the reality of God's existence?

4. Jesus said, "Anyone who has seen me has seen the Father" (John 14:9). Make a list of some facts we know about God that we wouldn't understand if Jesus had never come to earth.

5. When Pat describes "the exclusivity of Christianity," she's right. Jesus identified it this way: "Enter through the narrow gate. For wide is the gate and broad is the road that leads to destruction, and many enter through it. But small is the gate and narrow the road that leads to life, and only a few find it" (Matthew 7:13, 14).

According to the Scripture passages below . . .

How WIDE is the road?	How NARROW is the road?
John 3:16	John 14:6
1 Timothy 2:4	1 Timothy 2:5
2 Peter 3:9	Acts 2:38; 4:12
1 John 2:2	1 John 2:23

Note: for more help with this issue, see chapter twelve, "Truth, Freedom, and Tolerance," pages 183-192.

6. What do you think is the best way to try to lead someone like Pat to Christ? Why?

Respond

1. Focus your closing prayer time on these thoughts found in Psalm 139:

Praise God for his intimate concern about every detail of our lives (vv. 1-6).

Praise God for his consistent presence with us no matter where we go (vv. 7-10).

Praise God for giving us life and creating us to fulfill an important purpose (vv. 13-16).

Praise God for revealing his "precious thoughts" to us through the Bible (vv. 17, 18).

Ask God to search our hearts and lead us in his ways, especially as we reach out to others who don't know him (vv. 23, 24).

2. Before the group meets next, read chapters six ("Strange Ideas") and seven and prepare to talk about Matt's question, "What About Doubters Like Me?"

WHAT ABOUT DOUBTERS LIKE ME?

PLAN A (SEEKERS)

Relate

Seeing Is Believing. Have you ever met a well-known person, or been to some unusual or interesting place? Give everyone a note card and a pencil. Each person should write down the name of a famous person you've met or an interesting place you've been. After two minutes, the leader should gather and shuffle the cards, then read them one at a time and let the group guess who wrote each one. Briefly tell the group about your experience.

OPTION: *"I Doubt It."* Before the group meets, the leader should collect ten to fifteen recent newspaper headlines and write them down on note cards along with five to ten fictitious headlines the leader has made up. Read each one aloud, and let the group guess whether each story is true or false.

Reflect

1. What do you think about Matt's search for truth? What seems to have been his main problem?

2. Does it surprise you that he still struggled with doubt even after he became a Christian? Why, or why not?

3. Read James 1:2-8.

What does this Scripture say about the attitude a person should have when his faith is tested?

What word pictures found in this Scripture illustrate what it's like to struggle with doubt?

According to this Scripture, where does true wisdom come from (see also James 3:13-17)?

4. According to the author of this book, doubt comes in different forms, including
   - Lack of information (the doubter simply doesn't know the facts that could help him believe)
   - Perplexity (the doubter is plagued by uncertainty and indecision)
   - Weariness (the doubter is physically or emotionally exhausted)
   - Inadequacy (the doubter faces challenges that seem bigger than he can handle)
   - Disillusionment (the doubter has been let down by Christians in the past, and doesn't want to risk being disappointed again)
   - Unbelief (the doubter simply refuses to believe, no matter how much evidence others present to the contrary)
   - Unsubmissiveness (the doubter mentally agrees with a spiritual principle but refuses to change his lifestyle to comply with it)
   - Complacency (the doubter is so comfortable with the status quo that he'd rather not put forth any effort to resolve his doubts)

Have you ever experienced any of these doubts? If so, have you resolved them to your satisfaction?

5. How do you usually deal with your questions about faith?
   a. "I talk about them openly and seek to resolve them through conversation."
   b. "I keep them to myself, for my faith is a private matter to me."
   c. "I read books, magazines, or articles on the Internet and seek to resolve my questions through my own study and research."
   d. "I ask a trusted friend for advice."
   e. Other:

6. Read Jude 22. Does it surprise you that this verse is in the Bible?

7. The story of one of the most famous doubters of all time is recorded in John 20:19-29. Read this Scripture and discuss:

What and why did Thomas doubt?

Was he really all that different from the other disciples (compare Matthew 28:16, 17, and Luke 24:9-11)?

What evidence did Jesus give Thomas to help him overcome his doubts?

What was Thomas's response?

How do you feel about Jesus' words in John 20:29?

*What would it take for **you** to "stop doubting and believe," as Jesus told Thomas?*

Respond

Referring to Jesus' words on the cross ("My God, my God, why have you forsaken me?"—Mark 15:34), Matt says, "Think about it. Jesus even took our confusion to the cross with him." What do you think Matt means by this?

Before the group meets again, read the chapter about Bev in *Searching for Hope.* It's entitled, "Why Did God Let This Happen to Me?"

Close in prayer. (At this point in the group's life, perhaps someone in the group other than the group leader will be willing to voice a prayer.)

PLAN B (BELIEVERS)

Relate

1. *Strange Foods.* What is the strangest food you ever ate? Why did you eat it? Did someone have to persuade you to try it?

2. *Strange Ideas.* The Bible indicates that some spiritual truths can be "hard to swallow" at first (see John 16:12, 13; 1 Corinthians 3:1, 2; Hebrews 5:11-14). Can you think of a biblical truth that was hard for you to accept at first?

3. OPTION: *Jews and Gentiles.* Chapter six explains some of the cultural issues first-century Christians faced when they presented the

gospel to different groups, including the differences between a Jewish audience and a Gentile audience (see 1 Corinthians 1:22-24).

Before you became a Christian, was your mind-set more "Jewish" (familiar with God and the Bible, aware of God's principles of right and wrong) or more "Gentile" (unfamiliar with God and the Bible, unaware of God's ethical standards)? Explain your answer.

Reflect

1. What do you think about Matt's struggle with doubt?
   a. "I'm troubled that someone who claims to be a believer would seem so unsure about his faith."
   b. "I'm not surprised. Doubts like his are a Christian's normal part of developing a faith to call his own."
   c. "I think he was asking for something impossible: absolute assurance. Faith always needs to leave room for things we can't fully understand."
   d. Other:

2. Who is your favorite Old Testament character who asked hard questions of God? New Testament character? Explain your answer. (See pages 112-114 for ideas.)

3. Is it a sin to doubt? Explain your answer.

4. Read Matthew 14:22-33 and discuss:

Why did Peter say, "Lord, if it's you, tell me to come to you on the water?" (Wouldn't you want to know for sure who was calling you before you stepped out of the boat?)

Why did Peter begin to sink?

Why did Jesus say that Peter had only a "little faith"? Didn't Peter have more faith than the other men who remained in the boat?

What was the outcome of this incident? (See v. 33.) What does this miracle tell us about Jesus? About the nature of faith?

5. How can you help someone survive a severe bout with "faith stress"? What kind of attitude should you have when you get involved with this kind of problem? (See Galatians 6:1, 2; James 5:19, 20; and Jude 22, 23.)

6. What do you think was the main thing that helped Matt in his struggle with doubt? What can we learn from this?

Respond

What doubts have been holding you back in your service to the Lord? In the spirit of James 5:16 ("Therefore confess your sins to each other and pray for each other so that you may be healed"), share with the group some area of sin or stress that has been hindering your commitment to Christ.

Then select two volunteers to lead the group in a closing prayer. One person should focus on a prayer of confession, and the other on thanksgiving for God's gracious forgiveness (see 1 John 1:7-10 for ideas).

Before the next group meeting, read chapter eight and prepare to discuss Bev's question, "Why Did God Let This Happen to Me?"

WHY DID GOD LET THIS HAPPEN TO ME?

PLAN A (SEEKERS)

Relate

1. *Big Hurts, Little Hurts.* Tell the group about one of the following:
   a. The first time you ever broke a bone
   b. The first time you visited a hospital emergency room
   c. The worst pain you ever experienced
   d. Your most interesting scar

2. Which kind of pain seems worst to you? Explain.
   a. Physical suffering
   b. Emotional suffering
   c. Spiritual suffering
   d. They're all about equal; one is just as bad as the other

3. When you've experienced suffering in your life, what was the main question you asked?
   a. Why did God let this happen to me?
   b. How did I get myself into this mess?
   c. How (or what) can I get out of this experience?
   d. Other:

Reflect

1. What would you say to help someone like Bev?

2. Bev's question raises an issue that many of us find uncomfortable, but it's unavoidable; for eventually everyone experiences some kind of suffering or disappointment. The Bible is quite honest about life's unfairness and pain. Read and briefly discuss these verses:

Job 5:7
Ecclesiastes 9:11, 12
Habakkuk 1:2, 3

3. The author of this book says that "anger itself can be an expression of faith. You can't be angry with someone who doesn't exist! To feel angry with God is to admit, at least, that he is there." Do you agree with this statement? Disagree? Explain.

4. Ordinary people and philosophers alike have pondered the problem of evil. Many people say the key issue is reconciling these three statements: (1) *God is good,* (2) *God is all-powerful,* yet (3) *evil exists.* (All three of these statements, by the way, are supported by the Bible.) If God is good, wouldn't he destroy evil? And if he's all-powerful, *couldn't* he destroy evil? Yet evil exists and bad things happen on a daily basis. How do you suggest we resolve this dilemma?

5. Christians believe that Jesus, God's Son, holds the key to resolving the problem of evil. On the cross, he took our sins upon himself and suffered the penalty we deserve (1 Peter 2:24). *This demonstrates God's goodness.* When he rose from the dead on the third day, he gave us hope and proved that death doesn't have the last word (1 Corinthians 15:3-8, 55-58). *This demonstrates God's power.* And by his willingness to come to earth in person and suffer, he shows that God is not an absentee deity who's unconcerned and aloof while we suffer (Romans 5:1-11). *This demonstrates how seriously God takes the problem of evil.*
   • Read Jesus' words found in John 16:33. Was Jesus a realist about suffering? What do you think he meant when he said, "I have overcome the world"?
   • Read the description of Jesus recorded in Hebrews 2:14-18 and Hebrews 4:14-16. According to these passages, how does Jesus relate to us when we are suffering? What fear can he help us overcome?

6. In light of these Scriptures, how do you think God views the hurts you have experienced?

Respond

1. Bev didn't find all the answers about her dad's death and the other tragic events that happened in her life, but after becoming a Christian, she was able to find peace and release some of the anger she had been feeling toward God. Why do you think her faith helped her?

2. Read Philippians 4:4-7, 11-13. These verses were written by the apostle Paul, who experienced a great deal of suffering. How do you react to these Scriptures?

   a. They sound unrealistic. I don't see how I could ever live that way.
   b. They sound appealing. I'd like to be able to live that way, but I'm not sure how to do it.
   c. Other:

3. Before coming to the next group meeting, read the chapter about Yoshi and think about his question, "What About My Family Traditions?"

PLAN B (BELIEVERS)

Relate

1. *Painful Experiences.* If you had to endure something unpleasant, which of the following would you choose? Which one would you definitely *not* choose? Explain your answers.
   a. Spending two hours in a long, boring business meeting.
   b. Spending two hours in your car while stuck in a traffic jam.
   c. Spending two hours in the dentist's chair for a root canal procedure.
   d. Spending two hours waiting while your spouse shops at the mall.
   e. Spending two hours listening to a long-winded political speech.

2. OPTION: *Advice Giving.* Tell the group about one of the following:
   a. The best advice anyone ever gave you.

b. The worst advice anyone ever gave you.

c. The best advice you ever gave someone else.

d. The worst advice you ever gave someone else.

Reflect

1. Have you ever asked a question like Bev's? What circumstances caused you to question God's goodness?

2. Chapter eight mentions four counterproductive approaches (avoiding, minimizing, blaming, and pitying) that Christians sometimes employ with people like Bev. Do you agree that these approaches aren't helpful? Why, or why not? Did anyone ever use one of these counterproductive approaches with you?

3. What advice do you think would be more helpful to Bev?

4. Read 1 Peter 4:12-19. List at least four facts this Scripture teaches about suffering and how we should respond to it.

5. Chapter eight mentions the following steps that helped Bev overcome her anger toward God:

   Help your friend discover the fatherly love of God (Psalm 68:5; 103:13-18).
   Introduce your friend to the healthy fellowship of God's people (1 Corinthians 12:26; Galatians 6:2).
   Encourage your friend to focus on Christ (1 Peter 2:21-25).

Practically speaking, how can you do these things with a friend who is asking a hard question like Bev's?

6. Deuteronomy 29:29 says, "The secret things belong to the Lord our God, but the things revealed belong to us and to our children forever, that we may follow all the words of this law." And in Isaiah 55:8, the Lord says, "My thoughts are not your thoughts, neither are your ways my ways." Is it a cop-out to point to verses like these and say, "Sometimes we just don't know why bad things happen, but we can still trust God anyway"? Why, or why not?

7. In your opinion, what is the main lesson Bev's story illustrates?
   a. Life is short and uncertain, so we'd better be prepared to die at any time (James 4:14).
   b. Christian love is more important than elaborate answers, so we mainly need to make sure our church and group are safe places for hurting people to come (Romans 15:5, 6).
   c. Life is tough all over, so we'd better be prepared to suffer in a way that pleases the Lord (1 Peter 2:19).
   d. Jesus Christ is the only reasonable answer to the harsh realities of life and the only one who can give us hope (1 Peter 1:3).
   e. Other:

Respond

1. Romans 8:28 says, "And we know that in all things God works for the good of those who love him, who have been called according to his purpose." How have you discovered the truth of this verse in the midst of your own hardships?

2. Before the group meets the next time, read chapter nine, "What Is Faith, Anyway?" and chapter ten, "What About My Family Traditions?"

3. Close with prayer based on 1 Peter 5:7: "Cast all your anxiety on him because he cares for you." What anxiety-causing pressures and problems do you need to cast on the Lord today?

WHAT ABOUT MY FAMILY TRADITIONS?

PLAN A (SEEKERS)

Relate

1. My favorite holiday is _____ because _____.

2. How did you celebrate your birthday when you were growing up? What special memories stand out?

3. When you were growing up, did your family observe any unusual holiday customs?

Reflect

1. On a scale of one to ten, rate the importance of religious traditions . . .
   a. To your parents during your childhood
   b. To you during your childhood
   c. To your parents today
   d. To you today
   e. In today's culture as a whole

   0   1   2   3   4   5   6   7   8   9   10

   No   Utmost
   Importance   Importance

2. Specifically, what religious traditions (if any) do you observe? What makes them valuable to you? (If you don't observe any religious traditions, please explain why.)

3. Read and discuss Mark 7:1-23.
   a. *Verses 1-5.* Why did the Pharisees and teachers of the law criticize

Jesus' disciples? Why do you think ceremonial hand washing was so important to them?

b. *Verses 6-13.* What is Jesus' main point here? Do you think people violate this principle today? If so, cite some specific examples.

c. How can you tell the difference between a command of God and a human tradition?

d. *Verses 14-23.* What is Jesus' main point in these verses? Based on your past experiences, do you think most people really understand the distinction between outward religious acts and inward spiritual commitment? Explain.

4. In response to Yoshi's questions, the author of *Searching for Hope* makes the following points. What is your reaction to each of these ideas?

- Christianity isn't about a place; it's about a Person (Jesus Christ).
- Christianity isn't about luck; it's about faith.
- Christianity isn't just about what your ancestors believed; it's about what you believe.
- Christianity isn't about loyalty to one's ethnic group; it's about God's love for all people.
- Christianity isn't about money; it's about a relationship with God.
- Christianity isn't about leaving people out; it's about bringing them in.
- Christianity isn't about condemning people to Hell; it's about saving them from it.

Respond

1. There's an old story about a grocer who was known for his devotion to honesty. To make sure he treated his customers fairly and never overcharged them, he carefully weighed meat and other items on a large scale that stood on the countertop. The grocer's son always admired the way his dad handled the business, but after the older man died, the son was dismayed when he discovered the scale had been calibrated incorrectly and its measurements were wrong. When fifteen ounces of meat were placed on the scale, it read "One Pound." In other words, without realizing it, the well-meaning old grocer had been unintentionally overcharging his customers for years!

- Should the grocer's son fix the old, defective scale? Buy a new one? Continue to use the old one?
- If he decides to replace the old scale, would doing this dishonor his father who had used it for so many years?
- What do you think the grocer would want the son to do, based on the father's track record of honesty and the son's newfound knowledge about the scale's inaccuracy?
- How does this story relate to the religious traditions a family or ethnic group may hold dear?

2. Read John 1:10-13; 3:16-18; and Acts 2:36-41. How do these verses challenge you in your personal relationship with God right now?

PLAN B (BELIEVERS)

Relate

1. One tradition or custom our church frequently observes that I really *like* is _____.

2. One tradition or custom our church frequently observes that I really *dislike* is _____.

3. Considering nearly two thousand years of church history as a whole, I think . . .
   a. Most of the time, traditions have been a good thing and have served a worthwhile purpose.
   b. Most of the time, traditions have been a bad thing and have hindered the true exercise of Christian faith in its purest form.
   c. There's usually been a mixture of healthy traditions and unhealthy ones.

4. OPTION: *Agree/Disagree.* "Most religious traditions do more harm than good."

Reflect

1. Summarize your reaction to Yoshi's story and his questions. Are you personally acquainted with anyone like Yoshi?

2. Do you think this story might have a broader application? In other words, are there other religious customs that sometimes get in the way of one's devotion to God, even though a person may not care about Japanese traditions as Yoshi does?

3. Yoshi's daughter, Emiko, who is a Christian, observes, "I think Japanese Buddhists are like some Americans who go to church twice a year for Easter and Christmas. Whether they actually believe in Jesus' resurrection or not, it's a common practice."

In your opinion, is this a fair comparison? Why, or why not?

4. As time allows, read and discuss the following Scriptures. (Depending on the size of your group, you may want to ask several different individuals to look up these verses, or do it in pairs.) Make a list of some things these verses tell us God considers *important* and *unimportant* to our Christian faith.

   Romans 14:1-18
   Philippians 3:1-11
   Colossians 2:6-8
   Colossians 2:20-23
   2 Thessalonians 2:13-17
   1 Timothy 1:3-7
   1 Timothy 4:1-10
   2 Timothy 2:8-16
   2 Timothy 2:22-24
   1 Peter 1:18, 19

5. Do you think there's much hope that Yoshi will ever become a Christian? Why, or why not?

6. Chapter ten suggests the following steps for reaching out to someone like Yoshi. What do you think of these suggestions? Are there steps you would add to this list?
   • Be patient. (Someone like Yoshi may not be won to Christ quickly.)

- Be curious. (Ask questions, listen, and learn about your friend's beliefs and culture.)
- Be clear. (Kindly, but without compromise, make it clear what Christians really believe. See pages 162-166 for suggestions.)
- Be persistent. (Don't give up too soon. God's Word can penetrate even the most resistant heart.)

Respond

1. What happened when you gave the book, *Searching for Hope*, to your friends and neighbors? What problems and questions have you encountered? What victories (large or small) can you report?

2. How have your attempts at dialoguing with unchurched friends affected you personally?

3. Focus your closing prayer time on the freedom we enjoy in Christ (as described in Galatians 5:1).

4. Before your group meets again, read chapter eleven and prepare to discuss Tom and Danielle's question, "Why So Many Phony Christians?"

WHY SO MANY PHONY CHRISTIANS?

PLAN A (SEEKERS)

Relate

1. *Playacting.* Tell the group about one of the following:
   a. The outfit you wore in the last costume party you attended.
   b. A character you portrayed in a school play.
   c. A famous person or cartoon character you can imitate.

2. *Famous Phonies in the News.* Name some examples of hypocrisy you see in current events. In your opinion, what makes these people or situations so hypocritical?

Reflect

1. *Agree/Disagree.* "The church is full of hypocrites."

2. "I would find the church more appealing if _____."

3. Read and discuss the following portions of Jesus' exposè of hypocrisy recorded in Matthew 23.
   a. *Verses 1-15.* What did these people do that was inconsistent with their professed beliefs? How did their actions harm other people?
   b. *Verses 25-28.* How would you describe the tone of Jesus' words? Does this surprise you? Why, or why not?
   c. *Verse 37.* After all he said about the hypocrites, why does Jesus suddenly sound so eager to be kind to them?

4. Tom and Danielle felt disappointed when they visited churches that didn't seem to come close to the kind of Christianity they saw described in the Bible. Tom says, "I'd go into a church looking for real belief in Jesus and real worship. Instead, people would stand up

and sit down and kneel, and say the same words over and over like they're supposed to—but there didn't seem to be any heart in it at all."
    a. Have you visited church services that made you feel the same way?
    b. Read Acts 2:42-47. What was the New Testament church like in its earliest days? Does this sound appealing to you? Is it realistic to think that a church could be like that today? Why, or why not?

5. What do you think about the author's description of the way today's church should present the truth? (Pages 176-181.)

Respond

1. If this is the last time your group is meeting, discuss:
    a. What is the most helpful insight you have gained from these studies?
    b. How do you plan to continue your spiritual journey? In what specific ways could you continue to grow in your relationship with God?
    c. Should this group continue to meet? If so, what topic(s) would you like to study and discuss together?
    d. How would you suggest the group sessions could be restructured to make them more helpful?

2. Close with prayer. Ask God to grant each member of the group a satisfying conclusion to his "search for hope."

PLAN B (BELIEVERS)

Relate

1. *The Pretenders.* Give members of the group two note cards and a pencil. On one of the cards, each person should write a true but little known fact about himself (his place of birth, a nickname he used to wear, a hobby he enjoys, his middle name, etc.). On the other card, each person should write a "pretend fact"—something that *isn't* true—

about himself. The group leader should shuffle the cards and read them aloud. Let members of the group guess: (1) who wrote the information on the card, and (2) whether the information is true or false.

2. In *A Severe Mercy*, Sheldon Vanauken wrote, "The best argument for Christianity is Christians: their joy, their certainty, their completeness. But the strongest argument *against* Christianity is also Christians— when they are somber and joyless, when they are self-righteous and smug in complacent consecration, when they are narrow and repressive, then Christianity dies a thousand deaths." Do you agree with this statement? Why, or why not?

3. OPTION: *Definitions*. Give each member of the class a note card and a pencil. Ask them to write on the card either a definition of the word *hypocrisy*, or the name of a current person in the news who is an example of hypocrisy.

Reflect

1. Do you think Tom and Danielle's question is a common one in our culture? Have you ever encountered a friend who refuses to get involved in the church because "there are too many hypocrites in the church"?

2. Have *you* ever felt frustrated with the lack of authenticity you've found in the church?

3. Read Jeremiah 7:1-11; Ephesians 4:25; James 3:9, 10; and 1 Peter 2:1. How do these verses relate to Tom and Danielle's question?

4. *Contemporary Paraphrases of Matthew 23*. Divide your class into smaller groups of two or three people each. Provide paper and pencils, and ask one person in each group to be the writer for the group. Each group has eight to ten minutes to read and discuss one of the following sections of Matthew 23, and write their own contemporary paraphrase of it. *(Put the Scripture into your own words, trying to express what Jesus might say to hypocrites today.)*
a. Verses 1-7
b. Verses 8-14

c. Verses 15-22
d. Verses 23-28
e. Verses 29-33
After each group has finished, ask them to take turns reading their paraphrases aloud.

5. In chapter eleven, the author suggests several ways we can respond to the question, "Why So Many Phony Christians?" Briefly discuss each of these points, and look up each Scripture reference:

- Clarify *what hypocrisy means*. (A hypocrite is not simply someone who makes mistakes. It's someone whose actions belie his professed beliefs. Christians aren't the only ones who do this.)
- Clarify *what salvation means*. (The church isn't a club for perfect people. It's a hospital where the wounded admit our sin and find forgiveness and grace because of what Christ has done for us. See Ephesians 2:8-10; 1 John 1:9.)
- Clarify *what holy living means*. (As we grow in the Christian life, our outward actions and inner character should correspond more and more to the holiness of our perfect Savior. See 2 Peter 1:5-11. But during this growth process, we still make plenty of mistakes.)
- Clarify *what personal responsibility means*. (Even if the church were full of hypocrites, that still wouldn't excuse each of us from our own personal accountability to God.)
- Clarify *what the church means*. (The church may appear to be a flawed human institution, but the Bible makes it plain that the church is far more: it's the body of Christ, a group of people called out to follow the perfect Son of God and do his will. See Ephesians 2:19-22; 1 Peter 2:9, 10.)

6. Jesus Christ has never committed a single act of hypocrisy (see 1 Peter 2:21, 22). Can this fact help us answer Tom and Danielle's question? If so, how?

7. Tom says, "Where can I find a church where people truly love Jesus, and don't just get wrapped up in the social club and the institution?" What is your reaction to this question?
a. I wonder the exact same thing.
b. I think if he will read about the church in the book of Acts, he'll find the kind of church he's looking for.
c. Someone who feels that way ought to visit our congregation; he'd

see the New Testament church in action.
d. I think he's being too idealistic because . . .
e. Other:

Respond

1. How can we enthusiastically invite people to consider being part of a church we know is imperfect?

2. Since this is the final lesson in the series, please evaluate the effectiveness of this group.
   a. What is the main thing you have gained from this series of studies? Has it exposed any areas of weakness in your life? Has it helped you identify any areas of strength?
   b. What is the main thing you wish had been different about this series of studies?
   c. Where do you want to go from here 1) in your personal study of God's Word? 2) In your outreach efforts as you attempt to "take truth next door"?

3. Close by asking volunteers in the group to pray for lost people to come to Christ, for more workers in God's "harvest field" (Matthew 9:38), and that each member of the group will continue to "take God's truth next door."